MOON PHASE
ASTROLOGY

"Intuitive, poetic, and intriguing. More reverie than textbook, Raven
Kaldera's work makes for an enticing read."

SUE TOMPKINS, AUTHOR OF *ASPECTS IN ASTROLOGY*

"In *Moon Phase Astrology*, Raven Kaldera weaves a magical tale of
Moon lore, astrology, archetypes, and practical spiritual insight that
imparts deep knowledge and understanding of the Moon's impact
on our lives. The wisdom of the ages permeates this methodical col-
lection of information, enticing you to learn more about your dance
through the seasons and cycles of the Moon based on the lunar
phase at the time of birth. Highly recommended!"

SUSAN SELENE, INTERNATIONALLY
KNOWN PSYCHIC AND ASTROLOGER

"Raven Kaldera's *Moon Phase Astrology* is a much-needed addition
to astrology's literature on the Moon and how it affects our emotional and spiritual approach to life. By understanding the current
Moon phase and the phase we were born under, we can more easily
manage our responses to the ebb and flow of both stressful and joyful intervals. This book is an exceptional tool for keeping ourselves
on an even keel during these challenging times."

DONNA CUNNINGHAM, MSW, AUTHOR OF
MOON SIGNS AND *THE MOON IN YOUR LIFE*

MOON PHASE ASTROLOGY

THE LUNAR KEY TO YOUR DESTINY

RAVEN KALDERA

Destiny Books

Rochester, Vermont • Toronto, Canada

Destiny Books
One Park Street
Rochester, Vermont 05767
www.DestinyBooks.com

Text paper is SFI certified

Destiny Books is a division of Inner Traditions International

Library of Congress Cataloging-in-Publication Data
Kaldera, Raven.
  Moon phase astrology : the lunar key to your destiny / Raven Kaldera.
    p. cm.
  Summary: "A guide to understanding the phases of astrological Moon signs and
their effects on emotions and personality"—Provided by publisher.
  ISBN 978-1-59477-401-0
  1. Astrology. 2. Human beings—Effect of the moon on. 3. Astrology and
psychology. I. Title.
  BF1723.K35 2011
  133.5'32—dc22

                                                                    2011002150

Printed and bound in the United States by Lake Book Manufacturing

The text paper is SFI certified. The Sustainable Forestry Initiative® program
promotes sustainable forest management.

10 9 8 7 6 5 4 3 2 1

Text design by Jessica Johnson
Text layout by Virginia Scott Bowman
This book was typeset in Garamond Premier Pro with Trajan Pro, Bodega Sans,
Gill Sans, and Albertus used as display typefaces.

To send correspondence to the author of this book, mail a first-class letter to the
author c/o Inner Traditions • Bear & Company, One Park Street, Rochester, VT
05767, and we will forward the communication or contact the author directly at
www.ravenkaldera.org.

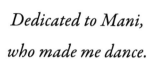

Dedicated to Mani,
who made me dance.

CONTENTS

1

IN THE BEGINNING: THE NEW MOON

CALL TO ACTION: THE CRESCENT MOON

INTERNAL CRISIS: THE WAXING QUARTER MOON

SOUL'S REDEMPTION: THE GIBBOUS MOON

CONSUMMATION: THE FULL MOON

THE GREATER GOOD: THE DISSEMINATING MOON

7

THE WOUND ON THE OUTSIDE: THE WANING QUARTER MOON

8

INTO THE EMBERS: THE BALSAMIC MOON

INTRODUCTION
THE ETERNAL DANCE

I like to think that the Moon is still there even when I am not looking at it.

ALBERT EINSTEIN

When a finger points to the Moon, the imbecile looks at the finger.

CHINESE PROVERB

The Moon is a dancer. That dance is sometimes seen as wayward, like the Norse Moon god Mani, who would stray from his nightly vigils to watch friends and rescue abused children, and had to be kept on track by a large wolf running after him through the sky. It is sometimes seen as reliable as clockwork, like the lunar Egyptian god Thoth, who ruled letters and numbers and invented the calendar. Sometimes the Moon is male, as in the previous examples; sometimes she is female, like the Afro-Caribbean Yemaya, or the Greek Artemis or Selene. Some traditions link the Moon with the woman's monthly menstrual cycle. Sometimes the Moon is seen as nurturing and maternal, sometimes as implacable and deadly. It is said to cause lunacy, and there is both a yearning for and a general mistrust of the half-hidden magical glow of moonlight . . . as opposed to the bright, revealing nakedness of sunlight.

Those are just some of the myths and perceptions surrounding Earth's heavenly companion. Our two most significant astrological planets, the Sun and Moon, come together in a conjunction—being in the same place in the sky—once every lunar month, during the New Moon. (For beginners, that means that if you're born on a New Moon, you'll probably have the Sun and Moon together in the same sign, perhaps even conjunct each other.) The rest of the time, they go their own way, touching and whirling apart again. If you're looking at the Moon from the solar perspective—which is the basis for our modern calendar, and most children are not taught anything different—the Moon looks annoyingly unreasonable, refusing to match up at any standard point. If you're looking astrologically at the Moon from the Sun's rational perspective (the Sun symbolizes the clear, rational "daylight" view), the same issues apply. To the left-brained identity, the moon's right-brained imagery must be nailed down safely in words and categories and solutions or ignored . . . which, of course, we do at our peril.

People tend to believe that the Moon's cycle is twenty-eight days long, and that number is actually listed frequently in books about lunar myths and magic. If it were twenty-eight days long, of course, thirteen lunar months would fit reasonably into the solar cycle of 365.25 days. It isn't, though. It's twenty-nine-and-a-half days long, and there are somewhere between twelve and thirteen moons per solar year. The Moon ignores the Sun's neat yearly cycle; it has its own agenda, its own pattern, its own dance. The pattern of Moon and Sun repeats over a period of 18.6 years. There's really no such thing as a "lunar year," because the 365-day concept of "year" is based on the Sun. The Moon may reflect the Sun's light, but it doesn't work on the Sun's schedule. It keeps spinning along, doing its thing, and annoying the solar-centered calendar-makers who would like for it to line up properly. Yet to attempt to make it fit the solar year is to deny the Moon's own nature, just as so many of us try to force our own erratic, annoying, feeling natures into a logical left-brained ego-control pattern.

Ancient civilizations handled the calendrical anomalies in various ways. Some, like the Hebrews, Egyptians, Greeks, and Hindus, went with twelve lunar months per year and added an extra month every three years to keep the calendar from slipping too badly away from the natural harvest cycle. The Celts went with thirteen months in their lunar tree calendar, but started the solar year on the first New Moon after the winter solstice, which truncated the last month more often than not. Some worked with two calendars side by side, and some used only the lunar or only the solar year.

The lunar month has eight phases—New Moon, Waxing Crescent Moon (here shortened to Crescent), Waxing Quarter Moon, Gibbous Moon, Full Moon, Disseminating Moon, Waning Quarter Moon, and Balsamic Moon (the waning crescent before the Moon goes into the dark again). The names that I use were made popular by noted astrologer Dane Rudhyar, one of the few astrologers to work extensively with the Moon phases. (For his take on the subject, try his book *The Lunation Cycle: A Key to the Understanding of Personality*.)

You'll notice, if you're the sort who studies calendars, that the Sun also has eight "phases," if you will, marked out by the solstices, equinoxes, and "cross-quarter" days of Imbolc, Beltane, Lammas, and Samhain, holidays named various things in various cultures but still found over and over again as markers of the solar year. I've speculated that the Sun's eight "phases" might echo, in some way, the phase tale of the Moon. If this were the case, then Yule (the winter solstice when the Sun is at its ebb) would correspond to the New Moon of beginnings. Imbolc/Oimelc (February 1 or thereabouts) would correspond to the Crescent Moon and its call to action. The stormy spring equinox, Ostara/Eostre, would echo the Waxing Quarter Moon and its crisis, and fertile May Day would echo the healing Gibbous Moon. The Full Moon would correspond, of course, to the bright summer solstice and its archetypal Sun God. Lammas/Lughnasad (August 1 or thereabouts, the holiday of the sacrificed Corn King) would echo the Disseminating Moon—one imagines the crops carried off the field and "disseminated" into seeds that would be ground or planted the following year. The fall equinox, the time of hunting and harvest, would correspond to the Waning Quarter, and Samhain/Halloween, holiday of ancestor worship and remembering the Dead, would echo the Balsamic Moon's gentle descent into old age. The Moon may not dance on the Sun's schedule, but its pattern is not so different after all, it seems.

When I started studying the Moon phases, it really took me aback when I realized that eight phases passing through twelve signs produced ninety-six different Moons. Ninety-six—now there's a magic number for you. It's a multiple of three, the original "magic number," and when you write it, it is entirely made up of circles and crescents. It is also eerily similar to the symbol for Cancer, which is the Moon's own sign. There's no such thing as coincidence, I say. It's synchronicity—or, in some cases, a divine set-up for those with eyes to notice. Irrational or not, the Moon has nothing against numbers. It just has its own patterns of mathematics, which should probably be studied by someone who is much, much more proficient at anything mathematical than I am.

I've already mentioned that the New Moon is the phase where the Moon and Sun line up. On the Full Moon, the Moon is in the sign opposing the Sun. In other words, if it's May and the Sun is in Taurus, the New Moon during that time will be in Taurus, but the Full Moon during that time will be in Scorpio. If you know that Leo and Aquarius are the signs that square those two, you'll also know that the Waxing Quarter will be in Leo (at a right angle to Taurus in the forward direction) and that the Waning Quarter will be in Aquarius (at a right angle to Taurus in the backward direction). For the actual times when the signs change, don't be ashamed to have to check an ephemeris or a calendar; even experienced astrologers do that. If you're trying to find out the Moon phase you were born under . . . well, sometimes it's easy and obvious; you can read the descriptions of the Moon phases in this book, look at your chart, and count signs and degrees. If your astrology chart includes a major aspect between your Sun and Moon, for example, it will be easy to tell. If your Moon is on one of the cusps of a phase, you might want to consult with an ephemeris or an astrologer to get it exactly right, or just read the two possible options and see which one "clicks" for you. (For nonastrologers, check the section just after this one: "How to Use This Book.")

The Moon sails through twelve signs, writing an eight-part story about the essence of the Moon in each sign. The archetypes of the New Moons are children or youths, whereas the Balsamic Moons star wise elders. Some of the Moons—namely the Quarter Moons—are more unpleasant than others. Moons in signs that don't harmonize well with the lunar energy also tend to be less "easy" to walk through. That's just the way of things. Every

Moon has its challenges, but some are more challenging than others. As any astrologer knows, if you've got planets squaring your Moon, you're in for some unpleasantries. The Quarter Moons contain the energy of the square aspect, so if you read them and wince, well, you'd be wincing just as much if you read a description of some planet squaring your Moon. The idea is to wince, but then to recognize the challenges and pitfalls and do something about them. Also, keep in mind that the Moon is only one part of your chart. An "easy" Moon sign and phase can be made more difficult by being in an afflicting aspect to other planets, while a more "difficult" Moon sign and phase can be supported by enhancing aspects. Then there's all the other cacophony going on with the rest of the planets and asteroids. Indeed, while it's close to your heart—and in a way, it *is* your heart—the Moon does not rule your life any more than any other single planet. Keep that in mind when you read the descriptions, and adjust accordingly.

Where did I get all these stories? I asked the Moon, and at the same time I scrutinized a lot of people's astrological Moons and experimented with the energy of each Moon as it passed. They are not written about specifically as Moon tales in any ancient literature, although they are echoed in myths and legends all over the world. After all, we are all human and have the same human experiences. I would never suggest that these are the only way that the Moon's tales could be told. The Moon is more versatile than that.

The twelve Moon stories affect us in different ways. First, there is the effect of our own natal Moon. The first thing anyone does when they get an astrology book is turn to their own information if they have the details to access it. In fact, you probably looked up your own Moon sign and phase (if you know it) before you even started reading this chapter. The Moon sign and phase that you were born under will haunt your emotional life and its attendant lessons. It's as if you were born to live and struggle with that moment in the story, over and over, until you've perfected it and ironed out all its wrinkles . . . until you play the story, and the story does not play you. If it's a more challenging Moon, find the positive aspects to it and concentrate on nurturing those instead of falling into the tempting negative traits.

Second, there is the effect of the actual transiting Moon in the sky, which touches every one of us regardless of aspects in our natal chart. Even if a particular Moon isn't giving us more than the lightest of touches, it is probably touching some of the people around us in heavier ways. When you're accustomed to looking, you can see the influence of the Moon in other people and feel it in the currents of the world around you. For those who want to make the most of the Moon's phases in their lives, I've suggested activities that are particularly useful to work on during any given sign and phase. If more than one person wants to try it, one could begin a Moon Story group, in person or through correspondence, doing the various activities and journaling about them. I've also provided a number of inspirational quotes for each Moon archetype to illuminate its meaning. These can be used to meditate on to gain a better understanding of the essence of each Moon.

Keep in mind that if the transiting Moon is in the same sign as your natal Moon, it's going to affect you more strongly regardless of the phase that it's in. It may have the effect of casting the "shadow" of a different phase of the transiting Moon temporarily over your natal Moon. The chart I'll use in my examples has a Rebel Moon (Waxing Quarter in Aquarius). When the Moon in the sky passes through Aquarius, but in the Waning Quarter, the bearer of this chart might experience the story of the Heretic's Moon (Waning Quarter in Aquarius) taking place in their life at that time. Since the Moon passes through your own Moon sign every month, in its various phases, you may find that you resonate with each of the other Moon phases in your Moon sign's story at different times—in fact, it would be surprising if you didn't. You've experienced those other Moon phases casting their "shadow" over your Moon hundreds of times since you were born. The sign energy is stronger than the phase energy; you will resonate more strongly with the other Moons as the Moon passes through your sign than as it passes through your phase.

Third, there is the effect of the other planets in your chart. While the Sun's aspect determines the main phase of your natal Moon, other planets will affect it as well. Another way that the "shadow" of another phase can be cast over your Moon is if the natal Moon and another planet align in a major aspect. For example, since the Moon is full when it is in opposition to the Sun, any planet in opposition to your Moon adds a bit of that Full Moon energy to your Moon, no matter what phase the Moon is in. In addition, it's likely that when the aspecting planet is being strongly energized by aspects to other planets, it will temporarily strengthen that "shadow" over your Moon.

In the example chart shown in the next section, the Moon is opposed by Mars. When this person's natal Mars is being strongly aspected and stimulated by other planets, its energy may strengthen the Full Moon shadow on the Waxing Quarter Moon. This person may feel a vague sense of the energy of the Full Moon in that sign throughout this period, in addition to their own Moon phase and the current phase of the Moon in the sky. This means that celestial forces will constantly push you through other parts of the story of your Moon sign, which can hold you back, help you mature, or at least give you new energies to work with. It's worth it to study all the phases of your Moon sign, to be aware of these energies. (Again, for those who don't have enough experience with astrology to understand most of the last paragraph, please see the next section: How to Use This Book.)

If you absorb these stories, you'll see them everywhere—in people, in events, in humanity in general. That's because they describe the emotional reality of being human. We know them all, instinctively, because the Moon keeps circling above us and affecting us. Some may be more alien than others, but none are more or less sacred and amazing—even the difficult ones. These tales are the ebb and flow of the human heart, the salty inner sea that beats like the wings of eagles. They are the astrological heartbeat. Take them into yourself and understand not only your own heart, but that of everyone around you.

HOW TO USE THIS BOOK
FOR THE COMPLETE BEGINNER

FINDING YOUR
MOON SIGN AND PHASE

The first step in finding your Moon sign and phase is getting a copy of your astrological chart. There are a wide variety of websites and computer programs that can generate an astrological chart, provided you have the *date, time,* and *place of birth.* (If you do not know the exact time of birth, find the Moon sign and phase for 12:00 a.m., 12:00 p.m., and 11:59 p.m. This will give you the range of possibilities. The exact place of birth has a much smaller effect.) Two good sites with free charts on the Internet are:

ASTROLABE: **www.alabe.com/freechart**
This is a good place for beginners to print out a chart. The descriptions given below the chart provide a computer-generated example of how some parts of your chart might be interpreted. They do not take into account the complex interactions between the various parts of the chart, so they may be contradictory or irrelevant.

ASTRODIENST: **www.astro.com/horoscopes**
At the bottom of the page are links for "Chart Drawing, Ascendant" (good for beginners) and "Advanced Chart Selection" (for advanced users).

Note: These and other websites suggested in this book also sell services to the public. I am in no way representing or advocating for these sites or their pay services. I am merely including them as possible resources. If these sites are no longer available, a web search for the terms astrological chart, birth chart, or natal chart should find similar sites.

By using one of these websites, some other computer software, or an astrologer, you'll end up with a chart similar to those on pages 10–11. An astrological chart contains a circle divided into twelve parts with a lot of lines and symbols on it, and perhaps a graph or tables of more detailed information. These tables show the most important symbols on the chart. Your chart may contain additional symbols, or your symbols (especially Capricorn) may look slightly different than these. Don't worry, you don't need to understand

☉	☽	☿	♀
Sun	Moon	Mercury	Venus

♂	♃	♄	♅	Symbols for the Planets
Mars	Jupiter	Saturn	Uranus	

♆	♇ or ♇
Neptune	Pluto

♈	♉	♊	♋
Aries	Taurus	Gemini	Cancer

♌	♍	♎	♏	Symbols for the Signs
Leo	Virgo	Libra	Scorpio	

♐	♑	♒	♓
Sagittarius	Capricorn	Aquarius	Pisces

it all. For now, we are only interested in the position of the Sun and Moon. *(In astrology, the Sun and Moon are commonly referred to as "planets" because they affect us in the same ways as the other heavenly bodies.)*

In Example A, the position of the Sun is shown as ☉ 4° ♏ 53 and the Moon is ☽ 9° ♈ 41. The first symbol is the planet, and the second symbol shows the sign. The first number tells us the position of the planet by indicating how many degrees the planet is from the beginning of that sign. (The last number gives greater precision, indicating a fraction of a degree.) The lines in the center show relationships between the planets, which you can ignore for now.

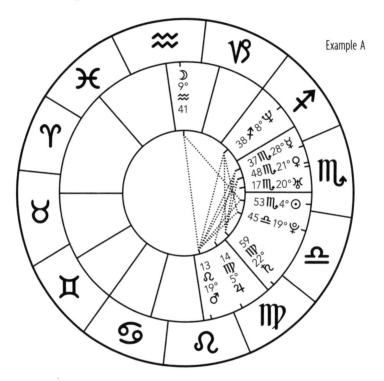

Example A

Example B shows a more complex style of chart for the same person. On the right is a table listing the positions of the planets with even greater precision, using a two-letter abbreviation for the sign, rather than the symbol. On the circular chart the positions of the sun and moon are noted as 4⁵³ and 9⁴¹, and the sign is assumed from the position of the symbol. Don't worry about the rest of the information. Just find the positions of the Sun and Moon. In our example, all we need to know right now is that the Sun is at 4 degrees Scorpio and the Moon is at 9 degrees Aquarius.

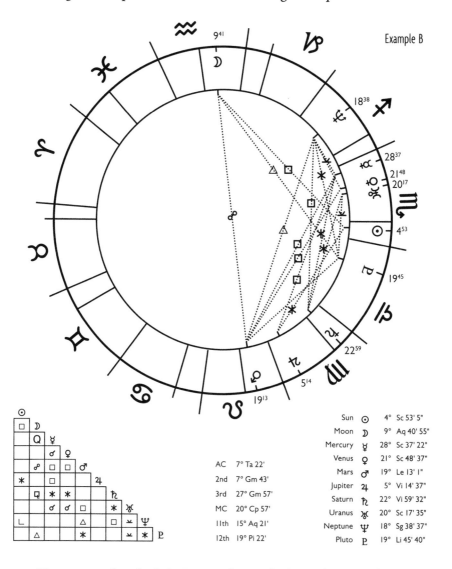

Example B

Sun	☉	4° Sc 53' 5"
Moon	☽	9° Aq 40' 55"
Mercury	☿	28° Sc 37' 22"
Venus	♀	21° Sc 48' 37"
Mars	♂	19° Le 13' 1"
Jupiter	♃	5° Vi 14' 37"
Saturn	♄	22° Vi 59' 32"
Uranus	♅	20° Sc 17' 35"
Neptune	♆	18° Sg 38' 37"
Pluto	♇	19° Li 45' 40"

AC	7° Ta 22'
2nd	7° Gm 43'
3rd	27° Gm 57'
MC	20° Cp 57'
11th	15° Aq 21'
12th	19° Pi 22'

Next, we need to find the Moon phase, which involves a small amount of math. To find the Moon phase, we need to know how many degrees apart the Sun and Moon are. Look up your Sun sign and your Moon sign in this table: this number will tell you how many degrees are between the two signs. In our example, the Sun is in Scorpio, and the Moon is in Aquarius; according to the table, there are 90 degrees from Scorpio to Aquarius.

FINDING THE DEGREES BETWEEN SUN AND MOON

		Aries	Taurus	Gemini	Cancer	Leo	Virgo	Libra	Scorpio	Sagittarius	Capricorn	Aquarius	Pisces
												MOON	
SUN	**Aries**	0	30	60	90	120	150	180	210	240	270	300	330
	Taurus	330	0	30	60	90	120	150	180	210	240	270	300
	Gemini	300	330	0	30	60	90	120	150	180	210	240	270
	Cancer	270	300	330	0	30	60	90	120	150	180	210	240
	Leo	240	270	300	330	0	30	60	90	120	150	180	210
	Virgo	210	240	270	300	330	0	30	60	90	120	150	180
	Libra	180	210	240	270	300	330	0	30	60	90	120	150
	Scorpio	150	180	210	240	270	300	330	0	30	60	90	120
	Sagittarius	120	150	180	210	240	270	300	330	0	30	60	90
	Capricorn	90	120	150	180	210	240	270	300	330	0	30	60
	Aquarius	60	90	120	150	180	210	240	270	300	330	0	30
	Pisces	30	60	90	120	150	180	210	240	270	300	330	0

Here is the math to get the full distance between the Sun and Moon: **Number from table + Degrees of Moon − Degrees of Sun = Degrees from Sun to Moon.**

In our example, with the Sun at 4-degrees Scorpio and the Moon at 9-degrees Aquarius, we get 90 + 9 − 4 = 95 degrees. Now, look up the number we just calculated in the table below to determine your Moon phase. In our example, 95 degrees indicates the Waxing Quarter Moon, and the Waxing Quarter Moon in Aquarius is the Rebel Moon. Look up your own number in the following table to get your Moon phase, and then look up that phase and sign in the Table of Contents to find your Moon.

DEGREES AND CORRESPONDING MOON PHASES

PHASE	DEGREES BETWEEN
New Moon	0°–44°
Crescent Moon (Waxing Crescent)	45°–89°
Waxing Quarter Moon (First Quarter)	90°–134°
Gibbous Moon (Waxing Gibbous)	135°–179°
Full Moon	180°–224°
Disseminating Moon (Waning Gibbous)	225°–269°
Waning Quarter Moon (Last Quarter)	270°–314°
Balsamic Moon (Waning Crescent)	315°–360°
New Moon	360°–390°

COMPARING METHODS OF DETERMINING THE MOON PHASE

There are a wide variety of tools for finding and tracking Moon phases, and these can be used as long as the method of determining the Moon sign is understood. There are three main methods used to determine the Moon sign. Most online tools will use an *astronomical method,* where the four primary phases of the Moon (New, First Quarter, Full, Last Quarter) are specific instants in time, and the waxing and waning phases describe the entirety of the transition between primary phases. For instance, if the Full Moon is on June 12th at 11:15 a.m. and the Waning Quarter Moon (Last Quarter) is on June 19th at 4:29 a.m., then by this method June 13th through 18th are likely to be listed as the Disseminating Moon (Waning Gibbous).

The *astrological method* of moon phase calculation divides the lunar cycle into eight equal parts approximately 3.7-days long. The four primary phases begin at the precise instant of the astronomical Moon phase, and the waxing and waning phases begin exactly halfway between. By this method, the Full Moon in the above example lasts from June 12th at 11:15 a.m. to June 15th at 7:22 p.m., and the Disseminating Moon lasts from June 15th at 7:22 p.m. to June 19th at 4:29 a.m. If you were born even a few minutes before the moon was at its fullest, then from an astrological perspective you were born under the Gibbous Moon. This is the method used in the calculations in the previous section.

To many people, this astrological method doesn't feel quite right. They may consider the Full Moon to be the three days when the moon looks the fullest. This can be called the *natural method* of Moon phase calculation, where the moon is considered to be in each phase for a day or so on either side of the astronomical Moon phase, and there isn't a specific moment when the phase changes from Gibbous to Full, or Full to Disseminating. This method of phase calculation can be useful for activities like gardening by the Moon, or doing magical rituals with Moon energy. However, this method can become complicated. For instance, some people consider the fully dark New Moon to have a very different energy than the first visible crescent or the last sliver of the "old" Moon. They might feel that the distinct energy of the Quarter Moons is only perceptible quite near the astronomical moment of the Quarter Moon, while the Gibbous and Crescent Moons occupy a longer period of time.

The presence of all these different methods may seem ambiguous and

confusing, but for the purposes of this book we are only going to con-
cern ourselves with the astrological method. Astrology is a practice that
attempts to make the cosmic cycles as clear and mathematically precise as
possible. From an astrological perspective this is the best way to calculate
the energy of the Moon as a part of the cosmic clock, as opposed to a
luminous rock that orbits the Earth and moves the tides.

The figure below compares the three calculation methods visually.

USING CURRENT
MOON PHASE INFORMATION

While this book focuses on interpreting the significance of a person's natal Moon, the current Moon phase also influences us. Because Moon phase information is so frequently provided in terms of percentage illuminated or days since the New Moon, I am providing the following table for you to get a rough conversion.

CONVERSIONS FOR MOON PHASES		
MOON PHASE	**APPROXIMATE PERCENT ILLUMINATED**	**DAYS SINCE NEW**
New Moon	0–15% (waxing)	0–4 days
Crescent Moon (Waxing Crescent)	15–50% (waxing)	4–7 days
Waxing Quarter Moon (First Quarter)	50–85% (waxing)	7–11 days
Gibbous Moon (Waxing Gibbous)	85–100% (waxing)	11–15 days
Full Moon	85–100% (waning)	15–19 days
Disseminating Moon (Waning Gibbous)	50–85% (waning)	19–21 days
Waning Quarter Moon (Last Quarter)	15–50% (waning)	21–26 days
Balsamic Moon (Waning Crescent)	0–15% (waning)	26–29 days

For instance, if the Moon phase is listed as Waning Gibbous with 98 percent of the Moon's visible disk illuminated, then astrologically, it is the Full Moon because it is just after the astronomical full moon. However, if it is listed as *Waxing* Gibbous with 98 percent illuminated, then astrologically it is the Gibbous Moon, because it is just *prior* to the astronomical full moon. You must get the waxing or waning part correct in order to get the correct phase.

If the Moon is listed as "24 days past new" then astrologically it is the Waning Quarter Moon. If it is listed as "7 days past new" then you would have to check the date and time of the First Quarter in order to determine when on that day the phase changes from the Crescent Moon to the Waxing Quarter Moon. Here are a few sites that provide current Moon phase information.

ZODIAC ARTS: www.zodiacarts.com/Calendar.shtml

This is a great site, providing a clear and useful monthly calendar showing the time and date of all eight current Moon phases as well as their astrological sign and position.

MOON CONNECTION: www.moonconnection.com

This site provides a monthly visual Moon phase calendar for any month you choose, as well as a current moon phase calculator you can include in your website or blog. It also provides information about the paid software QuickPhase Pro, which provides many features for working with the Moon.

NAVAL OCEANOGRAPHY PORTAL: www.usno.navy.mil/USNO/astronomical-applications

Hosted by the United States Naval Meteorology and Oceanography Command, this website provides detailed Sun and Moon data, as well as other dates of astronomical and meteorological interest. Select "Complete Sun and Moon Data for One Day" and enter your information. They also provide tables of the time and date of the primary phases of the Moon and tables of the percentage of the Moon that is illuminated on each day for a full year.

I realize that the Internet is an ephemeral place and that any website I list may be gone in a matter of months, but I would hope, assuming for some future other than the collapse of civilization, that a simple web search using the keywords *moon phase calculator* or *moon phase calendar* would turn up an equivalent to the ones listed above.

SHADOWING MOONS

Earlier, in the introduction, I mentioned that various planetary aspects in the chart can color, or "shadow," the story of one's natal Moon. This means that you don't have only one story; while our example chart has a Rebel Moon (Waxing Quarter Moon in Aquarius), other planetary aspects involving the Moon can give this story the additional flavor of other Aquarius Moons, other Waxing Quarter Moons, and to a lesser extent, any other moon which has a relationship to the planetary aspects in the chart or their relationship to the current sky. Figuring out which Moons shadow your own is a little complicated for the complete beginner, but I'll try to lay it out here as simply as possible. If it's too confusing, please do consult an astrologer; that's what we're there for.

Planetary Rulers

First, take a look at your Moon glyph in the big circle again. Does it have another planet right next to it, practically on top of it? Are they in the same sign? When you look at the degree marker of the other planet, are they less than 10 degrees apart? (You can have planets close together on either side of a sign cusp—the edge of a sign—so that they're less than 10 degrees apart but in different signs, but that's a more complicated situation and one I won't go into here.) If you've answered yes to all of the above, you have another planet *in conjunction with* your Moon. To understand the effect of that planet, look at the moon in the **same phase as your own Moon**, in the sign that is *ruled by* that planet. For instance, Jupiter rules Sagittarius, so if your Moon is in conjunction with Jupiter, you can look at the Sagittarius Moon in the same phase as your own. For planets that rule two different signs, you may feel the effect of either or both. Our example chart does not have any planets conjunct the Moon, but if yours does, refer to the following list of planetary rulers to see what other Moons may be shadowing yours.

The Sun rules the Leo Moon.
The Moon rules the Cancer Moon.

Mercury rules the Gemini Moon and the Virgo Moon.
Venus rules the Taurus Moon and the Libra Moon.
Mars rules the Aries Moon.
Jupiter rules the Sagittarius Moon.
Saturn rules the Capricorn Moon.
Uranus rules the Aquarius Moon.
Neptune rules the Pisces Moon.
Pluto rules the Scorpio Moon.

Major Aspects

Does your Moon have lines running out from it to various other planetary symbols? Those are *aspects,* places where planets click with each other because they're close in degree at specific angles. (Astrologers have different opinions on exactly how close the degrees need to be, so some versions of a chart may show more lines than others.) Not everyone will have these angles to their Moon, but most will. Some of those angles are beneficial, some challenging; some are major and some are minor. In our example charts on pages 10–11, A shows lines that indicate aspects but gives no detailed information. If you don't know how to determine aspects on your own, you will need a chart like Example B, which has a grid showing the aspects.

Look at the graph—yours may look slightly different, but find the long row or column marked with the Moon symbol. You'll see a new set of symbols in these boxes. The most important ones are listed below. In the example, you can see the symbols for *opposition* and *trine* underneath the Moon, as well as two other symbols (Q ⊡), which indicate minor aspects.

☍ Opposition, directly across from each other, six signs apart. Approximately a 180-degree angle.

△ Trine, a third of the way around, four signs apart. Approximately a 120-degree angle.

☐ Square, a quarter of the way around, three signs apart. Approximately a 90-degree angle.

✳ Sextile, two signs apart. Approximately a 60-degree angle.

If you find one of these four symbols under the Moon symbol, take note of the other planet involved (on the other axis of the graph; refer to the planetary symbol chart again if need be). In the example, the symbol for opposition (φ) is in the row marked with the Mars symbol ($\male$) and the symbol for trine ($\triangle$) is in the row marked with the Pluto symbol ($\womars$ or P), showing that the Moon is in opposition to Mars and trine Pluto. Your grid may include many minor aspects, and it may include aspects to things besides planets. Ignore these for now, and find only the four major aspects listed here. (If there are no major aspects to your Moon, move ahead to the section on Transits.)

Now go back to the circle chart and look at your Moon again. Look at the lines that radiate out from it, and try to figure out which planet is on the other end of each line by checking the symbol. The lines may be color-coded or marked with symbols. In the example chart, three lines radiate from the Moon. One goes to Mars, another to Pluto, and a third to the Sun. (Because the aspect between the Moon and Sun is what determines the Moon phase, we don't need to reexamine that aspect here.)

Once you've identified which of the lines represent which aspect from the graph, figure out whether the other planets are ahead of or behind your Moon. The chart is read counterclockwise. Planets that are sneaking up on your Moon from behind, aspecting it from the earlier parts of the chart, are called *approaching aspects*. Planets that are further ahead of your Moon, aspecting it from the later parts of the chart, are called *separating aspects*. Figure out what each aspect is and write that down. (The Sun does not count in this list, because its position determines the phase of the Moon. Here you're looking at the aspects of Mercury through Pluto.)

Now, refer to the following list. Here you'll be looking under the **same sign as your Moon**, in different phases. If your Moon and a planet have a

separating sextile ($\sextile$, further ahead), look at the Crescent Moon.

separating square ($\square$, further ahead), look at the Waxing Quarter Moon.

opposition (φ), look at the Full Moon.

approaching trine (△, behind your Moon), look at the
   Disseminating Moon.

approaching square (☐, behind your Moon), look at the Waning
   Quarter Moon.

approaching sextile (✶, behind your Moon), look at the Waning
   Quarter Moon.

In our example chart, the Aquarius Moon is in opposition to Mars, so
we'd look at the Full Moon in Aquarius, the Friendship Moon. The Moon
is also trined to Pluto. Since Pluto is behind the Moon (an approaching
trine) we'd look at the Disseminating Moon in Aquarius, the Apostle's
Moon. (The Moon is also squaring the Sun in this example. The natal
Moon phase is determined by the Moon's position relative to the Sun,
while these other aspects are determined by the aspecting planet's position relative to the Moon. (This is why the Sun in a square aspect behind
the Moon is the Waxing Quarter, not the Waning Quarter.)

*Note to astrologers: Use the Gibbous and the Disseminating for quincunxes
in either direction. You use the Moon to calculate these aspects in the way
that you use the Sun to calculate the Moon's phases. Aspects more minor than
the quincunx can be calculated in the same way.*

Rulers and Aspects

Still with us? To go a little further and find yet more "shadows," combine
the last two sections. (Conjunction is actually one of the major aspects.
Its symbol is ☌.) Take each aspect you have listed and look at the phase
indicated in the previous section (pages 20–21) with the sign ruled by
the other planet (listed in the Planetary Rulers section on page 18). In
our example, the Moon is opposing Mars, so you would look up the Full
Moon (opposition) in Aries (Mars), which is the Warrior's Moon. The
Moon is also in an approaching trine to Pluto, so you would look up the
Disseminating Moon (approaching trine) in Scorpio (Pluto), which is
the Witch's Moon. These should all give you a little more depth to your
exploration of your Internal Emotive Self.

Note to Astrologers: You might also look at aspects to the planet that rules the natal Moon (assuming that the natal Moon is not in Cancer), although I haven't explored this possibility much as of now.

TRANSITS

Determining the effect of transits—the way that the revolving planets in the sky periodically shadow your natal Moon—is trickier, but not impossible. Assuming you're not consulting an astrologer—if you are, you can just have them make you a nice neat list of transits to your Moon for whatever period of time you'd like—you will need to go to one of the free-chart websites and look for transits. Then plug in your birth data and how long a period you want to look at (a month, three months, six months, a year, and so forth), and the site will give you a list. That list will contain transits of all the planets to all your planets. Ignore most of them—just look at the ones marked natal moon. Then refer to the previous sections using that information.

Space prohibits a lengthy discussion of transits. Suffice it to say that if they involve inner planets, they move fast and can last a matter of hours. If they involve the outermost planets, they can go on for months or even years. That, too, an astrologer can help you with. However, if you want to get a feel for what's going on—what lunar lesson is being pressed on you—without the aid of an astrologer, try cross-referencing your Moon transits with the stories in this book.

1
IN THE BEGINNING
THE NEW MOON

We tend to think things are new because we've just discovered them.

MADELEINE L'ENGLE

THE NEW MOON is the time when you can't see the Moon in the sky. It is entirely hidden by the Earth's shadow, but its energy is like that of a seed in the ground, waiting to burst forth. During this phase, the Moon is often in the same sign as the Sun, having circled back around to meet its solar partner once more. Its energy begins when the Moon conjuncts the Sun, and this phase continues until the Moon is 44 degrees ahead of the Sun. The New Moon is the time of beginnings, and all twelve of these stories begin with the New Moon. Everything is just an unformed idea with no manifestation. The archetypes here are children and adolescents, not yet firm in their own identity, but already bearing qualities that will become the basis for what is yet to be.

People born under a New Moon are often childlike at heart. Whether that child is happy and trusting or wounded and feral depends on the sign, the aspects to the Moon, and the childhood of the person in question. It is not so much that they are emotionally shallow as that they are emotionally unsophisticated. The Moon is most powerful at the New and the Full, and the New Moon is especially powerful when it conjuncts the Sun. These people may be great at beginnings, but not so great at follow-up. Ironically, they may not blossom into emotional adulthood until later in life.

INFANT'S MOON
THE NEW MOON IN ARIES

The New Moon in Aries is the most primal of all beginnings. First of the first, Aries in this phase is the tiny Infant freshly come into the world, squalling and hungry, greedy for love and experience and happiness. The other New Moons all seem to start a little later, with a child or adolescent, but the Infant is so new that he barely has a personality. Well, he's an Aries, so of course he has a personality. An exuberant one, you can bet.

Astrologer Linda Goodman once exclaimed about how appropriate it was that the archetypal Infant of Aries was protected by the seasoned and powerful Warrior of Mars. Be that as it may with the Aries Sun, on the Aries New Moon the Warrior is hardly a glimpse on the horizon, barely believable, and the Moon—patron of the Inner Child—starts with the newly born. The story will end in a very different place, but the Aries Moon struggle will be about faith or distrust in the Universe, as well as the important lesson of learning self-control and honor. Right now, of course, he has neither. Infants don't. He does have a lot more trust than most signs, even in the beginning, and so this is the strong point we begin with.

On the Infant's Moon, we begin things. That's what it's for. It is the Fool card of the Tarot deck, blithely stepping off the cliff with unquenchable faith in the Universe's benevolence. We revisit our relationship with that state of utter faith and excitement for the grand unknown. Have we become too cynical for that kind of trust? That's part of the Aries Moon story too, somewhere in the distant future of the cycle, but if we are to get anything at all out of the Infant's Moon, we must at least suspend our disbelief long enough to feel what the Infant feels. The Infant hasn't been hurt yet; he suckles needily, trusting that it will be there again in an hour when he is hungry, and again, and again. We can't remember that far back, but we can imagine it. Or, rather, we need to be able to imagine it, if only for a few minutes.

People born on the Infant's Moon are in many ways a living archetype of Aries. This is made more salient by the fact that during the New Moon the Sun is very likely to be in Aries as well, and fairly likely to be in conjunction range with the Moon. Most Infant's Moon people are double Aries, with an Aries Sun sign and Moon sign. On top of that is the Ariesness of the New Moon being the first lunar position. They want to be first, in everything, and they act from instinct. Emotionally, they are very raw and primal; even if they have enough other aspects to cover it with a blanket of sophistication, the straightforward openness shines through in their emotional endeavors.

They may at their worst be intolerably infantile in their emotions as well. They want what they want, and often they don't understand why they just can't get it. Whether they are endearing or infuriating will have a lot to do with whether their Moon is afflicted, what their upbringing was like—were they indulged or disciplined or neglected?—and whether they still retain the Infant's trust in the Universe to take care of them. At their best, they can be a wonderful inspiration to the more cynical, who don't know how to trust anything, but will watch in fascination as people born under the Aries New Moon walk off the cliff smiling and live.

Quotes for the Infant's Moon

All glory comes from daring to begin.

EUGENE WARE

Psychoanalysis shows the human infant as the passive recipient of love, unable to bear hostility. Development is the learning to love actively and to bear rejection.

KARL STERN

We cannot put off living until we are ready. The most salient characteristic of life is its coerciveness; it is always urgent, "here and now," without any possible postponement. Life is fired at us point blank.

JOSÉ ORTEGA Y GASSET

I place my faith in fools. Self-confidence, my friends call it.

EDGAR ALLAN POE

Men often bear little grievances with less courage than they do great misfortunes.

AESOP

Resentment seems to have been given us by nature for a defense, and for a defense only. It is the safeguard of justice and the security of innocence.

ADAM SMITH

We need others. We need others to love and we need to be loved by them. There is no doubt that without it, we too, like the infant left alone, would cease to grow, cease to develop, choose madness and even death.

LEO BUSCAGLIA

He continued to be an infant long after he ceased to be a prodigy.

ROBERT MOSES

I had as many doubts as anyone else. Standing on the starting line, we're all cowards.

ALBERTO SALAZAR

That's what it takes to be a hero, a little gem of innocence inside you that makes you want to believe that there still exists a right and wrong, that decency will somehow triumph in the end.

LISE HAND

DRYAD'S MOON
THE NEW MOON IN TAURUS

The New Moon in Taurus is the Dryad's Moon. Here Taurus, the earthiest of Earth signs, comes forth in a form that is as close to Nature as it is possible for humankind to get. The Dryad is the shy, quiet spirit of a tree, innocent not in the human infant way of Aries, but in the way of a wild thing that does not differentiate between self and the rest of Nature. New Moons are beginnings, and this Moon calls us back to the earthly beginning, when we were not yet differentiated from the rest of the natural world, before the human identity began.

Nearly all Grecian dryads were seen as female, at least in art (which may have had less to do with mythology and more to do with the preferred subjects of artists), but in more northerly climes legend tells of the Green Man, the figure with face and beard made of leaves, literally singing greenery from his mouth, adorning church and inn and bookend alike. The Green Man was known in some locations as Jack-in-the-Green, a wild man running through the streets who ended up being sacrificed and beheaded, as we cut down trees and plants for our ever-expanding needs. Still, he was wild, not tame; he was our victim, not our collaborator.

The Dryad and Green Man are creatures of simple language and simple life; the complexities of human existence make no sense to them. They are strongly moved by seeing the suffering of the natural world under the hands of humankind, although they may be strangely at peace with the suffering that the natural world inflicts on itself, even if that is the more violent of the two. The Dryad has not yet learned to see Nature as Other and consequently has not yet learned to change the environment for personal purposes. The forest is just the forest, for good or ill, and that is that. To remove a tree or replant a shrub would be like robbing or murdering a neighbor.

During the Dryad's Moon, we struggle with our relationship to Nature, and especially to the Green World. This includes our relationship to the food we put into ourselves (and the ecosystem that may have been destroyed to grow it), the wood that made our coffee table, the paper that makes the pages of our books, the plants who were exploited to make our clothing, and all that we have killed in order to make our lives. It may also lead to an exploration of our relationship to "inanimate" objects of all kinds, as the Dryad's Moon is a time when animism creeps into our lives around the edges. It is an excellent time to do ecological work, especially for the purpose of protecting wild open land.

This is not an easy Moon to be born under, at least in our modern times. If there is not enough Nature in the life of those born under the Dryad's Moon, something in their emotional nature withers and sets up a great yearning, which they may try to fill with other Taurus coping mechanisms of food, sex, and apathy. The only cure is spending significant periods of time interacting with the natural world, ideally in an untamed state. While other Taurus Moons may be able to substitute symbolic forms of Nature to calm their inner spirit, the Dryad's Moon is the place where humanity touches most closely the Green World, and it is strongly suggested that Dryad's Moon people betake themselves to actual Nature whenever the yearning begins.

Dryad's Moon people often share the nonverbal quality of this Moon; touch is their real language, and they have trouble verbalizing emotions. Their intuition is strong but often silent; they have to learn to listen for it and not to worry if they can't explain "why" to others. Like Cancer Moons, they may be strongly moved by suffering, but unlike the weeping Cancerians they may keep it all private except for a single tear. They usually take well to solitude and probably need it frequently, unless there are serious lunar afflictions. They may tend to endure difficulties in their emotional environments rather than attempt to change them.

Quotes for the Dryad's Moon

My green thumb came only as a result of the mistakes I made while learning to see things from the plant's point of view.

H. FRED ALE

Some men go through a forest and see no firewood.

ENGLISH PROVERB

The clearest way to the Universe is through a forest wilderness.

JOHN MUIR

It is not so much for its beauty that the forest makes a claim upon men's hearts, as for that subtle something, that quality of air that emanates from old trees, that so wonderfully changes and renews a weary spirit.

ROBERT LOUIS STEVENSON

A woodland in full color is awesome as a forest fire, but a single tree is like a dancing flame to warm the heart.

HAL BORLAND

I am thought of all plants, says the Green Man
I am thought of all plants, says he . . .
It's off with my head, says the Green Man,
It's off with my head, says he . . .
I've paid for your pleasure, says the Green Man,
I've paid for your pleasure, says he.

WILLIAM ANDERSON

God is the experience of looking at a tree and saying, "Ah!"

JOSEPH CAMPBELL

Shall I not have intelligence with the Earth? Am I not partly leaves and vegetable mould myself?

HENRY DAVID THOREAU

I have always found thick woods a little intimidating, for they are so secret and enclosed. You may seem alone but you are not, for there are always eyes watching you. All the wildlife of the woods, the insects, birds, and animals, are well aware of your presence no matter how softly you may tread, and they follow your every move although you cannot see them.

THALASSA CRUSO

Remember me, try to remember.
I am that laughing man with eyes like leaves.
When you think that winter will never end,
I will come . . .
I'll come with daisies in my hands—
we'll dance among the sycamores
once more.

LAUREN RAINE

LITTLE BROTHER'S MOON
THE NEW MOON IN GEMINI

The New Moon in Gemini is the Little Brother's Moon. Gemini is linked to the third house, which rules siblings, and Gemini itself is the sign of the

Twins. Unlike the Cancerian children, whose primary relationship is with the Mother, or the Aquarian children, who must rebel against the Father, or the Dryad, whose relationship is with Nature itself, the Gemini child archetype is first and foremost a sibling, and specifically the male aspect of the sibling bond. He comes first because he matures a little slower than his twin sister, whom we will meet in the next phase.

The Little Brother is rambunctious, hyperactive, and mischievous, pulling his sister's pigtails and hiding dead frogs under the bedclothes. Think Dennis the Menace or Calvin of *Calvin and Hobbes*. He is curiosity incarnate, never happy until he's found out everything that catches his eye. Fortunately, he is easily distracted. He has a hundred ideas, approximately one every five minutes. Most of them are terrible, but he comes out with so many that by sheer volume he manages to come up with quite a few good ones inside of a day. He's brilliant, and he delights in his brilliance. He hates having to stop moving; for him, life should always go fast and never be boring.

He also lacks social skills and doesn't really understand that he lacks them. His twin sister has learned what behavior is appropriate and what's not, but he still doesn't think it's fair that he gets sent to his room after doing all the things that he was explicitly told not to do. Gemini is a mental rather than an emotional sign, and the Moon filtered through it can seem rather unfeeling at times. The Little Brother is terribly clever, but compassion is an unknown concept to him. He lives in the world of the mind, not the world of people. People are entertaining or annoying; a few he is beginning to care about, and he will happily help them out if it's a chance to prove his own cleverness and get petted for it. He'll do your homework when you're stumped and it's due in an hour, but he'll call you stupid for needing his help and expect you to ignore the insults, just like he does.

On the Little Brother's Moon we indulge our curiosity. We peek inside people's drawers, look under rotting leaves, glance into our files when the doctor leaves the room. There is a nervous energy about the Gemini New Moon that can affect already highly strung people to the point of hyperactivity or nervous shrieking. Concentration is difficult; perhaps this is a better time to go out with some (preferably wild and crazy) friends rather than work late at the office. It is possible to learn things—education is definitely part of the Little Brother's world—but academic work should focus on the interesting lecture part, not the boring homework part.

People born under the Little Brother's Moon have quick, active emotions and love to talk. Of course, they don't necessarily talk about their emotions; more often, they talk about things that get emotional reactions out of other people, for their own entertainment. Sometimes they can be real comedians; sometimes they just say nasty, witty things that cut deeply. Gemini's tool is the small knife, and a particularly nasty Little Brother (of either gender) can slice up your heart when he gets going. Since his curiosity has probably spurred him to find out a lot about you, he can use even more against you. Although he's pretty sure that he's hurting you, often he doesn't really realize how much; he just thinks he's being clever.

Men with the Little Brother's Moon are easy to pick out by their boyish good humor. They do tend to make a joke rather than talk about their feelings, and they can be surprisingly verbally cruel when they're angry or bored with you. Like the Little Brother, they may lack the social understanding to keep their mouths shut and not do clever but annoying things that make them enemies. If they lack social skills, they most certainly lack relationship skills. Charm and humor are their trusty tools, but they are often at a loss when those don't work.

Women with this Moon have the same problem that all the females with male-archetype Moons have. They don't respond emotionally like girls, and other girls often give them a lot of trouble for that. Some are outright tomboys and may hang out with the boys; others may wear dresses but don't think like their sisters, and often they have the same holes around social and relationship skills that their male counterparts struggle with. Since mischief-making boyish charm doesn't go over as well on a girl, they may have a hard time coping and may revert to a life of mistrust and intellectual sarcasm.

Quotes for the Little Brother's Moon

Nothing is interesting if you're not interested.

HELEN MACINNES

The important thing is not to stop questioning. Curiosity has its own reasons for existing. One cannot help but be in awe when he contemplates the mysteries of eternity, of life, of the marvelous structure of reality. It is enough if one tries merely to comprehend a little of this mystery every day. Never lose a holy curiosity.

ALBERT EINSTEIN

Most of the evils of life arise from man's being unable to sit still in a room.

BLAISE PASCAL

The cure for boredom is curiosity. There is no cure for curiosity.

ELLEN PARR

The best way to have a good idea is to have lots of ideas.

LINUS PAULING

To promise not to do a thing is the surest way in the world to make a body want to go and do that very thing.

MARK TWAIN

It is of the nature of ideas to be communicated: written, spoken, done. The idea is like grass, it craves light, likes crowds, thrives on crossbreeding, grows better for being stepped on.

URSULA K. LE GUIN

The highlight of my childhood was making my brother laugh so hard that food came out his nose.

GARRISON KEILLOR

There is a little boy inside the man who is my brother. Oh, how I hated that little boy. And how I love him too.

ANNA QUINDLEN

You send your child to the schoolmaster, but 'tis the schoolboys who educate him.

RALPH WALDO EMERSON

MOTHER'S DAUGHTER MOON
THE NEW MOON IN CANCER

The New Moon in Cancer starts very much like the beginning to the myth of Persephone and her mother Demeter. Persephone is the young girl who is undifferentiated from her mother; indeed, in that myth Father is not even present, and the mother-daughter dyad is tightly knit to the point where the daughter has not yet developed her own identity. She lives in a happy world, until the time when she has to learn to differentiate herself—and then everything blows up and goes to Hades, quite literally.

The same-sex dyad of mother-daughter is very hard for Persephone to break away from, and in order to do it she must rebel against her mother in a big way. Indeed, the rebellion would hardly have been possible at all without being swept away by Hades—some sources say against her will, some say otherwise. While sons also have to break away from their mothers—and that archetype will be explored next—there is a peculiar difficulty in being socially trained to the same role as one's (likely) first and primary caretaker, and then having to differentiate oneself against that tide. Since conflict with family members is always incredibly painful for people born under any phase of a Cancer Moon, one can imagine the trauma of being set up for this as a repeated karmic lesson. The Mother's Daughter must strike a balance between her need to be cared for in that same-sex dyad (Persephone spends half the year with her mother even after her marriage) and her desire to put energy into the rest of her life.

On the Mother's Daughter Moon we examine our relationships with others, especially those in which one person nurtures another. We also examine our early nurturing and our same-sex bonds. (If you don't have any, that's certainly something to examine.) We may also examine the issue of differentiating oneself from the same-sex parent, which usually happens in adolescence (as with Persephone) but sometimes waits until well into adulthood. This is a good time for those who need a rite of passage to plan or carry that out.

Those born under the Mother's Daughter Moon are deeply affected emotionally by the people they are close to, and they often have trouble discerning the emotional boundaries between themselves and those they love. (This is not the Pisces problem of having trouble defending boundaries against anyone, including store clerks and gas station attendants. Cancerians are quite able to slam their shell against people who are not Family or the Beloved.) Generally, they will defer for a long time, submerging resentment, until the blowup. Which, considering Cancerian levels of emotion (and considering that there is a good chance that they will be a double Cancer), will be significant.

While people's choice of lovers is a complicated thing and not dependent simply on the Moon (Venus and Mars and the entire contents of one's seventh house have a lot to say about it, too), I have noticed a few repeating trends with people born under this Moon. I've observed that heterosexual women born under the Mother's Daughter Moon tend to have male lovers with whom they share physical intimacy with but can't confide in, and they have close female friends with whom they share emotional intimacy, thus recreating that mother-daughter bond (although either woman could be "mother" or "daughter," and indeed they sometimes switch roles back and forth). This somehow echoes the myth of Persephone being carried off by Hades. The one exception I've seen was a woman who married a man who reminded her strongly of her mother. People I've met born under this Moon who were in a same-sex relationship, whether female or male, tended to end up in situations that looked very much like the tight parent-child relationship of Demeter and Persephone in many ways . . . one person nurturing the other, who was sometimes needier or "wounded."

When I've met heterosexual men with this Moon . . . well, one was a very "feminine" man with a caretaking wife, but the rest were protective, caretaking men with women who were younger or less emotionally mature. One such woman even called her partner "Daddy." It was as if the men identified with Demeter and married Persephone. In general, men with this Moon may well have been closer to their mothers than their fathers, but in a comradely way rather than a "Mommy's Little Boy" way, perhaps because the mothers themselves were not terribly maternal or feminine people.

Like those born on the Mother's Son Moon (Crescent Moon in

Cancer), childhood experiences are particularly "marking" for these people, and they may spend many years working out subtle nuances that might just brush by those less vulnerable to the emotions of their loved ones. Verbalizing their emotions is not easy for them, and loved ones should be patient with their need to verbally process in small portions.

Quotes for the Mother's Daughter Moon

If I nurture the newness while I have it, perhaps, I won't lose it—at least not for something less. And if I nurture what I keep, perhaps, I won't miss what I have lost.

JAN DENISE

We don't see things as they are, we see them as we are.

ANAÏS NIN

My mom is a neverending song in my heart of comfort, happiness, and being. I may sometimes forget the words but I always remember the tune.

GRAYCIE HARMON

Mother is the name for God in the lips and hearts of little children.

WILLIAM MAKEPEACE THACKERAY

A little girl, asked where her home was, replied, "where mother is."

KEITH L. BROOKS

Mothers and daughters are closest, when daughters become mothers.

AUTHOR UNKNOWN

He that would the daughter win, must with the mother first begin.

ENGLISH PROVERB

The woman who bore me is no longer alive, but I seem to be her daughter in increasingly profound ways.

JOHNNETTA BETSCH COLE

No river may return to its source, but all rivers must have a beginning.

NATIVE AMERICAN PROVERB

> The Demeter-Persephone narrative is complex. The myth hinges on the violence of young women's sexual initiation and the wrenching separation from the protective mother, social realities of many women's lives under male domination.
>
> ELINOR W. GADEN

SUN CHILD'S MOON
THE NEW MOON IN LEO

The figure of the Sun Child wends its way through folk mythology all over Europe. Sometimes a girl, sometimes a boy, these children are always creatures of smiling, radiant light. We see Lucia, the Kristkindl, the child born on the winter solstice. Their innocence is not shy; they rain their laughter down on everyone who stands dumbfounded and joyful before them. Their zest for life is contagious, and they love to be looked at, for what is the Sun when it is hidden? We see them also in many child movie stars throughout the ages, catching our eyes and hearts with their budding charisma.

That's where the New Moon begins for Leo. The Sun Child is the archetypal prodigy, amazingly creative and talented, good at everything, making people gasp and drop their jaws, and charming the pants off of them in the process. The Sun Child can sing with heart-wrenching sweetness or compose his own violin music or get them rolling with perfectly timed comedy performances. He loves the spotlight, and it loves him right back. It seems as if his job in the world is to spread light and joy, and he trustingly gives his whole soul to the audience. He models the instinctive and untrammeled process of creativity; he needs no Muse to pour it forth.

On the other hand, it's not hard at all for the Sun Child to get spoiled and turn into a demanding, insufferable brat or a little manipulator who tries to get everything he wants through charm. This is a trick also played by the Little Sister's Moon (Crescent Moon in Gemini), but where the Little Sister gets a rush from playing the adults, the Sun Child honestly believes that he is owed this worship. His attitude comes from a feeling of privilege, which is only added to by each round of applause. Someday that applause is going to be his downfall, but for now he has the unthinking sense of entitlement of the purely self-centered child. Self-expression, self-confidence, self-esteem—these things come easily for him, but empathy is not his strong suit. (You'll notice that all those hyphenated words start with *self.* Another might be self-absorbed, and not necessarily in the negative sense. The Sun Child can put out so much of himself only because he is so aware of that Self.)

During the Sun Child's Moon, we concentrate on creativity in any endeavor, and we try to reattain that childlike confidence of the era before we became conscious of the criticism of others. It's also a good time for people who are not performers—especially if it's because they are too afraid to perform—to tentatively get up on stage and try their best. If we can neither create nor perform, then the task is to focus on feeling joy and on spreading that joy to others by whatever means we have.

People born under this Moon contain the Sun Child's endless capacity for joy and self-confidence, and his trusting ability to express himself, even if they have trouble accessing that sunlight due to other factors. They have a well of creativity inside them, although because this is the Moon, the pump is best primed with their emotions rather than their intellect. They also have the ability to be almost naively arrogant and self-centered, and they may be emotionally clueless about such concepts as unselfish service and suffering for a greater good. "Why would anyone think that was worth the trouble?" they ask.

While many of the Leo Moons long for an audience and will get one however they can, people born under the Sun Child's Moon are inveterate scene-stealers, and they will get attention any way they can. While another Leo Moon phase will pout in the corner, the Sun Child will aggressively steal the center of attention by any means necessary. They are so engaging to watch that you'll forgive them for it . . . the first few times. Eventually it does get old. They may well need someone to sit them down and give them straight and honest talk about how one loses audiences, and for reasons other than a bad performance.

Quotes for the Sun Child's Moon

To him whose elastic and vigorous thought keeps pace with the Sun, the day is a perpetual morning.

HENRY DAVID THOREAU

Had I been present at the creation of the world, I would have proposed some improvements.

ALFONSO X

To love one's self is the beginning of a lifelong romance.

OSCAR WILDE

When I am grown to man's estate,
I shall be very proud and great,
And tell the other girls and boys
Not to meddle with my toys.

ROBERT LOUIS STEVENSON

Being a child prodigy is a curse because you've got all these terrible possibilities.

ITZHAK PERLMAN

The key question isn't "What fosters creativity?" but it is why in God's name isn't everyone creative? Where was the human potential lost? How was it crippled? I think therefore a good question might be not why do people create, but why do people *not* create or innovate? We have got to abandon that sense of amazement in the face of creativity, as if it were a miracle if anybody created anything.

ABRAHAM MASLOW

Thank goodness I was never sent to school; it would have rubbed off some of the originality.

BEATRIX POTTER

The moment when you first wake up in the morning is the most wonderful of the twenty-four hours. No matter how weary or dreary you may feel, you possess the certainty that, during the day that lies before you, absolutely anything may happen. And the fact that it practically always doesn't, matters not a jot. The possibility is always there.

MONICA BALDWIN

> All children are artists. The problem is how to remain an artist once he grows up.
>
> PABLO PICASSO
>
> Imagination is the beginning of creation. You imagine what you desire, you will what you imagine and at last you create what you will.
>
> GEORGE BERNARD SHAW

MAIDEN'S MOON
THE NEW MOON IN VIRGO

The Virgo Moon starts with the archetypal Maiden. There are many virgin goddesses in mythology, and all have different attributes, but their defining quality is the ability to be one-in-themselves, needing no other to complete them. This, by definition, implies a certain amount of reserve and distance, a preference for one's own company and personal space over getting involved with others. This is the heart of the matter, the reason why Virgo is called the Virgin. It has nothing to do with sex per se, but a great deal to do with intimacy. This is especially an issue with the Moon, without whose blessing no intimacy is going to happen.

We're all aware that some signs are harder than others for the Moon's energy to get through—Capricorn, Aquarius, and Gemini, for example. Virgo is also one of those. The Maiden puts up a wall of reserve and solitude, guarded by her concentration on the small details, and that's that. While later Virgo Moons must attend to the problem of all the other people in the world, the Maiden is still in her pristine state in which the other people hardly seem to matter. It means that she can bring fresh eyes to any new relationship, but it also means that she is very reluctant to get too close.

On the other hand, there is a great beauty in being at ease with solitude and aloneness. People do many stupid things to keep themselves from being lonely, and someone who rarely has to contend with that problem has freed up a lot of time to work, learn, and simply be. The Maiden comes to this from a different place than the tired elder; she has learned that if she sits still and contemplates, or works quietly and methodically, peace will come. She has not yet learned that this is not an acceptable or desirable or even comprehensible thing to most people. She simply is herself, without fuss or bother.

The fuss and bother comes when she is forced to leave her solitary walled garden. She becomes frazzled, trying to figure out what others want of her and how to do it. She is good at being obedient, but not so good at being "charming," and indeed she doesn't quite understand what it's all about. This means that she is ignored in favor of brighter lights, which makes her more likely to retreat back to her peaceful haven and lock the door behind her.

On the Maiden's Moon, we go alone to a beautiful place and work on being at ease without the presence of our fellow humans. How can we find solace in solitude rather than desperately trying to fill the room with other auras? It's a good time for solitary work, but an even better time for quietly observing beauty and "sitting with time," as my grandmother used to put it. If you work, let it be something repetitive that allows you to concentrate on a meditative space, turning the work into a background rhythm.

People born under the Maiden's Moon have a strong need for privacy and aloneness. The kind of invasive togetherness encouraged in modern romance and even family is grating on their nerves, and they may have done a good deal of hiding as children. They may have trouble living in shared space, and it takes them a while to get to know people well, and even longer for them to allow people to know them. If people leave their lives, they are sad, but move on more easily than many other Moons. After all, they always have themselves, and for them that is not a second choice. Even when they do let people into the garden and allow intimacy, conflict will tend to silently throw up the wall again. It's not that (like the Cancer Moons) they can't verbalize their feelings. It's that verbalizing them during conflict feels like a violation, forcing them to reveal guarded inner feelings in an environment that is less than safe, and they would rather remain silent and be thought cold. They may not be able to discuss things openly until the fire has died down, so those who deal with them should remember that.

Quotes for the Maiden's Moon

The ability to simplify means to eliminate the unnecessary so that the necessary may speak.

HANS HOFFMAN

I thank God I am endowed with such qualities that if I were turned out of the realm in my petticoat, I were able to live in any place in Christendom.

ELIZABETH I

Happiness is as a butterfly which when pursued is always beyond our grasp, but which if you will sit down quietly, may alight upon you.

NATHANIEL HAWTHORNE

Solitude is such a potential thing. We hear voices in solitude, we never hear in the hurry and turmoil of life; we receive counsels and comforts, we get under no other condition.

AMELIA E. BARR

Being solitary is being alone well: being alone luxuriously immersed in doings of your own choice, aware of the fullness of your won presence rather than of the absence of others.

ALICE KOLLER

The heart of a maiden is a dark forest.

RUSSIAN PROVERB

No padlocks, bolts or bars can secure a maiden better than the power of her own reserve.

DON MIGUEL DE CERVANTES

Solitude is not something you must hope for in the future. Rather, it is a deepening of the present, and unless you look for it in the present you will never find it.

THOMAS MERTON

I was passionate. I found something that I loved. I could be all alone in a big old skating rink and nobody could get near me and I didn't have to talk to anybody because of my shyness. It was great. I was in my fantasy world.

DOROTHY HAMILL

> A sheltered life can be a daring life as well, for all daring starts from within.
>
> EUDORA WELTY

WHITE KNIGHT'S MOON
THE NEW MOON IN LIBRA

The Libra New Moon dawns with the youth who is the romantic, idealistic White Knight. If anything, he is more saturated in ideals than the Aries Moon; Libra's Venus rulership keeps him looking for the perfection in things. The White Knight wants to do right, correct wrongs, and rescue people who then ought to be grateful. Fortunately for him (because people are so often ungrateful), he doesn't do it for the applause, but for the principle. He can be rather rigid in his principles, as he is young and sees everything as black and white. Gray areas aren't on his radar yet, and he largely ignores them or tries to sort them into one box of the other. Since this is a Moon sign, his principles will be ruled by his heart, even if he doesn't see that fact. They are not coldly calculated; they are deeply felt.

Libra is the sign of the Scales, and these continually swing back and forth, trying to find balance. On one side of those scales is the influence of Venus, and the Venus aspect of Libra wants things to be harmonious, loving, and beautiful; is invested in aesthetics; and doesn't like conflict. On the other side is the Air element, windy and contentious, that wants abstract justice at all costs. The force for justice doesn't care if things are pretty so long as they are fair. The problem is that beauty is often unfair, and justice is often unbeautiful. Only occasionally are the two balanced, and that means that Libra spends every day alternating between the two sides of the scale. Each phase of the Libra Moon story shows a different side of the scale. In the New Moon phase, the focus is on justice, but it will swing back soon enough. Unlike some of the other Sacred Children of the New Moon, the White Knight latches quickly onto the principle of Right and Wrong—at least as he is taught the distinction—and becomes heavily invested in it. He goes about correcting his chums when they are less than ethical or fair, and while some of them may roll their eyes when they see him coming, others will call on him when they are in trouble. While he dislikes conflict in and of itself, he will jump into a fight without hesitation when he sees the underdog being tormented.

The Venus side of the White Knight's nature manifests in love and romance. He comes to romantic love with permanent stars in his eyes. He can even put up with unrequited love so long as he can dream about the Beloved and do great deeds in her name. If he gets her, however, she will need to live up to his ideals of love, or she isn't going to work out, and he will fall for another possible True Love.

On the White Knight's Moon we reexamine our ideals. Are they still serviceable and proven? Do we have them as keepsakes of a more naive time, but don't really believe them? Do we actually hold to them? Have we been disillusioned, and how did that happen? Are we willing to fight for what we believe in, even if no one else believes it?

People born under the White Knight's Moon are keenly aware of injustice, and it infuriates them. They may well go around continually complaining of the unfairness of things, but if they try to do something about it, it will probably be a sincere attempt to get the unreasonable people to be reasonable, which may or may not work. They are peacemakers at heart and may start young as the family mediator whenever fights break out. As adults, they may get involved with law, politics, social work, or anything that tries to even the playing field of society.

Their idealism carries over into their love lives. They love to rescue people, but they often find to their dismay that the ones who most need rescuing are usually the least likely to live up to the White Knight's postrescuing relationship standards. They are terribly prone to crushes and following someone around with adoration in their eyes, and even when they become disillusioned by a failed relationship, they never really lose their faith in love. The next time, they tell themselves, will be the One . . . and often enough, it does happen. The partner of a White Knight's Moon person, even if he or she is the One, will have to remember to be not only tolerant but appreciative of the White Knight's need to fight injustice (even if some clothes or a reputation gets ruined) and rescue people in need (as long as the White Knight doesn't fall in love with every new rescue). Still, if that person is truly the One, he or she will automatically see the value in being loved by a White Knight.

Quotes for the White Knight's Moon

A true knight is fuller of bravery in the midst, than in the beginning of danger.

SIR PHILIP SIDNEY

Ideals are like stars; you will not succeed in touching them with your hands, but like the seafaring man on the desert of waters, you choose them as your guides, and following them you reach your destiny.

CARL SCHURZ

Apathy can be overcome by enthusiasm, and enthusiasm can only be aroused by two things: first, an ideal, which takes the imagination by storm, and second, a definite intelligible plan for carrying that ideal into practice.

ARNOLD TOYNBEE

Nothing ever perplexes an adversary so much as an appeal to his honor.

BENJAMIN DISRAELI

Those are my principles. If you don't like them I have others.

GROUCHO MARX

An idealist is one who, on noticing that a rose smells better than a cabbage, concludes that it will also make better soup.

H. L. MENCKEN

Idealism increases in direct proportion to one's distance from the problem.

JOHN GALSWORTHY

My specialty is being right when other people are wrong.

GEORGE BERNARD SHAW

Every form of addiction is bad, no matter whether the narcotic be alcohol or morphine or idealism.

CARL JUNG

> Idealism springs from deep feelings, but feelings are nothing without the formulated idea that keeps them whole.
>
> JACQUES BARZUN

RAGING MOON
THE NEW MOON IN SCORPIO

The New Moon in Scorpio is one of the most difficult of the New Moons to endure. We tend to think of the New Moon as a joyous place of beginnings, especially since by now readers will have noticed that the New Moon archetypes are all children and youths. Surely they should all be bright and wide-eyed and full of promise, unspoiled by the trouble that will come their way?

But not all childhoods are happy and comfortable, and for some life stories, the troubles start early, when the heart has not yet matured enough to understand and cope. Pluto ruling the emotional Moon lashes its sensitivity with stronger and more passionate feelings, and for the infant Scorpio those feelings include rage at the unfairness of his environment. The Plutonian energy of Scorpio is all about power, and for the children of this Moon, being powerless and unable to change your world is beyond frustrating, it is soul-wounding. To be dependent on the goodwill of others, especially flawed people who may make mistakes, is torture for a suspicious Scorpio heart that has not yet learned to trust. The Raging Child flings himself, again and again, at obstacles that he is not yet old enough to handle, and again and again he fails. Every time he is abandoned or ignored, he feels it keenly and screams with impotent anger. This is a Water sign, and Water sign Moons are not known for being realistic or for responding well to sensible ideas like "You'll have to wait and work for that; everyone else does." The fact that he cannot manifest his desires when he desires them is, to him, a deadly injustice, and one that he will not forget. It will color all his actions and beliefs when he is older, until he absorbs understanding at a level deeper than that of his feelings.

On the Raging Moon, we deal with our irrational desires and selfishness, all the parts of ourselves that we were taught to repress as early as kindergarten. It's important, during this process (which is probably best done alone and not inflicted on hapless others) to temporarily restrain the voice that says, "But that's irrational. That's wrong. That's not sensible. That's not the way it is. You need to be reasonable and think of others." That voice may well be right, but if we shove the unreasonable feelings into the basement and never look at them again except to shame them, they will still be down there years from now trying to saw through the floor and sabotage the rational voice that they have come to hate and resent. It's important to give space for those feelings to come out and be accepted as having some fair basis (if only from the point of view of the Raging Child), even if they can't be acted upon.

The Raging Moon is one of the best times for shadow work, that task of going down into one's psychological cellar and learning to love the most unacceptable part of oneself for what it is, with no attempts to change it. Healing is not the point here, although it may come about on its own in some way. Understanding is the point, deep understanding that leads to compassion in the end.

It's redundant to say that people born under the Raging Moon have anger management problems. If they've got an obvious monster of rage periodically leaning out of his prison window and flinging embarrassing things at passersby, it's actually easier to handle than if that monster is crouched down there in the subconscious, ignored and plotting, creating acts of self-injury and harm to relationships with others while the upper parts of the psyche are busily ignoring the damage and pretending that they have no idea where it came from. The heart of the Raging Moon person needs to be handled with care, but still held accountable for its actions. The more skills for self-awareness, self-propelled behavioral change, and handling crises in relationships they can learn, the more powerful and capable they will feel, and the less angry they'll be. Remember that with this Moon the anger is born out of helplessness and that teaching how to get around that helplessness in a way that is more effective than lashing out is the best possible medicine for the problem.

Quotes for the Raging Moon

The wailing of the newborn infant is mingled with the dirge for the dead.

LUCRETIUS

You fall out of your mother's womb, you crawl across open country under fire, and drop into your grave.

QUENTIN CRISP

In the beginning the Universe was created. This has made a lot of people very angry and been widely regarded as a bad move.

DOUGLAS ADAMS

It is surely a great calamity for a human being to have no obsessions.

ROBERT BLY

Seeing ourselves as others see us would probably confirm our worst suspicions about them.

FRANKLIN P. JONES

Every new beginning is another beginning's end.

SENECA

Anger is a killing thing: it kills the man who angers, for each rage leaves him less than he had been before—it takes something from him.

LOUIS L'AMOUR

Man is at bottom a wild, terrifying animal. We know him only in connection with the taming and training which is called civilization.

ARTHUR SCHOPENHAUER

Prejudice not being founded on reason cannot be removed by argument.

G. K. CHESTERTON

Being a Scorpio has a pretty steep learning curve.

JOSHUA TENPENNY

GYPSY'S MOON
THE NEW MOON IN SAGITTARIUS

The New Moon in Sagittarius kicks off with the Gypsy, wandering through life without a care in the world. (I don't necessarily see him as a Roma person; here the term is being used archetypally rather than ethnically.) In this phase Jupiter lends his luck to the lunar forces, and the Gypsy's Moon is one of the luckiest when it comes to lunar subjects. That luck can manifest as being born to positive parental figures, having an eternally childlike but not selfishly childish nature, or attracting miraculous circumstances that save the Gypsy from emotionally dangerous situations.

The Gypsy's job is to come into contact with as many different things as possible. He is in this life to gain experience after experience, and only later to attempt to put them together into a meaningful form. His greatest talent is his ability to go native—to put himself in the place of the people he meets who are exceedingly different from him, at least enough to be able to cheerfully accept their odd customs. When he's done sampling the interesting new sights, he hits the road again. There is no method to his travel; his destination is Wherever I End Up. He hates being tied down and likes to know that there's always a back door open in case he needs to run.

The ability to run is, of course, also the Gypsy's biggest temptation and—often—excuse. When things get hairy, it's so easy to slip out the back and leave the trouble behind, especially if this is the way you've been living your life. We mentioned how Jupiter will sometimes save him from emotionally uncomfortable situations? From the outside, that may look like luck, but what it really means is that he doesn't get many chances to learn how to cope . . . and then, on the inevitable day that Jupiter's luck isn't answering the phone, he doesn't know how to handle it. His only answer is to leave once again, often abandoning a great mess behind him. One of the drawbacks of this behavior is that he eventually runs out of friendly places to hole up where he hasn't created a mess. Other drawbacks are that he never really learns how to endure stress and never develops any discipline. The Gypsy manages to be the Eternal Youth better than the natives of almost any other Moon, but eventually he has to grow up and keep promises.

On the Gypsy's Moon, we go outside our homes and experience new cultures. Ideally, we should be experiencing cultures that stretch our ability to accept, that force us to confront ourselves and our own biases. It's best if a good deal of actual travel is involved, because the travel provides a buffer before and after for contemplation. Don't succumb to the temptation to just read about something—actually go breathe air you've never breathed, on ground you've never put your feet on.

To say that people born under the Gypsy's Moon have issues with commitment is an understatement. Learning to commit to any one thing long enough to get enough out of it will be a battle that will take them the rest of their lives. Of course, there may be a debate over the definition of *enough*—Gypsy's Moon people may make that *when it's done interesting me,* while others may want to point out that true understanding doesn't come from a shallow, entertainment-level study of the subject. Watching a docudrama is not the same as being there, and there are, unfortunately, ways of being there that limit the experience to little more than a docudrama about the hero. These folks need to learn about depth as well as breadth.

Breadth they'll have, though. They are consumingly curious and not easily shocked. They collect a varied dowry of odd friends and acquaintances in strange places, and are remarkably accepting of differences. People often instinctively like them, at least at first, and their perpetual wandering makes them interesting to talk to. They can get emotionally claustrophobic from promises, especially if those promises revolve around how they're supposed to act on their feelings. "But how can I possibly know how I'll feel next month?" they ask reasonably. "You can't expect me to plan for that!" Loved ones whose feeling natures are a little more security-based may not appreciate this viewpoint. Still, giving them an out makes it more likely that they will stay without panicking, and their deep need for change and interesting new scenery must be taken into account.

Quotes for the Gypsy's Moon

Tell me, what is it you plan to do with your one wild and precious life?

MARY OLIVER

All mankind is divided into three classes: those that are immovable, those that are movable, and those that move.

ARAB PROVERB

Do not worship, revere, or be afraid of any person, group, space, or reality. An investigator, an explorer, has no room for such baggage.

JOHN LILLY

As I watched the seagulls, I thought, "That's the road to take; find the absolute rhythm and follow it with absolute trust."

NIKOS KAZANTZAKIS

Hope is a good breakfast, but it is a bad supper.

FRANCIS BACON

He who chooses the beginning of a road chooses the place it leads to. It is the means that determine the end.

HARRY EMERSON FOSDICK

Remember what Bilbo used to say: "It's a dangerous business, Frodo, going out your door. You step onto the road, and if you don't keep your feet, there's no knowing where you might be swept off to."

J. R. R. TOLKIEN

A person often meets his destiny on the road he took to avoid it.

JEAN DE LA FONTAINE

There is something in October sets the gypsy blood astir,
We must rise and follow her;
When from every hill of flame,
She calls and calls each vagabond by name.

WILLIAM BLISS CARMAN

Endure pain, find joy, and make your own meaning, because the universe certainly isn't going to supply it. Always be a moving target. Live. Live. Live.

LOIS MCMASTER BUJOLD

FORGOTTEN ONE'S MOON
THE NEW MOON IN CAPRICORN

The Capricorn New Moon begins with the Forgotten One, the child who no one notices. He may be shy, or awkward, or slow to mature, but he is undervalued by most and underestimated by all. While other youths battle for the spotlight, he watches from the shadows.

Saturn-ruled Capricorn is one of the hardest Moon placements. Saturn puts huge restrictions on the Moon's natural expressiveness, creating deep repression and inarticulate sadness, perhaps even a chronically melancholic nature. He is not one of the beautiful people, and they let him know that in no uncertain terms. He watches the other youths pass him by, and where Cancer would retreat in sorrow and Scorpio would seethe in resentment, the Forgotten Child simply feels his heart go cold inside him. Better to repress those emotions than to deal with the pain of feeling them.

The Forgotten Child lives in a dark place, but it is a different sort of darkness than that of the Raging Child (New Moon in Scorpio). His darkness is silent, dulling, depressive. It threatens to rob him of many of the usual motivations for action: curiosity, wonder, enthusiasm, decisiveness, even rage. He can escape the shadowed closet of his despair only by disciplining himself and doggedly forcing his way toward a goal that is worth achieving. While one might assume that such a burden would simply press him down permanently—and this does happen sometimes—there is much more to him than limp sorrow. What no one sees about the Forgotten Child is that he nurses great ambitions under the quiet, withdrawn exterior. He watches as he is passed by, and he has choices: he can continue for the rest of his life under that same rock, or he can grit his teeth and decide to make something of his life, something that will impress the world in spite of its cruel indifference. The story that comes to mind is of the Greek god Hephaistus, who was flung off of Olympus to die, but survived and wrought a revenge on his rejecting family that forced them to take him back onto their holy mountain and count him as one of them.

On the Forgotten Moon, we remember our early experiences of being left out and the feelings and fantasies that we used to tide us over during that painful time. We look at the ambitions that may have been stunted or set aside because of early trauma, and we reexamine them. Perhaps we acknowledge that we have come to a place where they are no longer useful, or perhaps we realize that they might now actually be achievable. We also confront our feelings about the unfairness of the Universe, especially if we're the sorts who have been internally complaining about its unfairness for most of our lives, and seeing that unfairness as our reason for never getting ahead. It's a good time to sort out what we are really powerless against and what we might be able to change.

People born under the Forgotten Moon have difficulty expressing emotion; their feelings are instinctively repressed, sometimes to the point where they don't even know what they are. It takes a very safe place and a lot of work to get these people to a point of fully dealing with their Moon self, and then only if you can make them see the use of bothering with it. They tend to assume that people won't like them and that they will be betrayed by any emotional investment in a person. The first assumption is all too often painfully self-fulfilling, and as for the second one, they rarely give it a chance to be disproved.

Forgotten Moon people often had a childhood of neglect or of being ignored or worse. They may not have been a good "fit" for more outgoing parents and were given the clear message that they were not the child that was wanted. They may have been shy and thus overlooked or raised in a milieu of underprivilege so that it seemed like success was as far away as the sky. Inside, though, they want to succeed and be respected. More than being liked or even loved, they crave respect. They may let their melancholia overwhelm them and stay in their emotional cave forever, or they may turn to inappropriate and desperate ways to get respect . . . or they may grit their teeth, find a worthy goal on the horizon, and pull themselves out of their darkness by their own bootstraps.

Quotes for the Forgotten Moon

The fact of having been born is a bad augury for immortality.

GEORGE SANTAYANA

The mass of men lead lives of quiet desperation.

HENRY DAVID THOREAU

There was this weird little weaselly kid I went to elementary school with. If there was a fight he would hang around and if one or the other of the participants got pinned or held down this kid would leap in and kick him a few times and then run away shrieking as he was chased home. Anyone can get attention, but it doesn't ever really satisfy the need for respect.

GREG PARKINSON

Hermits have no peer pressure.

STEVEN WRIGHT

In talking, shyness and timidity distort the very meaning of my words. I don't pretend to know anybody well. People are like shadows to me and I am like a shadow.

GWEN JOHN

Many a man is praised for his reserve and so-called shyness when he is simply too proud to risk making a fool of himself.

J. B. PRIESTLEY

Shyness has a strange element of narcissism, a belief that how we look, how we perform, is truly important to other people.

ANDRE DUBUS

Everyone is shy; it is the inborn modesty that makes us able to live in harmony with other creatures and our fellows. Achievement comes not by denying shyness but, occasionally, by setting it aside and letting pride and perspiration come first.

KIRKPATRICK SALE

Treat people as if they were what they ought to be and you help them to become what they are capable of being.

JOHANN WOLFGANG VON GOETHE

Never underestimate the power of "I'll show *you!*"

BELLA KALDERA

FATHER'S SON MOON
THE NEW MOON IN AQUARIUS

The New Moon in Aquarius begins with the Father's Son. All the New Moon archetypes are children and youths, and there is a youthful quality to their emotional natures. The Father's Son is the Golden Boy, the Father's heir and hope. He has a strong feeling from his first days that he is special, and this impression is furthered by all the attention he gets. "This one could be President," says Father proudly, watching his son build towers out of blocks. The Father's Son is given special privileges and attention by the Father that the other children don't get . . . and may or may not want, depending on their natures. It's generally agreed, however, that the Father's Son is a genius, and eventually he learns to accept this idea. The Aquarius New Moon looks on the world with eyes that are fresh, enthusiastic, lively . . . and, since this is an Air sign Moon, he is very much out of touch with his own feelings. The lunar energies have a hard time manifesting through Aquarius. Those born under the New Moon in Aquarius can be fooled for a long time into thinking they don't actually feel the way that they do.

Aquarius is also the sign of one's relationship to the social group, of being the outsider or insider. While most astrological discussion about Aquarius stresses the sign's nonconformity, that's only half the story . . . and not usually the first half. Aquarius doesn't just rebel, it goes through cycles of belonging and rebellion. When the Moon and its subjective feelings are involved, the cycle is especially pronounced. Just as the Taurus Moon story is about moving toward and away from Nature, the Cancer Moon is about moving toward and away from Family, and the Pisces Moon is about moving toward and away from reality, the Aquarius Moon does that dance with society. One can't start with rebellion; one has to absorb the thesis fully before one can act on the antithesis. This is why the Father's Son, the starting point of the Aquarius New Moon, is happy and content—even desperate—to remain the Father's Son.

There are drawbacks to being the Father's Son, of course. First of all, to gain his approval, you have to do things his way. More often than not, this extends to everything you do. You have to value his rules and fit into society in a role that he finds appropriate. Deviation gets you reprimanded and possibly cast out of the limelight of his joy—and also of his help and aid, all the special privileges that the role bestows. As long as he is the Golden One, the genius, he's fine, but failure is not an option. Second, it's not uncommon for there to be more than one Father's Son in the family, and the Father may subtly encourage competition among them for his approval, or at least not discourage it. The son who loses is cast out of the role, temporarily or permanently. One is reminded of Zeus playing Apollo and Ares off of each other to ensure their rabid loyalty, using the crippled Hephaistus and the effeminate Dionysus as the bad examples.

Eventually, the Son is going to have to reevaluate the Father's rules and control, and it is going to hurt. Losing that approval is terribly wrenching and puts the Aquarius Moon in touch with all sorts of feelings that he would rather not have. It's easier, and so much more tempting, to just bury the dissatisfactions and keep going, ignoring the nagging feeling of constriction and injustice. But that can't last forever, and sooner or later the hard choice will have to be made: to follow one's own inspiration and lose everything or to stay and be ruled by the Father's ghost.

On the Father's Son Moon, we examine our feelings about our personal fathers (and our mothers if they were career-minded, externally oriented people who focused on the outside world instead of concentrating on the home base). We also look at our attitudes about the Fathers of society and how they decided things were to be, and how many of those values we've chosen to keep, or on the other hand have not yet rooted out even though we are discontented with them. We evaluate what we get for obeying social mores, and what we think is worth it.

It goes without saying that people born under the Father's Son Moon have father issues. Even the best father is going to have to put up with an eventual violent breakaway as sons separate themselves from Dad's shadow. If Dad isn't there, or refuses to play the Father, Father's Son Moon people may project their struggle onto the wider stage of society and its rules. Women with the Father's Son Moon may have had a dad who treated them like one of the boys or encouraged them to be brilliant at the expense of their femininity. While they had to follow the rules, unlike women born under the Father's Daughter Moon (Crescent Moon in Aquarius), they may never have felt second best and may hold all the sense of privilege of the men with this aspect.

Privilege is indeed a problem. On some level, people born under the Father's Son Moon have a strong need to feel that they are special geniuses and that the rules pertaining to "un-special" people oughtn't apply to them. They have a sense of intellectual entitlement that can interfere with their compassion for those trodden underfoot and that can also keep them chained to a desperate struggle for the few limited slots at the top of whatever totem pole they're worshiping, no matter what the personal cost. At least up there, geniuses get some slack. Sooner or later the Universe will give them humbling choices and show them where they aren't quite the geniuses they were told they were, so it's good for them to start considering it now.

Quotes for the Father's Son Moon

The surest way to corrupt a youth is to instruct him to hold in higher esteem those who think alike than those who think differently.

FRIEDRICH NIETZSCHE

It is impossible to begin to learn that which one thinks one already knows.

EPICTETUS

I seem to have been only like a boy playing on the seashore and diverting myself now and then finding a smoother pebble or a prettier shell than ordinary whilst the great ocean of truth lay all undiscovered before me.

ISAAC NEWTON

It behooves a father to be blameless if he expects his child to be.

HOMER

To bring up a child in the way he should go, travel that way yourself once in a while.

JOSH BILLINGS

If there is anything that we wish to change in the child, we should first examine it and see whether it is not something that could better be changed in ourselves.

CARL JUNG

When you teach your son, you teach your son's son.

THE TALMUD

The world . . . is only beginning to see that the wealth of a nation consists more than anything else in the number of superior men that it harbors. . . . Geniuses are ferments; and when they come together, as they have done in certain lands at certain times, the whole population seems to share in the higher energy which they awaken. The effects are incalculable and often not easy to trace in detail, but they are pervasive and momentous.

WILLIAM JAMES

What was silent in the father speaks in the son, and often I found in the son the unveiled secret of the father.

FRIEDRICH NIETZSCHE

To be nobody-but-myself in a world which is doing its best, night and day, to make you everybody else, means to fight the hardest battle which any human being can fight, and never stop fighting.

E. E. CUMMINGS

DREAMER'S MOON
THE NEW MOON IN PISCES

The New Moon in Pisces begins with the Dreamer, the child who walks around all the time in another world. We all know one of those. Perhaps we were one of those. To the Dreamer, reality is not fixed in one state. This is a reflection of Neptune's influence on the Moon. Neptune's influence on anything will blur its edges and prevent whoever is affected from figuring out where they end and anything else begins. Neptune likes the Moon, which is also watery, changeable, and heedless of boundaries.

When the two of them get together, the result is a story about people who will never quite know where all their edges are.

The Dreamer is especially naive about this process. He is barely able to figure out what's real and what's his imagination. The flowers and trees speak to him, and he takes this as normal. The animals might, any day, get up and start talking in English. Why not? When the leaves fall from the trees, he weeps for them. A bad dream can ruin his whole day, as he wonders if it is prophetic. Even if he knows it's not, he'll still jump at shadows.

To be blunt, his relationships with people are fraught with problems. He generally goes quietly along with what they want, and they think he's amiable enough until he opens his mouth. Then they generally decide that he's crazy. He's easily intimidated by people and easily pushed into doing things that he doesn't want to do. Most of them want him to listen to them, because there's something soothing about his nodding acceptance of whatever they spout, but they aren't willing to return the favor. He seems distant to them, off in his own world. The Dreamer himself has difficulty articulating his feelings in ways that can be understood. He writes poetry, but it's not anything that anyone can understand. He feels himself to be terribly misunderstood, and he's probably right.

As the Taurus story is characterized by movement toward and away from Nature, the Pisces story is about movement toward and away from Reality. The Dreamer lives half in and half out of the "real world" and finds it less desirable than his own internal reality. He seeks it out more and more, which impairs his relationships further. At the same time, he scatters behind him bits of inspiration that are picked up by others and made into fanciful art. He gets no credit, but doesn't much care. He was done with those things, anyway. He can always make more, if he wants to, which he probably won't. This is not a Moon for concrete planning; that will have to come from elsewhere in the chart. The Dreamer's emotional satisfaction comes from the castles in the sky, not necessarily requiring that they be made solid. After all, they are practically real for him.

On the Dreamer's Moon, we dream. It's a good time for reading and writing fantasy or for utopian politics. Spend all the time you can afford daydreaming. It's not a time for practical planning. Instead, write down what you wish was in the world without regard to pessimism or practicality. Picture the outcome in your head and meditate on it. Then wish hard, or clap your hands, or click your heels together three times, or whatever else comes to mind. Don't let the rational side of your mind get in the way. Whatever you do, have faith; the Pisces strength is believing.

People born under the Dreamer's Moon have emotional responses that are a little off from reality. They shed ideas all over the place, but unless there are practical aspects in the chart, they don't often do much with them. They do seem a little distant emotionally; they get that faraway look in their eyes, and their loved ones aren't sure that they're still on the same planet. Like all the Pisces Moons they have trouble drawing boundaries and keeping out from under the will of others, but Dreamer's Moon people are actually less vague about that than those born to other Pisces Moons. The Dreamers love their dreams too much to be routed away from them for too long by other people's desires, so they frequently slip through their fingers and go off to their own wondrous places. If their circumstances are bad, they will use dreaming as their coping mechanism and place to withdraw; like Walter Mitty, they can survive almost anything if they can spend enough time mentally chasing rainbows.

Quotes for the Dreamer's Moon

I shut my eyes in order to see.

PAUL GAUGUIN

We are the music makers, and we are the dreamers of dreams,
Wandering by lone sea breakers, and sitting by desolate streams,
World losers and world forsakers, for whom the pale moon gleams,
Yet we are the movers and shakers of the world forever, it seems.

ARTHUR WILLIAM O'SHAUGHNESSY

Sometimes you wake up. Sometimes the fall kills you. And sometimes, when you fall, you fly.

NEIL GAIMAN

Sleepers, awake. Sleep is separateness; the cave of solitude is the cave of dreams, the cave of the passive spectator. To be awake is to participate, carnally and not in fantasy, in the feast; the great communion.

N. O. BROWN

My life has no purpose, no direction, no aim, no meaning, and yet I'm happy. I can't figure it out. What am I doing right?

CHARLES SCHULTZ

The man who listens to Reason is lost; Reason enslaves all whose minds are not strong enough to master her.

GEORGE BERNARD SHAW

The man who has no inner life is the slave of his surroundings.

HENRI FRÉDÉRIC AMIEL

A dreamer is one who can only find his way by moonlight, and his punishment is that he sees the dawn before the rest of the world.

OSCAR WILDE

The dream was always running ahead of me. To catch up, to live for a moment in unison with it, that was the miracle.

ANAÏS NIN

If you are a dreamer, a wisher, a liar, a hoper, a pray-er, a magic-bean-buyer, if you're a pretender, come sit by my fire, for we have some flax-golden tales to spin.

SHEL SILVERSTEIN

2
CALL TO ACTION
THE CRESCENT MOON

Trust only movement. Life happens at the level of events, not of words.
Trust movement.

ALFRED ADLER

THE CRESCENT PHASE starts when the Moon semisquares the Sun at a separating angle of 45 degrees and lasts to 89 degrees past the Sun. The narrow Crescent Moon appears in the sky, and we go from a place of not-moving to one of motion. This is the time of the first step, and generally we go in the direction that we were pointed at during the New Moon, for good or ill. The time for changing direction is not yet here; we now hasten along the path in front of us, happy in our ability to be moving at last. The archetypes of these Moons have grown out of the New Moons; they are the logical continuation of those energies, learning to do and create as well as be. The Crescent Moon contains the Sun-Moon sextile angle; many people born under this phase will have that angle in their chart, and even if they don't, that friendly sextile energy shines through.

Where the New Moon archetypes simply felt, during the Crescent Moon the issue of values comes in to bother the Eden of simple wordless experiencing. What is this good for? Where can I go with this? How can it be done right or wrong? What's the possible end result? This phase often reminds me of the Two of Wands in the Rider-Waite Tarot deck, with the man watching his ships go out to sea, unsure of whether they will ever come back, but calculating the future odds of success in his head. The Crescent Moon is where we take risks that we've actually thought about, instead of ones that are pure impulse.

People born under the Crescent Moon want to act on their emotions, regardless of sign. While the New Moon people may remain still while experiencing their emotions, the Crescent Moon people are prodded into motion by them. Since these Moon archetypes are still young and inexperienced, that motion may feel as if it is beyond their ability to control or alter. They are propelled, driven, thrown into the currents of life, entirely through their feelings. One of their biggest lessons will be to learn to step on the brake—to realize a split second before their emotions trigger them to act, judge whether the action is in anyone's best interest, and squash it if necessary. The action they will do most instinctively will reflect the sign of their Moon: Arians will throw a fit, Aquarians will become verbally defensive, Cancerians will become insecure and weep (or want to), Pisceans will do something to reaffirm their inner fantasy, and Sagittarians will exit stage left.

The Crescent Moon is always the moment of action before the fall, and just as we can see the roots of the New Moon in the actions of the Crescent Moon, we can also see the shadow of the coming Quarter Moon, preparing to betray those roots. If the New Moon is primal innocence, the Crescent is the desperate attempt to hang onto that innocence. It is also a time of transition, perhaps unwitting, and people born under this Moon may feel all their lives as if Something Bigger Is Coming.

TORCH-BEARER'S MOON
THE CRESCENT MOON IN ARIES

During the Crescent phase of the Aries Moon story, the Infant grows into a fiery, enthusiastic Youth, full of ideals and vigor. She is the runner with eyes on the goal, single-minded and intense, but not in a grim way. She is the one who laughs while she runs, or fights, or struggles. No other Moon has quite the fire and verve of this one, not to mention the faith in her ability to Do. I picture the Grecian-style torch-bearer racing down the path with this archetype, and certainly that purity of focus is one of her resources.

The flip side of all that enthusiasm, however—and the first great drawback of the Torch-Bearer—is that the fire that burns here is young and somewhat unsteady, and it can be diverted by a new enthusiasm.

The Torch-Bearer isn't much for doing three things at once, and she tends to throw herself into something until the spark is gone, and then finds something else to throw herself into. She has not yet learned persistence and discipline in effort, nor the art of saving one's strength for the long term.

The watchword for this Aries Crescent Moon is *energy*. The Torch-Bearer has a huge amount of energy to put into her goals, and the goals must be idealistic. The ideals of the Infant Moon have solidified and intensified during this Moon; she now knows what she is racing for, but any one thing's worthiness to be her goal is dependent on it living up to her internal standards, and they are pretty high. Some might even say that they are too high, which is a recipe for failure—not in achieving the goal, but in finding it worthy once it has been achieved, or when one is halfway down the road.

This is the other great drawback of this Moon: that when idealism solidifies, it can become rigid in favor of perfection. Each goal is given a cursory once-over—patience is not the Aries strong suit—and if it looks shiny enough, all the considerable energy of the Crescent Moon is thrown into it. However, should it reveal any imperfections (including human ones) during the run, the Torch-Bearer may throw a fit and demand that things be changed, or perhaps she will swerve off and find another, less tarnished goal to work on. There is something naive about this Moon and her difficulty with imperfections and failings.

She also has difficulty with her own failings, and she refuses to acknowledge either the rocks in the road or the tenderness of her feet, until there is a stumble—and then the entire goal may be at fault and abandoned as unsatisfactory. This is why the Torch-Bearer may provide the enthusiasm but perhaps should not be in charge of the project. However, should the goal keep her interest, there is no one with greater access to that pure faith in one's ability.

During the Torch-Bearer's Moon, we focus on our goals and on our ideals. They may need to be polished up after being tarnished by the world. It's a good time to ask, "What do I really still believe in?" and if there isn't a good answer, it's time to go looking. It's a good starting-gate time for a project, but it's necessary to look ahead to the Moon that directly follows the Moon on which you begin, be that Crescent or Waxing Quarter. Will the energy of this next Moon directly conflict with the fiery ideals of this one? Like it or not, the Crescent leads to the Waxing Quarter, but one can hedge one's bets and choose a Crescent period when the sign transitions to Taurus before the Moon transitions to Waxing Quarter. Buffering the path with the Gardener (Crescent Moon in Taurus) is better for a project than leaping straight to the Woodcutter (Waxing Quarter Moon in Taurus), which is a betraying phase with an alien sign.

People with the Torch-Bearer's Moon have an emotionally youthful quality well into their old age, for better or for worse. They can't help wanting a pure goal, and they can't help being let down when the purity turns out to be tainted, like everything else. They also have tons of emotional energy that needs to go somewhere, into some cause, or it will explode outward in fits over life's little imperfections. While Aries is a cardinal sign (meaning that it is concerned with leadership), people with the Moon here are not ready to lead, and they honestly want to follow someone else . . . as long as that person is honorable and charismatic, with rules that are appealing enough to live up to the Aries Moon's inner standards. Finding the right leader may be as important as finding the right lover.

Quotes for the Torch–Bearer's Moon

We cannot hold a torch to light another's path without brightening our own.

BEN SWEETLAND

You still stand watch, O human star, burning without a flicker, perfect flame, bright and resourceful spirit. Each of your rays a great idea—O torch which passes from hand to hand, from age to age, world without end.

KAREL CAPEK

The man who strikes first admits that his ideas have given out.

CHINESE PROVERB

Obstacles are those frightful things you see when you take your eyes off the goal.

HANNAH MORE

Whenever the true objects of action appear, they are to be heartily sought. Enthusiasm is the height of man; it is the passing from the human to the divine.

RALPH WALDO EMERSON

The Greeks have given us one of the most beautiful words of our language, the word "enthusiasm"—a God within. The grandeur of the acts of men are measured by the inspiration from which they spring. Happy is he who bears a God within.

LOUIS PASTEUR

Enthusiasm is the element of success in every thing. It is the light that leads, and the strength that lifts men on and up in the great struggles of scientific pursuits and of professional labor. It robs endurance of difficulty, and makes a pleasure of duty.

BISHOP DOANE

The most enthusiastic man in a cause is rarely chosen as a leader.

ARTHUR HELPS

A life without cause is a life without effect.

DILDANO, FROM BARBARELLA

GARDENER'S MOON
THE CRESCENT MOON IN TAURUS

In the second part of the lunar Taurus story, the Dryad learns about the cycle of seed and growth in a practical rather than an instinctual way. She already knows in her soul that there is root and branch and seed again, but as the Gardener she learns the magic of putting a seed in the soil where she wants it to grow, rather than leaving it to chance. It's the wonder of making an impact on the world instead of merely experiencing it. In the Gardener's Moon, we learn that we can change the world with our hands.

She also shifts from seeing all land as merely land, the ground beneath one's feet that all walk on, and wanting to have a small piece of land that is hers and hers alone. After all, when you plant a garden, you don't want someone walking on it and ruining your hard work, crushing your delicate seedlings. You learn to guard your property, to fence it, to protect it. You learn, in other words, the beginnings of ownership. The Gardener builds the first fence and makes the transition from wild to tame.

It's an easy thing to overlook: when you plant a garden, you lose the wilderness. Weeds must be uprooted, even if in the Dryad's phase those weeds were no worse than any other plant. Trees must be cleared and the soil turned over. Human beings have a deep need to improve their environments so as to improve their chances, and we also tend to look upon the chaos of untrammeled Nature and compare it unfavorably with the ordered work of our hands. Taurus is the keeper of this transition, this prejudice . . . and yet the Gardener still truly loves the Earth; she delights in working it and takes joy in the tender green sprouts that leap upward from the soil. It is a different sort of love than the emotion felt when you see the first green of wild Nature. It is closer, more intimate, more possessive. The Gardener says, "*My* garden, because it is *my* work," and Taurus learns what it means to possess.

She also learns the highest quality of Taurus: patience. A garden does not bloom in a day, and sometimes you may have to wait years for certain fruits. People with a Taurus Moon already have the capacity for great patience, but during the Dryad's Moon that virtue may lie partially dormant. The Gardener's Moon helps it to blossom and become the best tool in their kit.

During the Gardener's Moon, we learn about the intimacy of small-scale work and cultivation. It doesn't matter what we make or work at, so long as it is done with love for the task—actual gardening, or cleaning the house, or caring for animals or children, or beautifying a public place. We experience the possessiveness we feel about the work, about the area we have altered, about the results. We experience boundary-setting as a way to protect our labor—"Don't track that mud in here!"—and we learn the pain of having others trample over those boundaries, unappreciative of all we've done.

If we are self-aware, we also feel a little remorseful about ruining what came before, especially if it was part of Nature. If we fully experience the dark side of this Moon, we may also make space—and boundaries—to protect that wilderness from us and our work. Fences, after all, have two sides. All creation is violation, in its own way, and this is a time for us to struggle with that paradox.

People born under the Gardener's Moon have a strong need to create peaceful domestic enclosures for themselves (and often to own land). This need is different from that of some people with Cancer Moons, who crave land and home for the family it represents; Gardener's Moon people want that peaceful enclosure for themselves, rather than for a family. Ideally it should be a place to work uninterrupted. Some may graciously extend it to beloved others; some may resent the interruptions of boundary-jumpers. They may need to guard against the tendency to be too self-enclosed or to react too angrily to the clumsy, unwitting feet of loved ones. Again, patience is the key, and one of the great life lessons for the Taurus Crescent Moon is learning of how little importance immediate gratification actually is.

Work is one of the most important things in the lives of people born under this Moon, but it can't be just any work. These folks literally wither without work that isn't personally meaningful. They should take more care choosing a career than, perhaps, even choosing a mate. If they do have the work they love, they may bring it home often enough that the boundaries blur, or they may even choose to work from home in their enclosed garden space.

Quotes for the Gardener's Moon

We don't consider manual work a curse, or a bitter necessity, nor even as a means of making a living. We consider it a high human function, a basis for human life, the most dignified thing in the life of the human being, and which ought to be free and creative. Men ought to be proud of it.

DAVID BEN-GURION

Be aware of wonder. Remember the little seed in the Styrofoam cup: the roots go down and the plant goes up and nobody really knows how or why, *but we are all like that.*

ROBERT FULGHUM

Of all the wonderful things in the wonderful universe of God, nothing seems to me more surprising than the planting of a seed in the blank earth and the result thereof.

JULIE MOIR MESSERVY

No man but feels more of a man in the world if he have but a bit of ground that he can call his own. However small it is on the surface, it is four thousand miles deep; and that is a very handsome property.

CHARLES DUDLEY WARNER

Show me your garden and I shall tell you what you are.

ALFRED AUSTIN

A garden is evidence of faith. It links us with all the misty figures of the past who also planted and were nourished by the fruits of their planting.

GLADYS TABER

All through the long winter, I dream of my garden. On the first day of spring, I dig my fingers deep into the soft earth. I can feel its energy, and my spirits soar.

HELEN HAYES

Gardening is civil and social, but it wants the vigor and freedom of the forest and the outlaw.

HENRY DAVID THOREAU

To forget how to dig the earth and to tend the soil is to forget ourselves.

MAHATMA GANDHI

Our England is a garden, and such gardens are not made
By singing: "Oh, how beautiful!" and sitting in the shade.

RUDYARD KIPLING

LITTLE SISTER'S MOON
THE CRESCENT MOON IN GEMINI

On the Gemini Crescent Moon, we meet the other twin—the Little Sister. She is every bit as mischievous, bright, sarcastic, and exuberant as the Little Brother, and she is his partner in crime—sometimes aiding and abetting, sometimes masterminding. However, she is a little more socially mature than he is, and has gotten more of a handle on her hyperactive impulses. Rather than climbing the walls or shooting rubber bands at people, she is more likely to try to win the world's record for jumping rope while singing dirty songs. The Crescent Moon takes the active, communicative Gemini urges that were mostly undirected at the New Moon and funnels them into effective action. The Little Sister gets more things done than the Little Brother, although she pays for that effectiveness by being a little less carefree.

Mostly, the mission of the Little Sister is to Work the Grownups. She has figured out the art of saying things a certain way in order to get what she wants, and she plays it for all it's worth. She's learned charm, and ingenuity, and the power of advertising. She watches the grownups carefully, observing their every frown and twitch of eyebrow, and tailors her spiel accordingly. Right now it's all a game, a test of her skill, a honing of her talents. It's not Leo's desperation for attention or Cancer's desperation to please the parent; it's just fun and games and seeing how far she can go with it.

While she does play with manipulation, the Little Sister is loyal and helpful when necessary. She may scold and cajole and express her disgust with stupidity, but when the chips are down she will come through and pull out of trouble siblings and friends who have gotten themselves stuck with their own ingenuity. She shares with the Little Brother a nonjudgmental ability to shrug off the moral mistakes of those she cares about, and she does not let their errors kill her affection for them. "We are all sinners," the Twins seem to say, and they laugh and move on. She is less nonjudgmental about those who have done something idiotic, but even then she will roll her eyes and help, and it will be forgotten in a few days. The sibling relationship—closer than friends, more equal than parents—rules her model of how things should be, and she casts her best friends as sisters and brothers.

On the Little Sister's Moon we examine our communication patterns as well as our nonverbal signals that are out-and-out advertising, messages we send in order to seem better (or, in some cases, worse) than we really are. How do we manipulate people's perceptions of us? If you have trouble with this, think about your behavior on a first date or a job interview. It's also a good time to look at our own siblings or at people with whom we have sibling-type relationships, and examine those dynamics. How much are we thrilled when they are like us and disappointed when they are not? How often is our banter a cover-up for unspoken affection or resentment?

People born under the Little Sister's Moon love to use their charm to get their way, but they are both more goal-oriented about it than the Little Brother and more at ease with letting it go should it fail. They are a little more emotionally mature than the Little Brothers, and their mischief is less vulgar and slapsticky, but their sarcastic tongues can be even worse, because they see people and their faults more clearly. Both of the siblings have a distaste for authority, but while the Little Brother people will try to undermine it openly through minor acts of rebellion, the Little Sister people will attempt to undermine it subtly, by arranging things so that the authority looks bad and loses social support. No one can set you up to look bad quite so well as someone born under this Moon.

The ideal partner relationship for them often has a brotherly or sisterly cast to it. That doesn't preclude sexual passion, but it needs to have the kind of "my sibling, right or wrong" loyalty to it, and a good deal of playfulness and intellectual stimulation. They will overlook all manner of faults if you provide them with interesting conversation, humor, and the loyalty of a brother or sister, and if you try not to take anything too seriously.

Quotes for the Little Sister's Moon

Sanely applied advertising could remake the world.

STUART CHASE

You know what charm is: a way of getting the answer yes without having asked any clear question.

ALBERT CAMUS

Our siblings push buttons that cast us in roles we felt sure we had let go of long ago—the baby, the peacekeeper, the caretaker, the avoider. . . . It doesn't seem to matter how much time has elapsed or how far we've traveled.

JANE MERSKY LEDER

Having a sister is like having a best friend you can't get rid of. You know whatever you do, they'll still be there.

AMY LI

Sisters don't need words. They have perfected a language of snarls and smiles and frowns and winks—expressions of shocked surprise and incredulity and disbelief. Sniffs and snorts and gasps and sighs—that can undermine any tale you're telling. . . . Sisters annoy, interfere, criticize. Indulge in monumental sulks, in huffs, in snide remarks. Borrow. Break. Monopolize the bathroom. Are always underfoot. But if catastrophe should strike, sisters are there. Defending you against all comers.

PAM BROWN

I don't believe an accident of birth makes people sisters or brothers. It makes them siblings, gives them mutuality of parentage. Sisterhood and brotherhood is a condition people have to work at.

MAYA ANGELOU

Of two sisters one is always the watcher, one the dancer.

LOUISE GLÜCK

All charming people, I fancy, are spoiled. It is the secret of their attraction.

OSCAR WILDE

The most important persuasion tool you have in your entire arsenal is integrity.

ZIG ZIGLAR

The universe, they said, depended for its operation on the balance of four forces which they identified as charm, persuasion, uncertainty and bloody-mindedness.

TERRY PRATCHETT

MOTHER'S SON MOON
THE CRESCENT MOON IN CANCER

After the Mother's Daughter comes the Mother's Son. The Crescent Moon in Cancer reveals itself to be the mother's male child, which is something of a different relationship than the mother-daughter dyad. The Mother's Son lives with the knowledge that he is different from the mother and that sooner or later that difference will vastly interfere with their relationship. Where the mother says unconsciously to her girl child, "You are like me—keep following my path and you'll stay in this bond where we are one," the boy child's message is often "You are not like me, and if you want to stay in this bond where we are one, you must work against your own nature." While that paradoxically makes it easier to rebel and differentiate oneself—the Son, after all, is a boy and will grow up to be a man—the rebellion is no easier just because it can be glimpsed sooner.

I remember watching the relationship dynamics between a young, inexperienced single mother who was briefly staying at our house and her three-year-old son. She was the sort who had trouble defending her boundaries, and I could tell that they had been violated (especially her physical ones) by men, many times, setting up a certain physical defensiveness. Her son was robust, physical, roughly affectionate, the kind of boy who wants to wrestle and use people as jungle gyms, and then get a great deal of cuddling when he becomes tired. He repeatedly tried, in the persistent and whiny way that three-year-olds have, to get physical interaction with her, and she would push him away, saying, "You have to learn to respect my space!" More than once, she snarled in disgust, "You're such a boy!" My stomach twisted when I heard that, because I knew that she had given him (and would continue to give him) the choice of either being "good" or being "a boy." Being as he was actually a male child, I knew with sickening certainty where that would go.

The Mother's Son wants the mother's love and attention just as the Mother's Daughter does, and they are both tied to a desire for love and nurturing and a safe home. He also has a little more courage than she does—not that he feels the removal of parental approval any less keenly, but he is more likely to retreat and brood than to weep copiously. He can bear being out of the approving parental spotlight just a little longer than the Daughter can, and this is a strength that he will later harness to make his transition to adulthood, which will come earlier and be more certain than hers.

On the Mother's Son Moon, we continue to examine our early nurturing relationships, but this time we need to pay closer attention to what didn't work out, especially in the area of "fit." If we didn't "fit" with members of our family for some reason, we probably got the message that parts of our basic natures were unacceptable and should be repressed or changed. These are the parts that we need to drag out, look at, and perhaps give some of the approval that they didn't get before. Just like the Mother's Son, who has to try not to be so much of a "boy" in order to please his mother, how did we change ourselves to please the people we were dependent on?

People born under the Mother's Son Moon also, like Mother's Daughter people, have boundary issues and may need a catharsis to break away from their parents. They struggle with giving themselves permission both to be who they are and to be loved—not just accepted or tolerated or respected; that's an Aquarius problem—but deeply loved and lovable. The Aquarius Moon says, "They don't accept me!" The Cancer Moon says, "They don't love me!" Since love is a very subjective thing, it is by definition harder to win than mere acceptance.

Men born under the Mother's Son Moon are going to have "mother issues"; if they are wise, they will deal with them at a young adult age and not inflict them on every partner they have, of any gender, forevermore. Women born under this Moon may well have a mother who differs from them in some intrinsic way—perhaps one of them was more feminine or more masculine, or perhaps the daughter was an older child who took on the "son's" role if there was no appropriate son. Either way, the "mother issues" they bring to future relationships will be about being rejected for difference, not breaking away from sameness.

Quotes for the Mother's Son Moon

He is a poor son whose sonship does not make him desire to serve all men's mothers.

HARRY EMERSON FOSDICK

The precursor of the mirror is the mother's face.

D. W. WINNICOTT

The desolation and terror of, for the first time, realizing that the mother can lose you, or you her, and your own abysmal loneliness and helplessness without her.

FRANCIS THOMPSON

You don't really understand human nature unless you know why a child on a merry-go-round will wave at his parents every time around—and why his parents will always wave back.

WILLIAM D. TAMMEUS

My mother protected me from the world and my father threatened me with it.

QUENTIN CRISP

Conscience is less an inner voice than the memory of a mother's glance.

ROBERT BRAULT

Traditionalists are pessimists about the future and optimists about the past.

LEWIS MUMFORD

They that can give up essential liberty to obtain a little temporary safety deserve neither liberty nor safety.

BENJAMIN FRANKLIN

We've begun to raise daughters more like sons, but few have the courage to raise our sons more like our daughters.

GLORIA STEINEM

It is no surprise to me that hardly anyone tells the truth about how they feel. The smart ones keep themselves to themselves for good reason. Why would you want to tell anyone anything that's dear to you? Even when you like them and want nothing more than to be closer than close to them? It's so painful to be next to someone you feel strongly about and know you can't say the things you want to.

HENRY ROLLINS

CLOWN'S MOON
THE CRESCENT MOON IN LEO

On the Crescent Moon, the Leo Sun Child realizes that what people want, even more than to be charmed, is to be made to laugh. While the Clown still looks for approval—after all, what would be the point if you didn't get some applause—he has learned to value something else as well. He has learned that if you just smile and charm people, they smile back, but then they go on with their lives . . . whereas if you engage them with a joke that hits home, and make them laugh uncontrollably, they will come back for more. You don't have to chase them; they'll pay to see you. People with this Leo Moon learn that you don't have to steal a spotlight; if you make people happy, they'll show up to see you. The Clown moves beyond his own needs to those of others; people count on him to make them laugh, and he now has a new responsibility. He learns a new virtue: pride in making a positive impact on people.

However, no one likes sad clowns, unless they're deliberately calling attention to their staged misery so that you can laugh at it. Clowns can get stuck in their role to the point where they don't feel that they can be serious with anyone or that they will be taken seriously. When they are despondent, people are uncomfortable. It's easy to get stuck in a role when people are now depending on that role for their joy. After all, you can't let them down, can't bum them out with your baggage! Clowns want desperately not to disappoint them; their disapproval not only means that Clowns won't get their fix, but that they are failures as well. Unlike Actors

(Waxing Quarter Moon in Leo), Clowns are not polished performers. While they are good at comedy, their big charm is in their sincerity, and if all they're feeling is down, that will show through and ruin their act.

There's a legend about a famous French clown from the early days of psychotherapy. The way it goes is that an early French therapist received a new client who said that he was only going to be in town for a few days, but he was so sad and full of despair that he was worried about being able to function for his job. The therapist suggested that since he would only be briefly in Paris, he should go see the performance of the famous French clown tomorrow night, as that would lift his spirits. The client informed him, weeping, that he *was* that clown.

On the Clown's Moon we try not to take ourselves too seriously. It's a good time to watch funny movies, kid with each other, do silly things where people can see them, or even get together with friends to talk about something serious in a humorous way. It's also a good time to think about your relationship with humor: Are you still the class clown, or are you the awkward, serious one who didn't know how to have fun and was mocked by the funnier kids? One man's good time can be another man's horror if there's no sensitivity in it.

People born under the Clown's Moon were probably a class clown in school, unless there were other factors that prevented them from doing it . . . in which case they probably secretly wanted to be the class clown, even if they felt that they couldn't. They have a great sense of humor, perhaps even a certain wackiness. Like the Sun Child, they thrive on attention, even to the point of desperation when they don't get it, but the mature ones do honestly want to make people laugh and feel better, because they've learned that they feel better when the people around them are happy.

Humor is their defense mechanism, which can be a problem when their loved ones want to talk about something serious and sensitive. Continually foisting it off with a joke can make people not want to confide in them. They may end up as the friend who you kid around with, but don't call when you're upset. Like performing clowns, people born under the Clown's Moon need to be able to take off their makeup and engage in all aspects of life and emotion.

Quotes for the Clown's Moon

I think of myself as an intelligent, sensitive human being with the soul of a clown which always forces me to blow it at the most important moments.

JIM MORRISON

If there are twelve clowns in a ring, you can jump in the middle and start reciting Shakespeare, but to the audience you'll just be the thirteenth clown.

ADAM WALINSKY

A man one on one is your equal and is himself; that same man within a group aims to be the king or the clown.

ANONYMOUS

There are two kinds of egotists: Those who admit it, and the rest of us.

LAURENCE J. PETER

Imagination was given to man to compensate him for what he is not; a sense of humor to console him for what he is.

SIR FRANCIS BACON

The most protean aspect of comedy is its potentiality for transcending itself, for responding to the conditions of tragedy by laughing in the darkness.

HARRY LEVIN

Clown and guru are a single identity: the satiric and sublime side of the same higher vision of life.

THEODORE ROZAK

I remember in the circus that the clown was the prince, the high prince. I always thought that the high prince was the lion or the magician, but the clown is the most important.

ROBERTO BENIGNI

You can turn painful situations around through laughter. If you can find humor in anything, even poverty, you can survive it.

BILL COSBY

> Comedy is an escape, not from truth but from despair; a narrow escape into faith.
>
> CHRISTOPHER FRY

APPRENTICE'S MOON
THE CRESCENT MOON IN VIRGO

On the Virgo Crescent Moon, the Maiden has guardedly come out of her walled garden, not because she craves human contact, but because she wants to do something interesting and useful. Virgo is ruled by Mercury, and Virgo Moons do need some sort of stimulation. The Crescent Moon is also a time of action, of wanting to take off and do something besides merely *be*. She apprentices herself to the master of a skill and sets herself to learn. This is her first introduction to working hard, and she finds that she is good at it and enjoys it. After the solitary garden, the hum and bang of the workshop is unfamiliar, but she takes comfort in the noise. They mean that tasks are getting done, and things are being created.

The Apprentice's attention to detail stands her in good stead, and she develops discipline and a work ethic. She works the extra hour when the order needs to go out, even though she may be tired and bored. She learns how to form proper habits; how to organize things, information, and people; and how to ensure good workmanship on the job. She also learns about taking pride in a job well done. Unlike the Leo Moon, Virgo needs no outside applause to be satisfied, although the appraisal of a master is always welcome for purposes of measuring her progress. If no one knows how well the backs of the drawers were sanded except her and the Powers That Be, that's enough for her.

At the same time, she forms the first human relationships that don't cause her pain and annoyance. Her fellow apprentices and working colleagues are people with whom she can control her level of connection. There are firm boundaries around their behavior with each other, and if she wants to withdraw back into her work, no one chides her—after all, that's what they are all there to do. The subject of the work is always something to talk about and a common interest to bond over. Many of her coworkers seem to be useful and skilled people, and she can respect that. She slowly warms up to them and takes the next step in the dance of the Virgo Moon story, which seeks a balance between working in solitude and developing human connections.

On the Apprentice's Moon, we learn new skills, polish old ones, work in groups (especially with handcrafts or with people who are all learning a new skill together), and in general educate ourselves. Any class or workshop will do, so long as it teaches something that might actually be useful. Virgo has little time for abstract theorizing. *Show me the work,* she says. This is also a time for developing discipline and good habits. It's not really a good time to plan a big party, though—save that for warmer Moons.

People born under the Apprentice's Moon are curious about how things work and meticulous with the things that matter to them. That can include relationships, although it may take them a while to warm up to anyone. They tend to be most emotionally drawn, in the beginning, to people who do the same work, or share an important interest, or to whom they owe a duty. If they do find themselves drawn to someone and want more intimacy, there may be an initial period where they poke at and tinker with that someone's mind to see what it will do, not so much like a new toy as like a new tool that they want to master.

Apprentice's Moon people like rules and boundaries and knowing what is expected of them; they hate being thrust into situations where they are expected to emotionally ad-lib for hours on end. Social situations can feel like being forced to do hours of painfully bad improv in an acting class they didn't want to take. Loved ones should give them their privacy, allow them to have plenty of space to do their beloved work (even if they hate their job, there's probably a hobby they delight in), and encourage them to get more education and training to refine their skills. Remember that some of the most intimate time you can spend with Virgo Moon people is simply quietly working shoulder to shoulder on a project that is important to them.

Quotes for Apprentice's Moon

Never suffer an exception to occur until the new habit is securely rooted in your life. Each lapse is like the letting fall of a ball of string which one is carefully winding up; a single slip undoes more than a great many turns will wind again.

WILLIAM JAMES

Perhaps the most valuable result of all education is the ability to make yourself do the thing you have to do, when it ought to be done, whether you like it or not.

THOMAS HENRY HUXLEY

The first rule of intelligent tinkering is to save all the parts.

PAUL EHRLICH

Motivation is what gets you started. Habit is what keeps you going.

JIM ROHN

The experience of the race shows that we get our most important education not through books but through our work. We are developed by our daily task, or else demoralized by it, as by nothing else.

ANNA GARLIN SPENCER

One day a student asked Ike Taiga, "What is the most difficult part of painting?" Ike Taiga answered, "The part of the paper where nothing is painted is the most difficult."

KYOKO KINOSHITA

Talent without discipline is like an octopus on roller skates. There's plenty of movement, but you never know if it's going to be forward, backwards, or sideways.

H. JACKSON BROWN JR.

Right discipline consists, not in external compulsion, but in the habits of mind which lead spontaneously to desirable rather than undesirable activities.

BERTRAND RUSSELL

Be not angry that you cannot make others as you wish them to be, since you cannot always make yourself as you wish to be.

THOMAS À KEMPIS

DANCER'S MOON
THE CRESCENT MOON IN LIBRA

The story of the Libra Moon is about going back and forth between justice and harmony. On the New Moon, the White Knight began with the side of justice; now, on the Crescent Moon, the call to action makes the Libra Moon dance and learn the side of beauty and harmony. The Dancer follows whatever she feels is beautiful, like a child chasing a butterfly. She responds to her moods with her whole body.

The Dancer chases beautiful things instinctively, because they make her feel happy when she sees them. She surrounds herself with pretty things for the same reason. However, she is still young, and she has not quite mastered the idea that what is beautiful is not necessarily always good, nor that what is ugly necessarily bad. She knows that when she is sad and depressed, her dance becomes ugly to her. Eventually, if she matures, she will learn to dance sorrow and anger in ways that are beautiful, and she will learn the value of depth. At first, however, she is suspicious of things that are aesthetically unpleasing, and she desperately clings to the attractive to keep her spirits up.

The difficulty is compounded by the fact that what is beautiful to her changes from week to week, month to month. The combination of Venus and the Air sign that is Libra is not known for its certainty and steadfastness. In fact, running from one interesting thing to the next, butterfly-like, is part of how she learns. Newness attracts her. Harshness repels her, and during bad times she may spend a lot of energy protecting herself from the nastier parts of life.

She must also learn—often the hard way—that lovely things, people, and situations can be deceptive and toxic. This is a great betrayal for her, and it sends her into a tailspin of self-evaluation. She wants so much to believe in the idea that beauty and good are connected that it feels like a failure to notice when they are not, including in her own actions. For the Dancer, the lesson is to learn what direction she wants to go, following not her eyes but her gut. She is cursed with the famous

Libra indecision, and she doesn't trust the gut. The gut is ugly. It grabs you when things are at their worst. The Dancer will need to see a lot of bad times before she has the experience to understand why that's what makes it true.

On the Dancer's Moon, we dance. Even if you can't dance, figure out a way to move your body that feels good to you. We also look at things that please us—it's a good time to go to a museum or art gallery, or to a place that makes you smile or gasp. Sit by a waterfall, walk in a botanical garden, go to the ballet or whatever works for you. It's a decent time for a party, too, but decorate the place nicely.

People born under the Dancer's Moon have a deep emotional need for aesthetic beauty and feel it with their whole bodies. They have unerring taste and a wonderful eye for how things look, sound, and feel, and they are likely to be on the cutting edge of style, if that's the sort of thing they're into. They surround themselves with aesthetically pleasing people and objects, but fluctuate between them. They try to beautify their friends and may end up annoying them. They are charming and artistic, although they tend to lack the attention span to finish artistic projects, unless there are other variables in the chart that say otherwise.

Dancer's Moon natives display a dramatic delicacy of feeling that tends to make them collapse gracefully in a fainting heap, hand glued to their forehead, when things become stressful. Actually, what's really going on is that they'd like to think that they are that delicate, when in reality they simply have a fine distaste for the circumstances and hope that when they open their eyes it will all be gone. Incurable romantics, they firmly believe in the trappings of love—roses, ships covered in lights with petals up the runway, and probably other stagings of love that we uncouth sorts haven't even thought of yet, but once they pull it off and have it photographed or written about, it will become an enduring part of "traditional" romantic gestures of the sort every schoolgirl dreams about.

Quotes for the Dancer's Moon

We live only to discover beauty. All else is a form of waiting.

KAHLIL GIBRAN

The only way to learn is by changing your mind.

ORSON SCOTT CARD

They don't have ethics, they have aesthetics.

KENAZ FILAN

The indispensable first step to getting the things you want out of life is this: Decide what you want.

BEN STEIN

Is this not the true romantic feeling—not to escape life, but to prevent life from escaping you?

THOMAS CLAYTON WOLFE

Dance for yourself. If someone understands, good. If not, then no matter, go right on doing what you love.

LOIS HURST

Movement never lies. It is a barometer telling the state of the soul's weather to all who can read it.

MARTHA GRAHAM

Indecision is debilitating; it feeds upon itself; it is, one might almost say, habit-forming. Not only that, but it is contagious; it transmits itself to others.

H. A. HOPF

I must have a prodigious quantity of mind; it takes me as much as a week, sometimes, to make it up.

MARK TWAIN

When you reach the heart of life you shall find beauty in all things, even in the eyes that are blind to beauty.

KAHLIL GIBRAN

BLOOD MOON
THE CRESCENT MOON IN SCORPIO

As the angry child of the Scorpio New Moon matures, she realizes that she is not going to get anywhere near the empowerment that she craves without knowledge—and not the kind of superficial knowledge that other signs look for. She senses the call of the Underworld and feels instinctively that Power lies there. She's right, although she doesn't really understand the true nature of that Power yet. But she takes her first steps on that path, which is to understand the darker emotions, the blood and guts of the human soul. Bravely and determinedly, she watches and asks and studies, gets up to her elbows in people's pain, and tries to figure out how it all works. After all, why shouldn't she want to study the nature of pain and fear? They're what seem to take people down more often than anything else. They are the obstacles that stop so many otherwise fine paths. To control those, in one's own life, would be a great Power.

Fear is especially fascinating. There are so many things to be afraid of, and the conquering of each one is such a triumph. The Bloody One takes risks, throws herself at mortal fears with steely resolve, glorying in the adrenalin rush and the amazing feeling of still being alive when it's all over. There's also the fascination of other people's fears. Scorpio loves to know what makes people tick, and the Scorpio Moon likes to track down what makes other people feel. That thing that is so frightening to them; why doesn't it frighten me? What about the thing that I can't stand that is so easy for them? If I can understand it from their perspective, will I no longer fear it? The study of darkness has a good chance of leading to a mature perspective, but it also may end up somewhere less wholesome.

The knife's edge that the Bloody One rests on has to do with ethics. So long as the study of darkness is undertaken with the sole purpose of empowerment of oneself, all is well, but as soon as it edges over into gaining power over others, it becomes messier. That isn't to say that power over others can't be held honorably and well, but that's not very likely when one is still full of one's own rage and pain, which the Scorpio Moon is. Her Plutonian nature will make using her knowledge as power over others very tempting, and her own inner darkness may prevent her from doing so from a compassionate and honorable place.

However, if nothing else, it helps her to get better control over herself and her more destructive passions, including her inheritance of the floundering rage of the New Moon. She learns about delayed gratification and about being willing to work and wait for one's power—including one's revenge. (This will come up again in the next lunar phase.) She learns about the rituals and structures that different societies create to contain, acknowledge, repress, and make sacred the dark places in the collective psyche.

On the Blood Moon, we study darkness. We search inside our minds and hearts for the fears and pain that we bear . . . but, more important, we compare them to the fears and pain of other people, and of collective society. We study the blood rites of the people—any people—and how they work to make dysfunction functional. Gathering together for the purpose of telling bloody tales would be appropriate here, as would a personal ritual to work with one's shadow side.

People born on the Blood Moon are fascinated with the things that most of society considers inappropriate. Sometimes their fascination is half-denied, like children peeking through their fingers in horror and compulsion; sometimes it is blatant. On the good side, they are not generally horrified about your darkness, either, and they can make good counselors, therapists, and confidants . . . the latter only if they are evolved enough not to want to use the information against you. It's best for them if they make a commitment to use the information they learn—and in some cases, instinctively know—to do two things: First, to improve themselves through self-knowledge and self-control. Second, to work toward understanding how different other people's darknesses are from their own, while acknowledging that we all experience stress and pain regardless of who we are. It's appreciation of our differences and compassion for our similarities, through the study of darkness. It's an honorable road to walk.

Quotes for the Blood Moon

Let the warriors clamor after gods of blood and thunder; love is hard, harder than steel and thrice as cruel. It is as inexorable as the tides, and life and death alike follow in its wake.

JACQUELINE CAREY

We must have books which come upon us like ill fortune and distress us deeply, like the death of one we love better than ourselves. . . . A book must be an ice axe to break the sea frozen inside us.

FRANZ KAFKA

What I give form to in daylight is only one percent of what I've seen in darkness.

M. C. ESCHER

You can discover what your enemy fears most by observing the means he uses to frighten you.

ERIC HOFFER

If a man harbors any sort of fear, it . . . makes him landlord to a ghost.

LLOYD DOUGLAS

I believe that anyone can conquer fear by doing the things he fears to do, provided he keeps doing them until he gets a record of successful experience behind him.

ELEANOR ROOSEVELT

Every man without passions has within him no principle of action, nor motive to act.

CLAUDE ADRIEN HELVÉTIUS

Of all that is written, I love only what a person has written with his own blood.

FRIEDRICH NIETZSCHE

Monsters are real, and ghosts are real too. They live inside us, and sometimes, they win.

STEPHEN KING

Never fear shadows. They simply mean there is a light shining somewhere nearby.

RUTH E. RENKEL

TRAVELER'S MOON
THE CRESCENT MOON IN SAGITTARIUS

As the Sagittarius Moon passes from New to Crescent, the aimless Gypsy is suddenly seized with the urge to be more directed in his travels. Perhaps someone offers him a job as a courier; perhaps he becomes a peddler with a regular route to support; perhaps he just feels a prodding to do something more than merely wander. Whatever the reason, his steps become purposeful, and he looks at the path beneath him as more than just another random stretch of road, and at the people he meets as more than just random experiences to be tasted and discarded.

The Traveler also builds maps of where he has been and writes about his travels. He is beginning to understand that not only were his prints in the dust not the first ones, they will not be the last, either. He remembers the places where he got lost, or found trouble, or could have used some knowledge of the local customs. He remembers how much he could have used the advice of a fellow traveler, and he determines to be that fellow traveler. His maps and travelogues become famous, and he grows to be a master of casually tossed-off trivia about exotic places and ideas.

This leads to other travelers wanting to travel with him, which pulls him in two directions, often literally. On the one hand, the gregarious Sagittarian Moon loves company and finds people interesting and fun, and he is tempted by the thought of engaging traveling companions. On the other hand, much of the emotional benefit he gets from his travels is in the solitary viewing of sights, where no one but himself need know his thoughts about what he is experiencing. And then . . . there is the issue of commitment, which he is only one step further toward than the Gypsy. He can commit enough, now, to agree to be in a certain place by Tuesday in order to deliver a message, or by December to bring Christmas goodies to a particular town, but traveling with a companion—and especially one who wants to be emotionally close to him—means taking that person's wishes and needs into account when it comes to his travels. It means not being able to run off when he wants to be alone or is annoyed with that companion. It means a restriction on his soul, and he's still not quite ready for much in the way of restrictions.

On the other hand, the Traveler also feels the stirring of circumstances that will come to a head in the Waxing Quarter phase. He wonders if there is more than a physical dimension to the path he is walking. He senses that something more profound is calling him, that just setting physical goals is not enough. Mostly, though, he shakes that off as impractical.

On the Traveler's Moon, as on the Gypsy's Moon, we get out the door and go someplace. However, unlike the Gypsy's Moon, where one might just as well throw a dart at a map and follow it, the Traveler's Moon journey should be for some actual reason—to visit a friend, to see a particular sight, to attend a yearly event, to experience the pyramids by moonlight like you've wanted to do all your life. Set your goal and make it happen. Afterward, write about what you did, and send it out where others can see.

People born under the Traveler's Moon have all the commitment problems of Gypsy's Moon people, but they are more purposeful with their lives. They tend to be more practical than natives of other Sagittarian Moons, and they are able to keep a fairly even keel so long as they have their back door to slip out when things get hairy. They have more of an ability to set goals and keep them, and thus more of a possibility of becoming able to commit. Alternately, they might use their goals as a reason not to extend their energy into further commitments. Their heart loves the road and new experiences, but their karmic lesson is to do more than just experience. They should be giving others the benefit of their acquired knowledge on the subject, even if only in occasional writing to friends. For Traveler's Moon people, while the road is home, burdens and aches do pile up, and the best way to let them go is to share their thoughts with others.

Quotes for the Traveler's Moon

When you travel, remember that a foreign country is not designed to make you comfortable. It is designed to make its own people comfortable.

CLIFTON FADIMAN

Absence extinguishes small passions, and increases great ones, as the wind will blow out a candle, and blow in a fire.

FRANÇOIS DE LA ROCHEFOUCAULD

One does not discover new lands without consenting to lose sight of the shore for a very long time.

ANDRÉ GIDE

Greatness is not in where we stand, but in what direction we are moving. We must sail sometimes with the wind and sometimes against it—but sail we must and not drift, nor lie at anchor.

OLIVER WENDELL HOLMES

At the slightest invitation
I bed down in strange cities . . .
Paris is my harem now
and Aberdeen and Amsterdam
and Bath and Berkeley too . . .
I have dallied with Chicago,
San Francisco and Tucson,
Puerto de la Cruz and Marrakesh,
I do not love you less
Because I made Atlanta mine.
If I cannot have lovers
I will have cities.

RUTH HARRIET JACOBS

All that is gold does not glitter; not all those who wander are lost.

J. R. R. TOLKIEN

One travels more usefully alone, because one reflects more.

THOMAS JEFFERSON

The world is a book and those who do not travel read only one page.

SAINT AUGUSTINE

A journey is like marriage. The certain way to be wrong is to think you control it.

JOHN STEINBECK

> All the pathos and irony of leaving one's youth behind is thus implicit in every joyous moment of travel: one knows that the first joy can never be recovered, and the wise traveler learns not to repeat successes but tries new places all the time.
>
> PAUL FUSSELL

MOUNTAIN CLIMBER'S MOON
THE CRESCENT MOON IN CAPRICORN

As the New Moon gives way to the Crescent Moon in Capricorn, the Forgotten Child decides to take action. Coming out of her hole, she sees the mountain of her ambition and determinedly begins to climb it. Her feat is not an act of faith so much as an act of will. Saturn-ruled Capricorn is not a lucky sign, and the Capricorn Moon doesn't believe in luck. She will make it to the top by her own efforts, not due to any favoritism by the Universe. Capricorn doesn't expect that, and she acts accordingly.

Sometimes she falls back and has to climb again over the same ground. Sometimes she gains her footing and manages to nimbly hop from one place to another. Sometimes it's an agonizing crawl over jagged rocks. One way or another, she will reach the top . . . and she does. Part of the wonder of the Mountain Climber's Moon is that you do actually reach the top. It's just that once you reach it, you realize that this wasn't the end at all. There's a bigger mountain beyond that, a mountain that you couldn't see until you got to the top of this smaller one. Beyond that is another, and another. The Mountain Climber first despairs, but eventually she realizes that it means an unlimited number of opportunities. Besides, if she made it up this one, she can make it up the next.

If she quits and gives up, something dies inside her. It's not the same as the Aries drive for adventure, where quitting means trapping yourself in boredom, or the Sagittarius quest for knowledge, where quitting means plunging into mediocrity. For the Crescent Moon in Capricorn, quitting means that you aren't competent to handle your own ambitions. It's a strike to the self-respect. Once she has her goal in sight and a few mastery experiences under her belt, Capricorn is better than most other signs at handling failure well, at getting up and trying again, perhaps an even bigger mountain. She is also better than the more fiery signs at planning and strategizing, owning her limits and finding ways to compensate for them. That's compensate, not transcend. Neptune transcends. Saturn compensates. It may sound unromantic, but sometimes there are limits we're not supposed to transcend this time around, because we're supposed to learn something from them. That's when the Saturnian art of compensation comes in—respecting your limits like you respect every other part of you, but never letting them stop you.

On the Mountain Climber's Moon, we attempt the impossible . . . or at the very least the dauntingly difficult. It's especially useful to try something that you have avoided because you were told that you, or the sort of person that people assume you are, would just never be able to handle that. Whatever you do, do it without help. This is a Moon of lone accomplishment, attempted for the mastery experience or to achieve a goal. Don't rely on luck—plan and prepare, train and attack. Make a strategic attack on the goal as if it was a battle you could not afford to lose. If you fail, prepare once more with the proper compensations and do it again.

People born under the Mountain Climber's Moon are doers who need real goals to achieve or they become depressed and self-loathing. Their goal-focused nature can alienate them from people who are more about feeling and process, and their priorities (often goal first; people second) can alienate the ones who would rather they were first on that list. If you're faced with this kind of Capricorn Moon, your best bet is to promise that the relationship will help to support the goal (and mean that with all your heart), but also make the reasonable argument that if the relationship supports the goal, working to maintain and improve the relationship is also in the best interests of achieving the goal. You'd be surprised how much loyalty you'll get once they've absorbed that message.

Mountain Climber's Moon people are sometimes in danger of becoming workaholics, assuming that they've found the right mountain to climb. A supportive loved one may try to get them to take breaks and concentrate on other parts of themselves, but to belittle the goal in the process—to imply that it is not worthy of their best and entire efforts—is to strike them in the heart, and that tactic will probably get you left by the trail as they stubbornly continue the climb. On the good side, they are patient and hard workers, and good at self-discipline. They are excellent helpers when you're in trouble and need a steady hand and practical advice to climb your own mountain.

Quotes for the Mountain Climber's Moon

Success is the brand on the brow of the man who has aimed too low.

JOHN MASEFIELD

There is only one sort of success—to be able to spend your life in your own way.

CHRISTOPHER MORLEY

One can have no smaller or greater mastery than mastery of oneself.

LEONARDO DA VINCI

If you do not raise your eyes you will think you are the highest point.

ANTONIO PORCHIA

The heights by great men reached and kept
Were not attained by sudden flight,
But they, while their companions slept,
Were toiling upward in the night.

HENRY WADSWORTH LONGFELLOW

I studied the lives of great men and famous women, and I found that the men and women who got to the top were those who did the jobs they had in hand, with everything they had of energy and enthusiasm and hard work.

HARRY S. TRUMAN

Greater health, wealth, freedom, fairness, and educational opportunity are not going to give us the egalitarian society of our philosophical heritage. It will instead give us a society sharply graduated, with ever greater innate separation between top and bottom, and ever more uniformity between families as far as inherited abilities are concerned, making the social ladder even steeper for those left at the bottom.

RICHARD HERRNSTEIN

> Whatever men attempt, they seem driven to overdo. I always repeat to myself, "Two and two still make four, and no one has ever invented a way of getting something for nothing."
>
> BERNARD M. BARUCH

> The best things and best people rise out of their separateness; I'm against a homogenized society because I want the cream to rise.
>
> ROBERT FROST

> *He who ascends to mountain tops, shall find*
> *The loftiest peaks most wrapped in clouds and snow;*
> *He who surpasses or subdues mankind*
> *Must look down on the hate of those below.*
>
> LORD BYRON

FATHER'S DAUGHTER MOON
THE CRESCENT MOON IN AQUARIUS

Where on the Aquarius New Moon we met the Father's Son, here we meet the Father's Daughter. I always envisage her as similar to the Greek goddess Athena, her father's favorite child and devotee to the point where she denies femaleness altogether, supporting the male principle and casting her vote for patriarchy in the trial of Orestes. The Father's Daughter is also present in the ultrafeminine Daddy's Little Girl, with the subtle and almost-incestuous (and sometimes more than almost) dynamic between them. Indeed, it seems like the Father's Daughter tends to go in one of these two directions; Athena is no romantic partner of her divine father, but she is a sworn virgin who dresses in men's clothes and does her best to be sexless. As a daughter-as-son, she can be his protégé in ways that Daddy's Little Girl cannot. Daddy's Little Girl gets told to stay home with Mommy and wait on Daddy's homecoming; to get out in the world with Father, she needs to prove that she can ride the tall horse without flinching.

Like the Father's Son, the Father's Daughter has cast her allegiance where she wishes, in a place pointing to the outside world rather than the internal homeplace. Because most people were raised (and are still raised) by women as primary caretakers, Mother ends up symbolizing the protective, boundaried home, while Father (or various Father substitutes) symbolizes the way out . . . if one is willing to play by Father's rules, which are just as rigid and irrational as Mother's, but perhaps look less so from the perspective of the stifling kitchen. In order for Father to unlock the door and take her with him, the Daughter must agree to his ideas about what women are and are not and should be, and where she is allowed to stand in that arrangement. Sometimes she is allowed to be an exception, like Athena, but even Athena had to take on a role that resembled something in Zeus's universe, if not the female one. The Father tells you how to interact with the outside world, and if you do it with his blessing, you do it on his terms.

Because of this, the Father's Daughter tends to mirror him with regard to ideals and politics, and indeed may replace her own intuitions and feelings with these ideals and politics. She focuses on the outside world and its people, and she invests her future with the people he values. She paradoxically has more freedom than the Father's Son because she is not his Heir and Golden Boy, but she will also never have as much of his support, and she will have to work harder and sacrifice even more of herself for what she does get.

The Cancerian Mother's Children both have rebellion and differentiation as part of their archetypes, as they break away from Mother. That's an earlier process, because one has to deal with the home caretaker before one addresses the custodian of external values. The Father's Children, while dissatisfied with the hard expectations laid on them, are not yet rebels. (That's what comes next.) They are wholeheartedly for his realm and his worldview, because at this early stage the only other choice they can see is . . . going back home to Mother. The Mother's circumscribed realm is often the threat Father uses to make them behave. Just ask any teenager who's been grounded.

The Father's Daughter is creative, ambitious, and idealistic (within Father's worldview). She wants to be part of society but not too close to anyone, intends to use the social order to get ahead, and believes in progress (however Father sees that). While she believes in the freedom of the people (which appeals to her repressed qualities), her overwhelming fixation on her one chosen authority figure leads her to lean to the side of the king rather than the mob. (This too is destined to change.) She is contemptuous of those who defy Father's rules, and continually looks for reasons why those miscreants have failed. She, herself, intends to succeed at whatever she does. The truth of the matter is that even though she and her brother are destined to rebel, the strength that she learns at Father's knee will carry her through that pain less scarred than her brother.

On the Father's Daughter Moon, we examine how our relationship with our fathers, as well as all the other adults who interpreted the rules of the outside society to us, still hangs on in our beliefs and goals. We look at our ambivalent attitudes toward custom and authority, and we move toward achieving our goals. It's a good time to look ahead and plan for the future.

Women born on the Father's Daughter Moon will have father issues just like their Mother's Son counterparts will have mother issues—an ongoing struggle with the problem of sublimating themselves in order to please the one on whom their future—rather than the Mother's present—depends, only to have that precarious acceptance torn away eventually. Men born on this Moon may be very unlike their fathers—so much so that they could not fill the role of Father's Son—and have to long for acceptance at a distance, nearly as disenfranchised by their differences as their sisters. Both will be ambivalent about whether to rebel or comply with any given thing, but unlike the Rebel Moon children, who wholeheartedly choose the path of difference, the Father's Daughter people will go back and forth a great deal, depending on how solid their goals are.

Quotes for the Father's Daughter Moon

The defect of equality is that we only desire it with our superiors.

HENRY BECQUE

A lively and lasting sense of filial duty is more effectually impressed on the mind of a son or daughter by reading King Lear, than by all the dry volumes of ethics, and divinity, that ever were written.

THOMAS JEFFERSON

There's something like a line of gold thread running through a man's words when he talks to his daughter, and gradually over the years it gets to be long enough for you to pick up in your hands and weave into a cloth that feels like love itself.

JOHN GREGORY BROWN

As a rule people are afraid of truth. Each truth we discover in nature or social life destroys the crutches on which we used to lean.

ERNST TOLLER

If a person loves only one other person and is indifferent to the rest of his fellow men, his love is not love but a symbiotic attachment, or an enlarged egotism.

ERICH FROMM

The art of progress is to preserve order amid change and to preserve change amid order.

ALFRED NORTH WHITEHEAD

When the people have no tyrant, their own public opinion becomes one.

EDWARD GEORGE BULWER-LYTTON

The gentle bearded young men
have gone into the corporate offices
or are driving taxis
toward the graveyard
of their dreams for social change.
The long-haired women in ragged jeans
have cut their hair and hopes
and joined the . . . data processing pool.

RUTH HARRIET JACOBS

Athene is a goddess I once loved, entirely and innocently as perhaps one can only love in adolescence. She was all I wanted to be, and I gave my soul to her—self-confident and accomplished, judicious and fair. . . . Her dedication to the world of art and culture, of clear thought and realized accomplishment, were important testimony to me of how a woman might order her life. I coveted for myself the love and respect she was given by her father and her ease in the world of men, her erect carriage and her long proud stride.

CHRISTINE DOWNING

> Athene's ambivalence towards her father Zeus is . . . determined by the ambiguities inherent within fatherness itself. The power that fathers have for their daughters lies at the very heart of patriarchal culture. . . . To understand ourselves . . . means trying to comprehend as fully as we can how our creativity is released, distorted, and inhibited by the power of the father—not primarily his outward power but his power in our own imagination. . . . Indeed, she initiates us into the difference between repression and sublimation.
>
> CHRISTINE DOWNING

MERMAID MOON
THE CRESCENT MOON IN PISCES

The New Moon in Pisces gives way to the Crescent Moon, and the Dreamer chooses a direction and moves . . . in the direction of unreality. Well, of course she did. What did you expect? The more tempting option must always be explored first, and believe me, the Pisces Moon does not see this world as the more tempting option, ever. The Dreamer slips into the ocean of fantasy, where she becomes the beautiful Mermaid.

What do we know about mermaids? They are pretty, fishtailed creatures, daughters of the sea, who dance upon the waves and yearn for handsome land-born princes, or so the idealized modern stories would have it. The older tales, however, are not so pretty. The earliest mermaids were, indeed, beautiful water spirits who sat on rocks and combed their long locks and sang beautiful, irresistible songs . . . so they could lure sailors to their death. In the cold north of Europe, they were the daughters of the sea gods, of the same breed as giants and trolls, and bore sharp fangs and claws with which to feast on their victims. They took down ships and caused storms at sea and dragged unwilling lovers away with the undertow. They were seen as half fish for a reason: they were colder than human beings.

We think of Pisces as being malleable and gentle and perhaps victimized. What we don't understand is that a planet in Pisces makes its owner adept at doing those sacrificial gyrations through leading them into altered states. When you're living in an altered state, you are not quite human. That's part of Neptune's gift. There's a part of the Pisces person that can become a cold fish, and an elusive one, who slips away from the more human watchdogs, through the bars of passive ignoring, perhaps even into insanity and catatonia. *You can't catch me. I can always get away. I don't care how much it hurts you.* One is reminded of the legends about the selkie-wife whose seal skin had to be locked up or she would just slip into the ocean and never return . . . which, of course, inevitably happens in the end.

The Mermaid is the Pisces Moon in the grip of her own fantasy world. The challenge for these people is to retain enough access to their fantasy world to keep themselves sane, but also to anchor enough of themselves in the mundane world to keep from going insane, slipping away into the ocean and floating there forever in a small white room where no one stops their internal explorations. The Mermaid's world can pull you down; perhaps you come back with treasure that will be remembered forever; perhaps you simply get devoured. Growing legs and walking in the gravity of dry land is incredibly painful to the Mermaid, but never coming back from the ocean is a dead end, and the Powers That Be don't like dead ends. She is meant to go through this struggle, of realizing that as seductive as the ocean of fantasy might be, the real things of worth—including real love— are to be found on land.

On the Mermaid Moon, we explore our internal fantasies. Could you dedicate a whole day to daydreaming? If not, perhaps dedicating it to reading fantasy novels would be a better thing. Escapist movies will work too. Ask yourself, though: What appeals to you and why? What pulls you back to the mundane world; what are your anchors there? Remember to eat and take care of physical needs; these are often forgotten on the Mermaid Moon.

People born on the Mermaid Moon are chronic daydreamers who spend much of their time somewhere else. Like the New Moon's Dreamers, one can be sitting right next to them and feel like they're a million miles away. But the Dreamer's Moon people will good-naturedly come back when you drag them; Mermaid Moon people own serious real estate in their dreamworlds and are often very angry when they are forced to return in order to wash dishes or pay rent.

Balancing a life lived in fantasy with a life lived in the mundane world will be their own special struggle. If they do it right, they can come out of the ocean carrying amazing ideas that will benefit them and others, but they have to value the world that other people live in enough to bother. They also need to be willing to accept the full reality of another human being in order to fully love them, instead of loving the fantasy mask that they place on them, made in an image that came out of their own heads.

Quotes for the Mermaid Moon

It is not that I think or believe (in spiritualism) but that I *know*.

SIR ARTHUR CONAN DOYLE

God and other artists are always a little obscure.

OSCAR WILDE

Fantasy love is much better than reality love. Never doing it is very exciting. The most exciting attractions are between two opposites that never meet.

ANDY WARHOL

Artists can color the sky red because they know it's blue. Those of us who aren't artists must color things the way they really are or people might think we're stupid.

JULES FEIFFER

All the other colors are just colors, but purple seems to have a soul. Purple is not just a noun and an adjective but also a verb—when you look at it, it's looking back at you.

UNIEK SWAIN

When my daughter was about seven years old, she asked me one day what I did at work. I told her I worked at the college—that my job was to teach people how to draw. She stared at me, incredulous, and said, "You mean they forget?"

HOWARD IKEMOTO

Dreams pass into the reality of action. From the actions stems the dream again; and this interdependence produces the highest form of living.

ANAÏS NIN

It is hard to get one's heart's desire. Whatever it wishes to get, it purchases at the cost of soul.

HERACLITUS

My whole life is a movie. It's just that there are no dissolves. I have to live every agonizing moment of it. My life needs editing.

MORT SAHL

The gift of fantasy has meant more to me than my talent for absorbing positive knowledge.

ALBERT EINSTEIN

3
INTERNAL CRISIS
THE WAXING QUARTER MOON

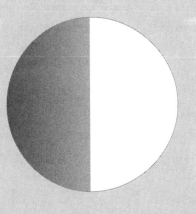

In the game of life, it's a good idea to have a few early losses, which relieves you of the pressure of trying to maintain an undefeated season.

BILL VAUGHAN

How did I get here? Somebody pushed me. Somebody must have set me off in this direction and clusters of other hands must have touched themselves to the controls at various times, for I would not have picked this way for the world.

JOSEPH HELLER

THE WAXING QUARTER MOON begins when the Moon squares the Sun at 90 degrees and continues to 134 degrees, and many people with this Moon will actually have a Sun-Moon square. Even those who don't will feel the square energy coming through the Moon phase itself. At the Waxing Quarter Moon, things reach a period of crisis. Sometimes it's because we realize that our former path has gone as far as it could go, and perhaps it went somewhere that we didn't expect or want. Oftentimes we find ourselves in a situation where we have betrayed and compromised the ideals of our New Moon period, or where we must betray them in order to keep from falling into stagnation. The Waxing Quarter Moon is the difficult place, the point of tears and treachery and mutiny. In each archetype of this Moon, the earnest youths of the Crescent period find themselves in painful and intolerable situations for the first time. They learn about suffering and taking responsibility for one's bad decisions. It's the time where we scream, "Why do I deserve this? How did I get here?" and we scramble, panicked, for a way out, even if that way out means justifying some means that will later come back to haunt us.

While there is a lot of talk about the higher rate of insanity on the Full Moon, when statistics were actually assembled, car accidents and assaults were seen to be highest on the Quarter Moons. These Moon phases have a shadow of the square aspect to them, and as such they create tension, turn the screws, and set you up for a crisis . . . usually of identity. That means that the Quarter Moons are the hardest Moon phases of all.

Modern astrologers have tried to soften the concept of "afflicting" aspects by calling them "challenging" and emphasizing that they can bring growth. While this is true, they still feel pretty much like an affliction when they're happening to you or when you have to get up and deal with them every day in your natal chart. (Even the most starry-eyed and euphemizing astrologers have been known to blanch when confronted with a seven-planet grand cross.) Being born on a Quarter Moon can be very like having a square to your Moon, even if nothing is actually squaring it. That means that when you read those entries, they are by their nature less pleasant than some of the other angles. That's life. The Quarter Moons are not a curse, any more than any other single aspect of the chart, and the afflictions that these phases bless us with can be overcome.

Yet there is hope on the horizon of the Waxing Quarter—the trine angle also appears during this phase, toward the end of it. This describes the energy of this quarter as well—you can get to the good stuff, but only after going through the bad stuff first. A trine angle between Sun and Moon can also ease the pain of the Waxing Quarter's process, although no one gets a free ride, and even those with Sun-Moon trines will still feel the echo of that square. First the fight, then the harmonious resting period, during which the heart can figure out how to get out of the predicament and forge ahead.

BRIGAND'S MOON
THE WAXING QUARTER MOON IN ARIES

They say that the three most idealistic signs are Aries, Libra, and Sagittarius. Actually, all signs start out idealistic in their own way, but it seems that Aries has the greatest capacity to stay that way the longest . . . and when he crashes, from the general betrayal of the world, he goes down hard. The Brigand is what is left of the Torch-Bearer after he has been pummeled by the world too many times. Instead of giving up, he becomes enraged and cynical, and he lashes out. It is the first part of the Infant's transition to Warrior, and that ride is a bumpy one.

The Waxing Quarter Moon is a time of betrayal, in two directions. The personal world (family, friends, job, etc.) has betrayed people in some way by being imperfect, and in return they betray the original innocent ideals of the New Moon archetype. The Brigand is the archetypal high-wayman, jumping out at bystanders and robbing them—in the tales he robbed them of their money, but in the astrological world it's more likely to be their dignity or peace of mind. The Brigand isn't above whacking people because they are self-important and need, in the Brigand's mind, to be taken down a few notches. That always delights him.

The truth is that under all the wrath and cynicism, part of the Brigand still believes in all those ideals and desperately wants them to be true. He's just lost trust in people to live up to any of them . . . and this is the way out of the pit for this Moon. Like the Torch-Bearer, choosing a leader the Brigand can follow and really believe in is key to his emotional maturity. He'd better choose carefully, though, because a second betrayal after he's placed his trust in someone (who then turns out to be rotten) can thrust him deeper into the hole and make it even harder to trust the next time. Unlike the Torch-Bearer, who will follow gladly, the Brigand will test the possible leader, trying to goad that person into wrong action. He won't follow until he's sure that the leader is stronger, more moral, and has better self-control than the Brigand.

On the Brigand's Moon, we work with our anger—at people, at institutions, at the world, at the gods. This is something that's likely to happen whether we will or not, because this Moon tends to trigger blowups—and the kind of no-fault accidents that lead to the worst blowups. Breathe, a lot. Remember that this too will pass, and use the time to really look at how you handle your rage, healthily or unhealthily.

For those born under the Brigand's Moon, anger management is one of their ongoing issues. Actually, anger management is an issue for any Aries Moon (and a few of the Scorpio Moons as well), but it is particularly a problem for the Aries Waxing Quarter Moon. Because they came into the world with a lingering sense of betrayal (and a good deal of anger) already following them, they will tend to automatically distrust people and assume the worst, attacking before anyone actually gets around to striking them. They will need to focus on other parts of themselves to keep themselves in check. There can be a dashing quality to Brigand's Moon people that some folks find romantic, but relationships are often the most likely place for their issues to play out. There's so much room for perceived betrayal in a love affair, after all.

I should explain that Brigand's Moon people aren't necessarily more likely to be criminals than other signs; their anger may end up betraying them into assault if other planets give them an extra lack of impulse control, but they aren't the career criminal type. In the end, they do want people to like them; a Brigand Moon gang member probably joined up because it gave him a place to put his anger and offered an opportunity to gain the like and respect of other members, and they probably goaded him into his worst crimes. One of the worst fights I ever saw in school was a Brigand's Moon bully provoked into striking by his friend and sidekick, a Little Brother's Moon boy (New Moon in Gemini), facing down an enraged Black Knight Moon loner (Waxing Quarter Moon in Libra). (I knew their Moon signs because I got my start as an astrologer doing other kids' charts during lunch hour.)

One of the most stellar examples of a Brigand's Moon came from a conference where I gave a workshop on the Moon phases and their stories. After the workshop ended, when I was on my way to the next one I was slated to teach, one of the audience members from the Moon phase workshop stopped me. She told me in no uncertain terms (and in a rather shrill voice) that my assessment of the Waxing Quarter Aries Moon was entirely wrong. She resented being associated with the archetype of a thug, and she informed me that she had no problems with anger at all, and she wasn't cynical, she had plenty of ideals and . . . Luckily, some friends came along at that moment and rescued me, carrying me off to my next workshop. I never did get the chance to ask her whether waylaying and attacking strangers during conferences was her regular modus operandi for dealing with disagreements.

Quotes for the Brigand's Moon

We are all ready to be savage in some cause. The difference between a good man and a bad one is the choice of the cause.

WILLIAM JAMES

I'm just starting to scratch the surface of what really makes me happy and it's taken me a while to admit that acting like a little child and being a jerk and a punk is fun.

LEONARDO DiCAPRIO

The bit of truth behind all this—one so eagerly denied—is that men are not gentle, friendly creatures wishing for love, who simply defend themselves if they are attacked, but that a powerful measure of desire for aggression has to be reckoned as part of their instinctual endowment.

SIGMUND FREUD

What is a cynic? A man who knows the price of everything and the value of nothing.

OSCAR WILDE

Watch what people are cynical about, and one can often discover what they lack.

HARRY EMERSON FOSDICK

He that is conscious of guilt cannot bear the innocence of others: So they will try to reduce all others to their own level.

CHARLES JAMES FOX

"I am a brigand; I live by robbing the rich."
"I am a gentleman; I live by robbing the poor."

GEORGE BERNARD SHAW

Gamesters and highwaymen are generally very good to their whores, but they are very devils to their wives.

JOHN GAY

Blood-red were the spurs in the golden noon,
Wine-red was his velvet coat,
When they shot him down in the highway,

Down like a dog in the highway,
And he lay in his blood in the highway
With the bunch of lace at his throat.

ALFRED NOYES

I am a fighter. I believe in that which is right, and the truth is, I have been the Lone Ranger for the past thirty years and I will not give up the fight. I love my public and I'll fight for you.

CLAYTON MOORE

WOODCUTTER'S MOON
THE WAXING QUARTER MOON IN TAURUS

The Waxing Quarter Moon in Taurus finds the Gardener of the last phase deciding that he needs more space for his gardens . . . and the only way to do that is to start cutting down trees and clearing the woods. This is, again, the moment of betrayal; in order to do this he must forget about the Green Man he once was.

In many poems and songs about the Green Man, he is spoken of as a sacrificial king whose head is cut off for us. The songs are all written from our very human point of view, expressing hope in our own self-centered way that the trees would want to give themselves for our needs and whims. Perhaps they would, if we had a reciprocal relationship of some kind with them, but it seems that in order to cut them down, we have to separate ourselves entirely from the Dryad's world. The Woodcutter's Moon is the moment of that separation. Whatever the Woodcutter once was, he is now fully human and detached from his genesis as a tree spirit . . . and that is why he can cut down the woods that were once his birthplace and life, without shedding a tear.

He also discovers another benefit that was heretofore hidden, but will now define much of the rest of Taurus's story: money. The cut trees can go into his warming fire or make furniture for him . . . or he can sell them to others and get comforts he did not have before. The Woodcutter is poor—a little garden won't make much—and he has come to realize, and resent, just how poor he is. The only way out of that is to sell what you have. "It's no shame to be poor," says Tevye the milkman in *Fiddler on the Roof,* "but it's no great honor either." The Woodcutter does not cut for excess profit—that will come later—but to feed his family. It's the devil's bargain that the poorer human beings are often given a choice between the survival of Nature and their own survival. He chooses the human side, as nearly all of us do, every day, far more often than we choose Nature.

On the Woodcutter's Moon, we think about those devil's bargains that we are forced into. Do we drive cars with low or no emissions? What if there's no way for us to afford such a thing, but the old clunker is necessary to get us to work? Do we buy organic, or does the extra ten dollars it costs to buy a bag of organic food instead of a bag of sprayed, processed food mean two more meals for our children? Do we recycle? What if our town won't recycle half our trash because the only trash company the town can afford without raising property taxes to levels we couldn't afford will take just certain items? How do I justify my decisions to all the people who have social or emotional power over me? This Moon phase isn't a time to feel superior or beat our breasts; it's a time to honestly and painfully look at the compromises we make, and what those say about our priorities, our society, and our own power (or lack of it).

People born under the Woodcutter's Moon spend their emotional life being faced with devil's bargains that have to do with the Taurus areas of food, money, survival, and profit. The Universe will constantly offer them choices of short-term comfort, or even survival, and long-term abstract value, and perhaps suffering with either choice . . . and then the Universe stands back, watching how they handle the struggle and the compromise. They may also end up choosing between their roots, the place that they were born and grew up in, and financial comfort or business success.

The key to dealing with the Woodcutter's Moon is learning about values. We think of Taurus (and the second house) as being about possessions, but really the bottom line is values. What the Universe wants for people born under this Moon is to develop a deep and thoughtful code of values, whatever those may be, rather than simply unthinkingly reacting to either upbringing or circumstances. Once they have carefully thought through their values and have shown themselves willing to follow through even if that means inconvenience, the Universe may let up.

Quotes for the Woodcutter's Moon

Man shapes himself through decisions that shape his environment.

RENÉ DUBOS

If poverty is the mother of crimes, want of sense is the father of them.

JEAN DE LA BRUYÈRE

Our country is wherever we are well off.

JOHN MILTON

Ay me! ay me! the woods decay and fall;
The vapours weep their burthen to the ground.
Man comes and tills the earth and lies beneath,
And after many a summer dies the swan.

ALFRED, LORD TENNYSON

Long life o man, you hope to gain, till flattened by a cunning wrench,
Your temperate weather turns to rain, your sun is strangely made to blench;
So here's a thought your teeth should clench: "All greenness comes to withering."
Alas! There is no queen nor king whom draught of Death shall fail to drench:
Before you tumble off your bench, all sinning quench.

THIRTEENTH-CENTURY POEM

Thank God men cannot fly, and lay waste the sky as well as the Earth.

HENRY DAVID THOREAU

We do not inherit the earth from our ancestors, we borrow it from our children.

NATIVE AMERICAN PROVERB

It is not easy for men to rise whose qualities are thwarted by poverty.

JUVENAL

Money can't buy happiness, but neither can poverty.

LEO ROSTEN

> There are a handful of people whom money won't spoil, and we always
> count ourselves among them.
>
> MIGNON MCLAUGHLIN

LIAR'S MOON
THE WAXING QUARTER MOON IN GEMINI

The Gemini Waxing Quarter Moon is the Liar's Moon, also called the
Moon of the Evil Twins. Where before we met the Little Brother and Little
Sister at their most ingenuous, we now meet them at their worst. During
the last two Moons, they both experimented with the power of words—
Gemini's gift of communication—and using their intelligence to affect
people and things. Now their experimenting reaches a crisis as they decide
that words can mean anything they want and can be used to get anything
they want. At first their imagination creates bigger and bigger whoppers,
but eventually they get the hang of telling smooth and polished lies, convincing enough to reap rewards and reinforce the idea that it's all right to
stretch the truth.

The Twins finally get to the point where there is no more naked,
straightforward truth, because there is no statement that can't be improved
on, painted up, even twisted. They justify their actions with other small
lies—people are easily hurt by the truth, and they are happier when you
soften it. Where's the line between truth and imagination anyway? Isn't it
a gray area? Isn't all fiction lies, all art lies, all poetry lies? And those are
respected, even revered, right? Storytelling is just another form of lie, and
everyone loves it. (Their relationship with Truth has not yet gotten to the
point where they can understand the Truth in storytelling—that will come
later.)

The other insidious part is that the Twins have started to lie to each
other, and—even worse—to themselves. They discover how difficult it is
to remember the web of untruths and half-truths that they've spouted,
and they must now keep consistent or get caught, which often requires
even more dissembling. They discover that while dissembling is useful

when they don't want to share their feelings, it means that people don't take them seriously when they do. They learn about the dangers of crying wolf, especially after getting caught a few times.

The Quarter Moons are where we need to hit bottom with our personal habits so that we can really appreciate getting out of the pit. It's Gemini's destiny to play with words and intellectual concepts and to work toward more effective communication, but sometimes we have to immerse ourselves in doing it wrong before we can really understand how to do it right. The Evil Twins won't really be able to see either the harm in their lies or the line between imagination and untruth until they've made a wreck of things, and then they can move ahead.

On the Liar's Moon, we examine—painfully and honestly—the ways we slant our words to more effectively get what we want . . . and the consequences both for doing and for not doing that. This is also the time to look at the ways we lie to ourselves. That's always easier said than done, so the best approach is to come up with one single lie that you've told yourself over the past month and concentrate on that. What weakness made you do it, and how can you make yourself strong enough to face that truth?

People born under the Liar's Moon will spend a lifetime struggling with the gray areas of truth and falsehood, and the most crucial part of that lesson will be the art of being completely honest with themselves. It's not that they're all liars, all the time . . . but they compulsively play with those dangerous areas, pushing them to see how far they can go. Sometimes it's all in the name of imagination, since they likely have good imaginations that can come up with all sorts of scenarios. The demons sitting on their shoulders are experts at justifications—"It's better to say that, it won't hurt her feelings"—and it will take a lot of willpower to ignore their blandishments.

A few of the Liar's Moon people I've met have gone into a field like advertising or other creative work, directing their urge to make imaginative whoppers into "acceptable" areas. While one could theoretically argue that aiding and abetting such larger social lies is also a form of harm, it's probably better for them than making up stories to bewilder their significant others with.

Quotes for the Liar's Moon

The devil is easy to identify. He appears when you're terribly tired and makes a very reasonable request which you know you shouldn't grant.

FIORELLO LA GUARDIA

The truth is often a terrible weapon of aggression. It is possible to lie, and even to murder, with the truth.

ALFRED ADLER

Get your facts first, and then you can distort them as you please.

MARK TWAIN

If one is to be called a liar, one may as well make an effort to deserve the name.

A. A. MILNE

And after all, what is a lie? 'Tis but the truth in masquerade.

LORD BYRON

Society can exist only on the basis that there is some amount of polished lying and that no one says exactly what he thinks.

LIN YUTANG

Lying to ourselves is more deeply ingrained than lying to others.

FYODOR DOSTOYEVSKY

If you do not tell the truth about yourself, you cannot tell it about other people.

VIRGINIA WOOLF

It wasn't lies. It was just bullshit, that's all.

ELWOOD BLUES

I would never lie. I willfully participate in a campaign of misinformation.

FOX MULDER

WEEPING MOON
THE WAXING QUARTER MOON IN CANCER

The Orphan Moon is also known as the Weeping Moon. As Cancer moves into the Waxing Quarter phase, the unthinkable happens to the Mother's Children: they are orphaned and made homeless, and sent crying out into the world. It is, for them, the worst of all fates. Home and Mother are taken from them, and nothing remains but the empty road, the unloving foster home, and the cold pillow. The Orphan is consumed with sorrow and—it must be said—self-pity, and spends every day weeping.

The challenge for the Orphan is to go on and learn to bring herself to a place where she can leave her self-enclosed room of grief and reach out again to others. It will take a long time and a lot of work, because Cancer is the Moon's own sign, watery and feeling. She does not recover quickly from blows so close to home. She pulls herself into her shell and refuses to come out; she may walk around in a gray dreamworld, unresponsive to outside stimulation, or she may act as if everything is normal, but it is a mask over a gaping, bleeding wound. Eventually she gets used to the walls around her and does not want to give up their safety, even though part of her admits that she put them up not only to protect herself, but to see if anyone cared enough to try to get through them.

While all the Waxing Quarter Moons are painful, when the Moon's own sign of Cancer goes into this difficult phase, it is especially traumatizing. There are other, alternate paths that this sad story can take, of course. In some versions of the story, the family reveals itself not to be loving but dysfunctional, and drives the Orphan away due to some perceived fault. The Orphan is no Gypsy, and she continues to cling to the family's negative opinion of her, because to reject that opinion would be to reject the entire world she was born into. In other versions, the Orphan stays in the dysfunctional family or continually returns to it after having been repeatedly driven away. She grows up knowing only harsh words and abuse, and she closes up into herself in the same way. Whichever it is, the betrayal of the Cancer Waxing Quarter Moon is that the idealized image of Family is shattered, and it will never be the same again to the child's mind. While the Capricorn and Scorpio Moons start with neglect and rage, Cancer has known that perfect ideal—if only for a short time—and feels her loss deeply.

The only way out from behind the walls is to become brave enough to look for small bits of happiness, a little at a time, until they nourish the soul enough for it to open up. Cancer goes sideways like a crab, making small moves. Large sweeping changes aren't the answer; large sweeping changes are what brought her to this point. But she must loosen her grip on the idealized image of what was lost before she can really look for anything new.

On the Orphan Moon, we weep. If your life is so good that you have no carefully hidden sorrow to pull out and weep over, weep for the sorrows of your loved ones. If you can't weep at all, go help someone who is mourning a loss. For those who can do so, plugging into the Universal Sorrow and experiencing it may be a strongly fulfilling act at this time.

People born under the Orphan Moon have strong issues around family love. They may have had dysfunctional families of the petty, needling variety, or parents who died or abandoned the family, or were alcoholic or addicted or depressed. Even if the parents were present throughout their childhood, it's not unusual for the bulk of their caretaking to have been pushed off on other figures. Cancer Moon children are more sensitive than most to not having enough attention from parents, and if they've fixated on the parents in that peculiarly Cancerian way, no one else's attention will be good enough.

As adults, they must learn to find their way through the morass of need, sorrow, self-pity, and unresolved abandonment that remains in their psyche. Those feelings will taint all their relationships until they have dealt with them. Those relationships might well be attempted replacements for the lost parental ideal; how well that works depends partly on whether the partner is mature, aware, and willing to be that for them, and partly on how idealistic and too-perfect-to-be-human the Orphan Moon partner's image of family may be. The goal, of course, is for people with Orphan Moons to learn to give themselves enough of that nurturing that the gifts of loved ones are enough, and they need not be pressured into taking care of the Orphan's needs.

Quotes for the Weeping Moon

When one door of happiness closes, another opens; but often we look so long at the closed door that we do not see the one which has been opened for us.

HELEN KELLER

Family quarrels are bitter things. They don't go by any rules. They're not like aches or wounds; they're more like splits in the skin that won't heal because there's not enough material.

F. SCOTT FITZGERALD

There is no greater sorrow than to recall, in misery, the time when we were happy.

DANTE ALIGHIERI

Sorrow is a fruit. God does not make it grow on limbs too weak to bear it.

VICTOR HUGO

One cannot be deeply responsive to the world without being saddened very often.

ERICH FROMM

When we honestly ask ourselves which person in our lives means the most to us, we often find that it is those who, instead of giving much advice, solutions, or cures, have chosen rather to share our pain and touch our wounds with a gentle and tender hand. The friend who can be silent with us in a moment of despair or confusion, who can stay with us in an hour of grief and bereavement, who can tolerate not knowing, not curing, not healing and face with us the reality of our powerlessness, that is a friend who cares.

HENRI NOUWEN

I have come to realize more and more that the greatest disease and the greatest suffering is to be unwanted, unloved, uncared for, to be shunned by everybody, to be just nobody to no one.

MOTHER TERESA

> You can clutch the past so tightly to your chest that it leaves your arms
> too full to embrace the present.
>
> JAN GLIDEWELL
>
> We must embrace pain and burn it as fuel for our journey.
>
> KENJI MIYAZAWA
>
> In three words I can sum up everything I've learned about life: it goes on.
>
> ROBERT FROST

ACTOR'S MOON
THE WAXING QUARTER MOON IN LEO

The Leo Moon story finds itself in the Waxing Quarter phase with a crisis of self-identity. Where the Clown was clumsy but sincere in his efforts to please an audience, the Actor has learned skill and polish. He can become whatever it is that people want to see, and he prides himself on his flexibility and talent for donning each mask of persona and letting it permeate his whole being. He is rewarded for this by more and more applause, more appreciation from the audience, and fame as well. The fame means that he is now observed in his "ordinary" life, and he creates a persona for going to the grocery store or talking to passersby. He has very little privacy, and people frown if he is seen grumpy and disheveled.

All this means that he has become desperately fused to his masks. On his best days, he is the master manipulator, making people laugh and cry whether they intended to or not. On his worst days, the applause is like a drug, and he is a puppet performing for his fix, craving more and more and willing to obscure himself in any way for it. The mix of power and helplessness pulls him further and further away from himself, until he's really not sure where the masks and the puppet strings end and he begins. The Waxing Quarter Moon in Leo forces the Actor to a point of terrible decision: For what would you sell yourself? How much applause is worth handing over your heart and going on without it?

The other hard part about the Actor's job is that he continually loses pieces of himself to the acting. It's not just that he closes his real self off, dons a mask, and doesn't let it touch him internally. It's not that simple— Leo is a Fire sign, not a detached Air sign or cold Earth sign. In order to give depth to a part, he pulls out a piece of himself that is similar to that part and uses it. Eventually, that part can become so changed by the acting process that it's not really his any more. When enough pieces of himself get prostituted to support the acting, the line between the mask and the soul truly begins to blur, and he may feel like there's not much of himself left to himself. His performances are his works of art, including the ones done in front of fans on the street while buying new sunglasses, but the characters he portrays are someone else's ideas. If he is to break free of the cycle, he needs to learn to retreat, gather up the last bits of himself, and reevaluate the importance of pleasing (and manipulating) people in his life.

On the Actor's Moon, we meditate on what we give up for the approval and applause of other people, including people we don't even know. Consider such things as the way that you dress, the sort of clothing you wear when you want to "look nice" or "look sexy," the way that you move and hold your body in public, on an interview, on a date. Consider the ways you act in public that aren't really you, and what purpose they serve. Go out doing something different for a change. Whether it's more you or less you will depend on your choice and calculations.

People born under the Actor's Moon crave the good opinion of others in a way that can drive them to new heights of creativity or destroy their self-esteem and put them at the mercy of anyone with a frown. This is a hard Moon to own. If there are other, more independent aspects to the chart, the Actor's Moon may be kept in check. But the temptation is always there: to pretend to be something you're not, and to fear that who you really are won't get you what you need. Some Actor's Moon people can't even get their relationships past the dating phase—as soon as someone is around long enough to notice that they're always wearing a mask and wants to know what's under it, they break up. When the whole world tells you that they like your masks better than you, it's hard to believe that anyone else would think otherwise.

Being alone for long stretches of time is incredibly painful for this gregarious Moon, but it might actually be useful for Actor's Moon people who are having trouble controlling their responses to others. In order to keep yourself from being a chameleon, you have to be alone long enough to figure out who you really are. Then you have to hold onto that hard enough to believe that it's worth sacrificing the applause. This will be the hardest task for Actor's Moon natives: believing that the few out there who want them for who they are will be enough to make up for the thousands who won't.

Quotes for the Actor's Moon

We are afraid of truth, afraid of fortune, afraid of death, and afraid of each other.

RALPH WALDO EMERSON

For an actress to be a success she must have the face of Venus, the brains of Minerva, the grace of Terpsichore, the memory of Macaulay, the figure of Juno, and the hide of a rhinoceros.

ETHEL BARRYMORE

All the world's a stage and most of us are desperately unrehearsed.

SEÁN O'CASEY

The deepest principle in human nature is the craving to be appreciated.

WILLIAM JAMES

Nothing makes one so vain as being told that one is a sinner. Conscience makes egotists of us all.

OSCAR WILDE

All my life I wanted to be somebody. Now I realize I should have been more specific.

LILY TOMLIN

Ordeal by Publicity is the legitimate grandchild of Ordeal by Fire, Water, and Battle. The physical harm of those ancient adjuncts of trial was more direct and severe than that of their present-day descendant, but it is likely that the mental and spiritual injury to the litigant and the damage to society generally resulting from the violence of unnecessary publicity are immeasurably greater.

GEORGE H. BOLDT

Vanity is so secure in the heart of man that everyone wants to be admired; even I who write this, and you who read this.

BLAISE PASCAL

People often become actresses because of something they dislike about themselves: They pretend they are someone else.

BETTE DAVIS

Tell me I'm clever, tell me I'm kind, tell me I'm talented, tell me I'm cute, tell me I'm sensitive, graceful and wise, tell me I'm perfect—but tell me the truth.

SHEL SILVERSTEIN

COUNTING MOON
THE WAXING QUARTER MOON IN VIRGO

The Waxing Quarter Moon in Virgo shows the Apprentice moving up in rank and skill, and finding work that he finds valuable and that he is good at. He is put in charge of the accounts, which shows his detail-oriented skills to good measure, and the work is solitary, which he also enjoys. For Virgo Moons, emotionally fulfilling work is healing to their hearts. However, it is all too easy for people with Virgo Moons to put work as a shield between their hearts and human contact. In the case of the Virgo Waxing Quarter Moon, the former Apprentice chooses to lock himself into a small and ordered world where everything is numbered, organized, and entirely free of chaos. His nerves need not be burdened, and everything is where it should be. Relief at last!

Free of chaos, of course, means that it is free of Art, Spirit, Nature, and other people. It is a sterilized space where nothing ever needs to change except for the work, which consists of ever more elaborate and efficient forms of Counting. Virgo is often symbolized by grains of sand, the smallest particle of land, a tiny detail of Earth itself that, when it becomes innumerable, can swallow up whole swaths of terrain in sterility. The Counting Moon is a time of the sterile desert, when each grain of sand must be counted, even when the sand irritates and gets in the eyes. The Mercury-ruled Virgo Moon is prone to irritability and poor nerves, which is one reason why the Accountant closed himself into his little room to begin with. However, the sand builds up in his isolation and makes him more irritable, not less. He has not yet learned that close relationships can be a balm as well as an annoyance.

There is one sort of human interaction that the Accountant does indulge in, however, and it is criticism. He mentally counts up every fault that he can see in other people, and the list is nearly endless. After all, people are so imperfect. Often, he starts sharing his list with them, which is not usually well received. It isn't all grumpy and malicious; he does actually want to help people and see them improve. It's just that the most natural way for him to do it, from his rather distant and uncompassionate place, is to criticize them. Since he hasn't learned much about more emotional and outgoing types of people, he doesn't understand why his approach never seems to help them, and he can't think of anything better to do that won't try his nerves further. He becomes generally disliked, which is more of an excuse to keep the door closed.

At night after the lights are out and he is sitting over his numbers with his frugal candle burning, the Accountant also tallies up his own faults, which are legion. There are so many that he despairs of fixing them all, and so he covers them up again and tucks the book away. For some people, acknowledging their own faults is a way to empathize with the faults of others. For the Accountant, the one does not lead to the other. The mental wall he builds between himself and others prevents that leap of empathy. There are his faults, and their faults, and they are entirely separate from each other, just as he feels separated from everyone else, just as each number is separate from every other number. There is no three that is almost four; even 3.9 is still separate from four. This is how he measures his life, and he hardly knows how lonely he is.

On the Counting Moon, we do our accounts. This is a good time to balance your checkbook and figure out how much you really owe, how much you really spend on groceries, how much electricity your house really uses. Pay attention to detail and bother to do it right.

People born under the Counting Moon really prefer abstract ideas to everyday life, and they like concrete facts better than fuzzy human feelings. They like to be regimented and orderly to a fault; their obsessive organizing seems brittle, as if it hides a great fear of the chaos that would ensue if the dark socks migrated to the white socks' side of the drawer. They criticize people almost compulsively and criticize themselves just as hard—the secret self-loathing of Counting Moon people beating themselves up for not being perfect enough may not be seen by others, but be sure that it exists anyway, to the exact same degree that they are invested in criticizing others. This is a very challenging Moon to have, and it requires that they force themselves to accept chaos, human connections, and that life cannot always happen on their terms. This requires accepting the imperfection of the Universe and that this is not a bad thing. Until they can let people in through that wall and love them even when they mess up the workbench and spill food on the account book, they will struggle alone and never make any progress with their own secret chapter of faults.

Quotes for the Counting Moon

Skepticism is chastity of the intellect.

GEORGE SANTAYANA

The problem with people who have no vices is that generally you can be pretty sure they're going to have some pretty annoying virtues.

ELIZABETH TAYLOR

Man is fond of counting his troubles, but he does not count his joys. If he counted them up as he ought to, he would see that every lot has enough happiness provided for it.

FYODOR DOSTOYEVSKY

If we had no faults we should not take such pleasure in noting those of others.

FRANÇOIS DE LA ROCHEFOUCAULD

Faults are thick where love is thin.

JAMES HOWELL

The man who makes no mistakes does not usually make anything.

BISHOP W. C. MAGEE

I have diligently numbered the days of pure and genuine happiness which have fallen to my lot; they amount to fourteen.

ABD-EL-RAHAM

I've met them down in the Cost and Accounting Department, clean-shaven and in white collars. They can't see a damn thing ridiculous about themselves . . . only about you.

JEAN SHEPHERD

If you want an accounting of your worth, count your friends.

MERRY BROWNE

He has a right to criticize, who has a heart to help.

ABRAHAM LINCOLN

BLACK KNIGHT'S MOON
THE WAXING QUARTER MOON IN LIBRA

On the Waxing Quarter Moon, the focus of Libra turns from beauty to justice yet again. The idealism of the White Knight and the Dancer has soured and turned to anger. The hopes of the White Knight have been betrayed, over and over, by the cruelty of unjust people. The Dancer has come, hopelessly, to the understanding that beauty cannot cover up the ugliness of the world, nor be used to pretend that it isn't there. Anger explodes in the Libra Moon's heart, and he comes out of the woods as the Black Knight, the Adversary, who takes justice into his own hands. Since the world has failed to keep the score even, he will be the one to even it.

The Black Knight does not consider himself evil, although he knows that he is not working for the Man, as it were. He is aware that he is outside the law, but he considers the law corrupt and intends to force people to live by his codes. If they don't, he strikes them down. This is a hard thing for him to do, at least the first time. The Dancer would not have been able to pick up a sword and strike down a perceived wrongdoer, but the Black Knight pushes himself to do it in the name of justice, and of principle.

That latter point, principle, means that he must dispense with mercy. After all, if you're really being fair, if you're really adhering to the principle, you can't grant mercy even when the opponent is on his knees begging to be spared because he has five children at home who will be traumatized and possibly homeless if they lose their father. It means that you can't grant mercy even if the insult happened out of ignorance or if the perpetrator is only thirteen years old. Principle is black and white, and that's what Libra knows about justice at this stage. He's been the White Knight and now he is the Black Knight. Shades of gray make him nervous, because they're all about that middle ground of compromise that is so tempting to him. When he stops to consider shades of gray, he starts thinking about things from the other fellow's point of view, and then . . . why, before long, he'll be in a bar drinking with the bad guy. And that's not sticking to principle. Really, Libra is not cut out to be a sticking-to-principle sort. Those inner scales, the part of him that he thinks is the inspiration for the justice-seeking Black Knight job, are just as likely to foul him up when he tries to be implacable. The dirty truth of what this means, in the long run, is that the principle of this week may not be the principle of next week. That's kind of hard for people to keep track of, and it means that anyone can become an enemy when he was a friend just a short time ago.

To be the Adversary is a hard job. First of all, it requires that you not care about social harmony, which is painful for Libra. It means that you need to get used to the idea that most people are not going to like you. In fact, you will probably be well and truly disliked. The Black Knight usually harbors a fantasy, at first, that people are going to come around to his point of view and see how right he is, and then they'll be grateful that he took on the vigilante role and saved them from themselves. When it becomes clear that this isn't going to happen, he becomes quite bitter. This leads to an internal debate over whether the people he's trying to protect are worth protecting if they all exile him, and so on. If you ever wondered why the

Black Knight in the fairy tales always seemed so cranky, now you know.

On the Black Knight Moon, we argue and debate. If that isn't something that you want to get into, read intelligent opposing views on an issue about which you are undecided, and let your own internal scales have the debate. It's also a good Moon for political action, for being the Adversary who wants justice.

People born under the Black Knight Moon are compulsive arguers. They are hyperalert for any sign of injustice, and they tend to attack without considering their target. Whether it's the counter clerk at the DMV or their own partner's innocent comment, it's hard for them to rein in the impulse to play the devil's advocate to anything. They are the Librans most likely to do the famous trick of arguing any point, even if they violently disagree with it, just to make sure that it's heard in a room of overwhelming agreement by the opposition. They are a challenge to live with, but at least they keep their loved ones questioning things. It gives their heart joy to win even one little victory for justice, so try to keep them pointed in the right direction. If they have a real enemy, they are less likely to turn on inappropriate targets.

Quotes for the Black Knight's Moon

No matter what side of an argument you're on, you always find some people on your side that you wish were on the other side.

JASCHA HEIFETZ

I never make the mistake of arguing with people for whose opinions I have no respect.

EDWARD GIBBON

A quarrel is quickly settled when deserted by one party; there is no battle unless there be two.

SENECA

You might consider whether running roughshod over people's stated experiences and feelings is a good way to advance an argument, if indeed you have one.

KATHRYN HUXTABLE

The best argument is that which seems merely an explanation.

DALE CARNEGIE

Learn to reason forward and backward on both sides of a question.

THOMAS BLANDI

We're both civilized. We just use different civilizations as our standard.

JEFF SHAEVEL

People are usually more convinced by reasons they found themselves than those found by others.

BLAISE PASCAL

I am unjust, but I can strive for justice,
My life's unkind, but I can vote for kindness,
I, the unloving, say life should be lovely,
I, that am blind, cry out against my blindness.

VACHEL LINDSAY

That most dangerous of opponents: the one who took pains to comprehend the position of his adversary.

PIERS ANTHONY

EXECUTIONER'S MOON
THE WAXING QUARTER MOON IN SCORPIO

The Bloody One of the Scorpio Crescent Moon gives way to the Waxing Quarter, and due to his special knowledge he is given a job by the frightened people: to be an Executioner and slay the people who are given to him by the forces of law. It is a job that no one else wants, and one that he is glad to have, because it introduces him to the heady wine of Vengeance. All his life he has harbored strong negative emotions and had nowhere to put them. Now he has a place to aim his wrath and pain, and he does not care very much about whether it is really a true place . . . at first.

The Waxing Quarter Moon is a time of crisis and betrayal of self. The

Bloody One's studies could have brought the Scorpio Moon to a point of understanding the darkness and being a counselor to others, but in this phase the tempting offer to focus on the internal rage and pain was made, and the Scorpio Moon finds it impossible to ignore. He revels in his job—after all, they are wrong-doers! They deserve to die! He cannot only indulge his love of revenge, he can even feel morally superior for the deaths he causes. What better place could there be? As the Executioner, he becomes quicker and quicker to condemn, and slower to forgive . . . if indeed he ever does. People fear him, and he sees this contemptuously as a mark of their weakness, as he is contemptuous of the people who were weak enough to commit crimes.

He lives in his haze of vengeance and glory for a long time. Eventually, though, he notices that the people who are sent to him to die may or may not be all that guilty. He kills them anyway, but it eats at him. He also observes, in his regular life, that some of the people he assumes are guilty, and attacks as such, later turn out to have extenuating circumstances. Some even seem to be completely innocent, and it was by mistake that he assumed them guilty. Sooner or later he unbends enough to apologize . . . and then, suddenly, he notices more and more mistakes, and more and more extenuating circumstances. This is very uncomfortable to Scorpio. Unlike Libra, whose experiment with black-and-white thinking didn't get very far, Scorpio is honestly more comfortable with everything sorted into good guys and bad guys, easily discernable by an unchanging visible standard. The hard truth that it isn't always (or, perhaps, ever) that way infuriates him and makes him unsure of himself.

Then comes the day when someone is sent to him to kill, and he disagrees with the guilty ruling. He tries to work himself into a mood of vengeance, but compassion—or at least a sense of justice that is greater than his own pain—keeps intruding. In spite of himself, he must stand up to the authorities and speak for mercy. Their response is to tell him to do his job or to put down his axe and let someone else do it. This is where the decision moment of the Quarter Moon comes in, and it is the Executioner's choice as to where he goes with it. This is one of the most painful Moons to have, for this moment alone.

On the Executioner's Moon, we remember all the times we have done things to "get back at" someone. Perhaps we feel that our actions were justified; perhaps they taught a good lesson; perhaps they were simply wasteful hatred. In retrospect, how might we have handled the situation differently? What actions might have brought us further along our own evolutionary path? These are hard questions to answer, and they require us to look at the anger and hurt that lie behind our actions.

Those born under the Executioner's Moon live with the smoldering rage of the last two Moons, but they are quicker to jump and strike, and they are very judgmental. Part of their life's lesson is to learn to forgive, and it may take decades for them to come to the point of doing that even once. At the very least, they need to compensate for their judgmental heart by becoming more emotionally objective, so that their strikes are at least reasonably appropriate and well thought through.

Executioner's Moon people, however, tend to be the ones who can do the hard thing that needs to be done—quickly and cleanly bashing in the head of the wounded, mangled sparrow in its death throes on the sidewalk while more fragile types stand around paralyzed while it suffers, for example. People tend to expect it of them, and they tend to end up taking it on as their job. This can harden them—or teach them more compassion—depending on the direction they choose to go in order to protect their own feelings. If they can be brave and expose themselves to pain, doing the hard but right thing while appreciating the sorrow of the situation can become a source of pride for them.

Quotes for the Executioner's Moon

The best way of avenging thyself is not to become like the wrong-doer.
MARCUS AURELIUS ANTONINUS

I write as one who spent far too much energy devoted to fantasy wish fulfillment scenarios of painful death to my enemies, and can say for certain that indulging in these fantasies did no harm to my enemies, and a great deal of harm to myself.

BOB LODENKAMPER

Every normal man must be tempted at times to spit on his hands, hoist the black flag, and begin slitting throats.

H. L. MENCKEN

After decades of raging against injustices—personal and communal, ephemeral and substantial—I have come to see that the more I take on the enemy's passion, the more I become just like him until finally the shared rage obliterates any distinction between his cause and mine—the means becomes the end and we are essentially indistinguishable in hatred.

JACK CARROLL

All cruelty springs from weakness.

SENECA

Something of vengeance I had tasted for the first time; as aromatic wine it seemed, on swallowing, warm and racy: its after-flavor, metallic and corroding, gave me a sensation as if I had been poisoned.

CHARLOTTE BRONTË

Never does the human soul appear so strong as when it forgoes revenge, and dares to forgive an injury.

E. H. CHAPIN

When you hold resentment toward another, you are bound to that person or condition by an emotional link that is stronger than steel. Forgiveness is the only way to dissolve that link and get free.

CATHERINE PONDER

The remarkable thing is that we really love our neighbor as ourselves: we do unto others as we do unto ourselves. We hate others when we hate ourselves. We are tolerant toward others when we tolerate ourselves. We forgive others when we forgive ourselves. We are prone to sacrifice others when we are ready to sacrifice ourselves.

ERIC HOFFER

To forgive is to set a prisoner free and discover that the prisoner was you.

LEWIS B. SMEDES

SEEKER'S MOON
THE WAXING QUARTER MOON IN SAGITTARIUS

The Traveler becomes the Seeker when he knows, paradoxically, that what he is actually traveling to find is some deep truth, but he does not know what it is or what direction to take in order to find it. This is a hard place to be in for the Sagittarian, who desperately wants to be Right in all things. (It's said that of the three Fire signs, Aries wants to be First, Leo wants to be Big, and Sagittarius wants to be Right.) She becomes incredibly frustrated with the elusive goal that dances before her, just out of reach of her intellect. If I can only find the right experience, she reasons, it will come into my grasp. So she stuffs herself with experiences of all kinds, throwing herself into worldview after worldview, experiment after experiment, all of which leave her feeling as if she found something but not what she was looking for.

The Waxing Quarter Moon is a time of crisis, and the Seeker's Moon is the crisis of faith. *Everything you know is wrong, or not enough. You must find what is True, greater than all these little truths that conflict with one another—and if you do not do it soon, you will die having lived a useless life.* After wandering the roads for so long, it feels to the Seeker that too much time has been frittered away . . . and yet she does not know any other way than to keep wandering. At the same time, her own skepticism turns her away from many truths that might help her to go deeper; her own biases trip her up in her Search.

The positive quality that she has going for her is that she is honestly drawn to find greater meaning in life. It is possible that she might quit the Search, but if she bucks her destiny in this way, she will settle down to a life that shows itself to be somehow hollow and empty. Eventually the Search reasserts itself, and she is swept again onto the road. The lesson and goal of this Moon phase is not to get to the eventual spiritual finish line, but to allow the process of Seeking to be a glorious thing rather than a frustrating grind due to the wrong expectations. It is all right to spend a lifetime Seeking, and it is necessary for the Seeker to give herself permission to do so.

It is also a lesson of this phase that she must learn to discern which experiences are going to be useful to her and which are not. She must learn not to err by turning away from something that is personally distasteful due to her existing biases or by throwing herself into injurious situations. She must learn to tell the difference soon enough to keep from destroying herself or missing too many important opportunities.

On the Seeker's Moon, we allow ourselves to yearn. We allow ourselves to look at the pain of all we do not know and at the slim likelihood of our ability to know—not all of it, but enough to satisfy us. It is a good time to seek out new spiritual experiences, but only with an attitude of open-minded curiosity, nothing goal-oriented, or you've missed the point. If you get nothing out of the experience, this too can teach you something about yourself.

People born under the Seeker's Moon either spend a good portion of their everyday lives on the Search or put the Search aside and have unsatisfying lives with the little nagging voice constantly in the corner of their mind. Sometimes they alternate between the two. Some end up adrenalin junkies, rushing about distracting themselves with spiritual thrillseeking; some hide their heads under the pillows in their "safe" houses and desperately try not to hear the call that drags them away. Some fear the Search because it may lead to something they fear, that will lose them their "safe" lives and force them into a wider but more challenging world. Some follow gurus or teachers who are not right for them, only to be disappointed. These are the pitfalls, but there is still plenty of hope. Seeker's Moon people need to cultivate a great deal of hope to get through their Search. For them, hope is more than a luxury: it is necessary for their heart's survival.

Quotes for the Seeker's Moon

I know well what I am fleeing from but not what I am in search of.

MICHEL DE MONTAIGNE

If we find nothing of interest where we are, we are likely to find little of lasting interest where we wish to go.

EDWIN WAY TEALE

Perhaps he knew as I did not, that the Earth was made round so that we would not see too far down the road.

ISAK DINESEN

Do not say, "I follow the one true path of the Spirit," but rather, "I have found the Spirit walking on my path," for the Spirit walks on all paths.

KAHLIL GIBRAN

The truth knocks on the door and you say, "Go away, I'm looking for the truth," and so it goes away. Puzzling.

ROBERT PIRSIG

A cynic is a person searching for an honest man with a stolen lantern.

EDGAR A. SHOAFF

Skepticism is a hedge against vulnerability.

CHARLES THOMAS SAMUELS

Doubt is a pain too lonely to know that faith is his twin brother.

KAHLIL GIBRAN

The folly of that impossible precept, "Know Thyself," can be translated into this partially possible one, "Know what thou canst work at."

THOMAS CARLYLE

There is nothing like looking, if you want to find something. You certainly usually find something, if you look, but it is not always quite the something you were after.

J. R. R. TOLKIEN

MINER'S MOON
THE WAXING QUARTER MOON IN CAPRICORN

The Mountain Climber reaches the top of the mountain and sees that it is only one in a long chain of mountains that could be climbed. Each one is higher than the last, and he can see the tallest of all wreathed in clouds in the distance. He stands there wondering, trying to decide whether to go on or give up and go back . . . and then he is distracted. At the top of the mountain is a gleam of gold in the rock, a streak of silver. He chips some out with a hammer, makes a fire, and smelts it . . . and discovers that the mountain is, indeed, riddled with precious metals. All thoughts of the quest for ascendancy go out the window as he goes back for pick and shovel, cart and mule, and begins to mine.

The Waxing Quarter in Capricorn begins with a distraction from the upward goal, and that distraction is often financial in origin. The problem of making money can distract us for many reasons, including the very justifiable one of "I need to pay my rent or I'll be out on the street." The problem occurs when the search for money beyond simple necessity or even comfort becomes the whole of one's personal quest. Both Taurus and Capricorn are very invested in money, valuable objects, and the general quest for resources, but their motivations are different. Taurus loves having things, and hoards them in order to look at them and be pleased. Taurus also loves comfort, and may be unwilling to sacrifice it in order to get that last bit of cash.

Capricorn, on the other hand, sees financial gain as a way to get social importance. Wealth makes you respected, wealth makes you an Authority. People treat you differently if you're visibly wealthy. You can make people do things with money, too; it is a tool to grease your path and help you achieve your goals. These are the things that the Miner tells himself as he toils alone in the dark, filthy, cramped tunnels. *This will make me important. This will make people do what I say.* It is easy to see the echo of the Forgotten Child, whispering up and down the cramped darkness. Even reaching the top of the mountain has not given the Capricorn Moon a feeling of self-respect strong enough to keep him from desperately needing that respect from the outside world. The tragedy of the Miner's Moon is that if he had continued on his climb and taken the other mountains with his own effort, respect for him would have been assured. Instead, he plans to circumvent the problem by buying it.

The Miner's Capricorn energy resonates with the stone he moves through, the metal and gems that he pulls out and hoards, but he does not see them as entities with value all their own, but only as a means to an end. His efforts tear the Earth, and in his hope and greed he does not see how much permanent damage he does. His salvation, if he chooses to take it, could be in noticing the beauty and worth of the materials themselves, and seeing it as a valuable job to share their beauty with others. Another way out could be taking up the interrupted journey of the Mountain Climber. However, the likelihood is that he will continue to dig in his darkness, counting up the prestige that will come.

On the Miner's Moon, we consider all the ways we want respect from other people and the methods that we use to achieve it. We also think about the ways we have interrupted and sabotaged our own success to chase after quicker and less ethical roads.

People born under the Miner's Moon have problems with getting stuck in negative mental patterns. They are kept in darkness by their own pessimism, and their self-esteem suffers from it. There are always excuses for why they can't have the goal they want by simply working for it. The reasons are legion, and they twist themselves downward into a spiral of helplessness. At the same time, they dream of the respect they could have if they could just acquire Impossibility A, B, or C, and they resent those who seem to have it easier. Getting out of the trap requires mastery experiences that have nothing to do with outside opinion. When they can do something valuable to them and know that it is worthy even when no one sees it—and it doesn't matter to them that no one sees it—then they will be getting somewhere. In the meantime, changing the negative mental patterns of self-sabotage is the first step.

Quotes for the Miner's Moon

The sun, the moon, and the stars would have disappeared long ago, had they happened to have been within the reach of predatory human hands.

HAVELOCK ELLIS

In his private heart no man much respects himself.

MARK TWAIN

How rarely I meet with a man who can be free, even in thought! We all live according to rule. Some men are bed-ridden; all are world-ridden.

HENRY DAVID THOREAU

You may be sure that when a man begins to call himself a "realist," he is preparing to do something he is secretly ashamed of doing.

SYDNEY HARRIS

There are only two ways of getting on in this world: by one's own industry, or by the weakness of others.

JEAN DE LA BRUYÈRE

And it won't make one bit of difference if I answer right or wrong.
When you're rich they think you really know.

SHELDON HARNICK

Self-respect is a question of recognizing that anything worth having has a price.

JOAN DIDION

Whatever you have forgotten, you can remember. Whatever you have buried you can unearth. If you are willing to look deep into your own nature, if you are willing to peel away the layers of not-self you have adopted in making your way through the tribulations of life, you will find that your true self is not as far removed as you think.

MEREDITH JORDAN

Self-respect is nothing to hide behind. When you need it most it isn't there.

MAY SARTON

The worst loneliness is to not be comfortable with yourself.

MARK TWAIN

REBEL MOON
THE WAXING QUARTER MOON IN AQUARIUS

On the Waxing Quarter Moon in Aquarius, the Father's Children get up and spit in the Father's face. This phase is characterized by betrayal of the original goals, and the Rebel stands up and casts off all the rules, values, and ambitions that had heretofore been so important. Everything is questioned, and damn near everything is rejected. Often a great deal of possibly useful things are also rejected because they bear a subjective association with the Father's world. There may be a lot of babies thrown out with the dirty bathwater, and a lot of casualties as the Rebel throws himself into Change for Change's Sake, allowing no one to stand in his path.

When things get too rigid, it's good to have Rebels. They are the ones willing to stand in the line of fire, to speak up even when the gun is pointed at them, to die bravely for their cause and inspire others. However, it's not uncommon for a Rebel to not only throw out useful things, but to fail to extract the worst of the Father's rules—the ones about intolerance that will, eventually, cause the Rebel to set himself up as an authority that will be just as ruthless and uncompassionate as the one he grew up with. A lot of Angry Young Men (and their female counterparts) grow up to be Intolerant Oldsters just like the ones they overthrew. To avoid this fate, the Aquarius Moon must do something that it finds very, very hard in any phase: truly care about people on a personal level and learn to empathize with them rather than simply deciding their ideal fates from a safe distance. For this Moon, that means finding friends, real friends, people who the Rebel likes and respects so much that they can disagree with him and keep the friendship strong. If they can do that, they also might be able to make him listen when he's being rebellious to no good end rather than creating real change.

The Moon rules childhood and conservatively sticks to its first childhood impressions, even when we tell ourselves that it is silly. It is not impossible for the Rebel to settle down, become part of a group again, adhere to group rules, and even—horrors!—faithfully follow an authority figure once more. It just has to be a group that does not resemble in any way the one that he grew up with. In a sense, dedicating oneself permanently to a subculture whose underpinnings are opposite to those you grew up with— and actually being happy and content!—is the biggest and best rebellion of all. It's also the secret that will put an end to the Rebel's destructive thrashing about. *Are you really happy with your new rules?* the voices ask. *Are you happy with your life?* If the answer is not an honest yes, then the detractors can say, *Why should we listen to you, if your road clearly makes you unhappy?* A wise Rebel, once the dust has settled and he realizes that he is well and truly alone, will figure out that finding real happiness—and, more important, joy in purpose—among like-minded people who value him on his own terms is the best revenge a Rebel can buy.

On the Rebel Moon, we take social structures to task. This is the best time of all for activism. Even if there is no cause that makes you burn or that you'd burn for, there is certain to be some injustice that you would like to see cleared away, and no matter what it is, other people are probably already working for that. Put your back, and not just your words or money, into the cause. Keep in mind, however, that tempers run high on this Moon, and tread carefully.

People born under the Rebel Moon have all the group-love and do-I-belong issues of any other Aquarius Moon, but they are constantly moved to play devil's advocate and push against ideas that have been unquestioned for too long. They don't do it for Libra's reason—keeping a balance—because they don't much care if the applecart is upset. In fact, that would probably be good for people. The fact that this might be hungry people's lunches rolling down the street may not occur to them, and they need friends they respect to tell them otherwise. Yes, that's *respect,* not just *like;* just because they like you doesn't mean that they won't decide your fate for you. Rebels may move through a lot of groups and a lot of identities before they find something that works for them emotionally—and remember that this is the Moon; the process is subjective rather than rational no matter how hard they protest otherwise. (The Aquarius Moon doesn't like to admit that it's a Moon, in charge of feelings instead of abstract thought.) Even when ensconced in a like-minded community, Rebels may feel like outsiders . . . and they may subtly and unconsciously (or openly and blatantly) encourage those feelings in themselves in order to feel like their ideas are superior, and thus were worth rebelling over. It will take them a while to get over continually justifying their rebellion to the inner Father, and it will necessitate a great deal of humility on their part to realize that they need others as much as they honestly do.

Quotes for the Rebel Moon

Those who profess to favor freedom, and yet depreciate agitation, are men who want rain without thunder and lightning. They want the ocean without the roar of its many waters. Those who profess to favor freedom and yet renounce controversy are people who want crops without ploughing the ground.

FREDERICK DOUGLASS

Is it so bad then to be misunderstood? Pythagoras was misunderstood, and Socrates, and Jesus, and Luther, and Copernicus, and Galileo, and Newton, and every pure and wise spirit that ever took flesh. To be great is to be misunderstood.

RALPH WALDO EMERSON

Anybody can become angry; that is easy. But to become angry with the right person, and to the right degree, and at the right time, and for the right purpose, and in the right way—that is not within everybody's power and is not easy.

ARISTOTLE

Idealistic reformers are dangerous because their idealism has no roots in love, but is simply a hysterical and unbalanced rage for order amidst their own chaos.

WILLIAM IRWIN THOMPSON

The first duty of a revolutionary is to get away with it.

ABBIE HOFFMAN

It is easier to fight for one's principles than to live up to them.

ALFRED ADLER

Revolutionary movements attract those who are not good enough for established institutions as well as those who are too good for them.

GEORGE BERNARD SHAW

It is necessary for the welfare of society that genius should be privileged to utter sedition, to blaspheme, to outrage good taste, to corrupt the youthful mind, and generally to scandalize one's uncles.

GEORGE BERNARD SHAW

It is a tragic paradox when the path of righteousness becomes the road to lawlessness. But the right to rebel is an elemental human right, just as the right to repress rebellion is an elemental public right.

ISRAEL ZANGWILL

Since it is now fashionable to laugh at the conservative French Academy, I have remained a rebel by joining it.

JEAN COCTEAU

MARTYR'S MOON
THE WAXING QUARTER MOON IN PISCES

The Pisces Moon struggles with conflicting desires—the desire to dissolve into another world and the urge to give of themselves to others. (It's actually the same urge—losing one's boundaries—but it can feel like conflicting urges sometimes.) In the Waxing Quarter phase, the Pisces Moon gets her chance to take the latter course, with a vengeance. The magical Mermaid is captured and bled of her energies for the good of others. As she does not have a lot of experience with defending herself and putting up walls, she simply lets it all be passively taken from her. She has only enough energy to keep herself alive, but seeing the people go from the pool of water where she has been imprisoned looking and feeling better than they had been, she feels as though her suffering has been worth it.

Eventually she rises from her pool and walks about the land on legs, now giving of herself more actively to others. She now offers them her energy freely, still barely keeping enough for her own life. Her health suffers for it, but she has learned the positive feeling of self-sacrifice. She's also learned a secret negative side: it's not hard at all to feel secretly superior to those you sacrifice yourself for. In fact, if one isn't careful, the act can develop into a downright self-satisfied feeling. You're so much more giving than they are, so much more moral, such a better person than those helpless, pitiful people who need you so much. And while you're needed so badly, you have a certain amount of power and leverage. From the perspective of someone who has felt tossed by the whim of the world all her life, the sacrifices may seem worth it. Not to mention that one can then wait for the guilt to set in when you ask things of them.

On the other hand, it's not a healthy relationship for any pair where one isn't a small child. The needy recipients are not unaware that this dynamic puts them in a supplicatory and obligated position, and they may feel the need to lash out at the Martyr in order to take back some of their power while still getting their needs met. Also, Martyrs often make people feel worse about themselves in comparison, which can compound people's suppressed resentment and its inevitable escape. There are also those who just don't care at all and will take everything that they can get and more, with no thought for the Martyr's health or sanity.

On the Martyr's Moon, we sacrifice ourselves for the good of others. This entails giving of our energy and resources past the point of inconvenience. If it didn't make you writhe just a little, it isn't a real sacrifice. While we make that sacrifice, we watch ourselves for our reactions. Some of us will err on the side of wanting to hold back, justifying our unwillingness to give with a variety of excuses. Some of us will give too much and not know where to set boundaries, or we will set them but feel terribly guilty about it.

Those born under the Martyr's Moon are strongly drawn to self-sacrifice, for reasons both worthy and unworthy. The first struggle for them will be to learn to set proper boundaries, which is more than just not giving so much that there is nothing left for them at all. It's also keeping enough for themselves to put energy into bettering their own lives and following their own path. They are not a public utility, and they will have to make hard decisions about who gets cut off. That's literally the way they will have to think of it: *Which of my children do I starve? I can feed only so many, or I will starve myself, which is a sin against the Powers That Be, who want me to do more than just this.*

The next struggle for Martyrs is giving what they can give cleanly and with no hidden agendas. Giving should be done with a whole heart and no expectations, or else it should be done with honest expectations laid out at the beginning. If receiving gifts makes people feel smaller—which an astute giver can tell by the subtle smell of resentment—then sometimes it's a kinder gift to cut them off and let them help themselves. Similarly, someone who is simply sinking deeper into neediness may need a somewhat harsher gift. It's often true that when Martyr's Moon people figure out how to give cleanly, they find more energy in their lives to give.

Quotes for the Martyr's Moon

The term *Satyagraha* was coined by me in order to distinguish it from the movement then going on under the name of Passive Resistance. Its root meaning is "holding on to truth," hence truth-force. I have also called it love-force or soul-force. In the application of Satyagraha, I discovered in the earliest stages that pursuit of truth did not permit violence being inflicted on one's opponent, but that he must be weaned from error by patience and sympathy. For what appears truth to the one may appear to be error to the other, and patience means self-suffering. So the doctrine came to mean vindication of truth, not by the infliction of suffering on the opponent, but on one's self.

MAHATMA GANDHI

If blood be shed, let it be our blood. Cultivate the quiet courage of dying without killing. For man lives freely only by his readiness to die, if need be, at the hands of his brother, never by killing him.

MAHATMA GANDHI

Once in a while it really hits people that they don't have to experience the world in the way they have been told to.

ALAN KEIGHTLEY

I have found the paradox: that if you love until it hurts, there can be no hurt, only love.

MOTHER TERESA

The stoical scheme of supplying our wants by lopping off our desires is like cutting off our feet when we want shoes.

JONATHAN SWIFT

Love seeks one thing only: the good of the one loved. It leaves all the other secondary effects to take care of themselves. Love, therefore, is its own reward.

THOMAS MERTON

Sacrifice, which is the passion of great souls, has never been the law of societies.

HENRI FRÉDÉRIC AMIEL

I have found that among its other benefits, giving liberates the soul of the giver.

MAYA ANGELOU

If nature has made you a giver, your hands are born open, and so is your heart. And though there may be times when your hands are empty, your heart is always full, and you can give things out of that.

FRANCES HODGSON BURNETT

It is more difficult, and it calls for higher energies of soul, to live a martyr than to die one.

HORACE MANN

4
SOUL'S REDEMPTION
THE GIBBOUS MOON

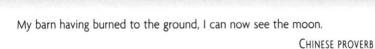

My barn having burned to the ground, I can now see the moon.

CHINESE PROVERB

AFTER THE PERSONAL CRISIS of the Waxing Quarter Moon, the soul finds itself in a pit created by its own response to hard choices. On the Gibbous Moon, we tend to the work of personal redemption, doing whatever we have to do to climb out of that pit. The Waxing Quarter Moon is the Mess We Make, and the Gibbous Moon is the Price We Pay to Clean It Up. The archetypes move into a role that is both something they have the aptitude for and something that is a challenge for them, and in moving through it they will find their way upward; they will work hard to perfect something precious to them. We are still struggling on the Gibbous Moon, but it is a struggle toward a goal and not merely a fight to keep from slipping backward into a pit. It is a time of applied, conscientious effort in the face of obstacles.

There is a focused feeling to the energy of the Gibbous Moon. After all the bad-and-good thrashing about of the Waxing Quarter, the heart begins a slow climb to a calmer and steadier place. Nothing is all-good or all-bad now, it's just . . . necessary. Doing what is necessary is the hallmark of this phase.

The Gibbous Moon begins at 135 degrees past the Sun and continues to 179 degrees, just short of the opposition. It contains the quincunx aspect with its odd half-positive, half-negative deeply karmically affecting energy. The Gibbous Moon nature does seem to reflect a combination of both of those: *It's good for me, but it's irritating. It's a good thing to do, but boy does it piss me off to have to do it.* Redemption is never a pleasant thing until you actually see what kind of progress you're making and how much better off you are.

ADVENTURER'S MOON
THE GIBBOUS MOON IN ARIES

The Aries Gibbous Moon begins with the Brigand of the Quarter Moon saying, in effect, "I can do better than this." Pitting himself against other people in surprise attack may have been gratifying, but it did little for self-esteem. The Adventurer pits himself against bigger things—feats of endurance, courage, and indomitable humor. There's more risk of loss and death in attacking a mountain or a monsoon or a jungle than a shivering traveler, but there's a lot more honor in it. In a sense, the Adventurer's Moon is a time when the Aries Moon learns that honor is not only valuable, but that one must build up a fund of it.

Many ancient cultures have considered that there is a fund of personal power earned by giving one's word and keeping it, by making great boasts and actually carrying them through. The greater the deed, the greater the power, and the greater one's confidence in accomplishing the next great deed . . . and, from the spiritual point of view, the more power that the Universe will grant you to get behind the oath and push. The first part is that bit about keeping one's word, if only to oneself. In fact, oneself is the most important person not to cheat. Aries is often all about Me, but then that's where most of the work lies.

The Adventurer has found a way to redeem all that rage—throwing it at worthy obstacles—and to retrieve some hope. If he can climb a mountain that looked impossible, perhaps other things aren't so impossible either. This Moon is about making one's own hope from scratch, not waiting for it to be bestowed. By not giving up on himself, he is slowly learning how to have faith again in other people.

On the Adventurer's Moon, we go adventuring. Really. Not vacationing, not popping off to the beach for a good time. Not even seeing new sights. If there's no risk, it isn't an adventure. The risk can even be that you aren't sure you'll like whatever it is, but if that's the case, try to get yourself into a space where you have the most chance of liking it. Stretch yourself. If there's a little fear involved (or perhaps more than a little), all the better.

People born under the Adventurer's Moon may be secret adrenalin junkies. If they don't have a way in their lives to get that fix, they will get it by starting arguments with other people. They are at their best when they are terrified and exhilarated and facing down the thousand-pound dragon. Getting that experience regularly will keep them on an even keel. It may be useful for them to take up an extreme sport of some kind. The adrenalin rush cleans out their system.

Novelty is important to them, and if you're boring, they will not stay around. Partners of Adventurer's Moon people have two choices: be the hearthkeeper who they come back to, ideally with a life of your own so that you don't have to be lonely when they're off scuba-diving in Madagascar, or be the sort who can keep up with them and be a companion on adventures . . . preferably one who keeps smiling when things are terrifying or uncomfortable, which adventures always are. Wet blankets will get relegated to hearthkeeper status all too quickly. Appreciate that adventuring is an emotional need for them, and it keeps their aggression from going bad.

Quotes for the Adventurer's Moon

However brilliant an action, it should not be esteemed great unless the result of a great motive.

FRANÇOIS DE LA ROCHEFOUCAULD

Bite off more than you can chew, then chew it.

ELLA WILLIAMS

Security is mostly a superstition. It does not exist in nature, nor do the children of men as a whole experience it. Avoiding danger is no safer in the long run than outright exposure. Life is either a daring adventure or nothing.

HELEN KELLER

It is nice to make heroic decisions and be prevented by "circumstances beyond your control" from ever trying to execute them.

WILLIAM JAMES

It is often the failure who is the pioneer in new lands, new undertakings, and new forms of expression.

ERIC HOFFER

It is only in adventure that some people succeed in knowing themselves, and finding themselves.

ANDRÉ GIDE

An adventure is only an inconvenience rightly considered. An inconvenience is only an adventure wrongly considered.

G. K. CHESTERTON

When you're safe at home you wish you were having an adventure; when you're having an adventure you wish you were safe at home.

THORNTON WILDER

It is not because things are difficult that we do not dare; it is because we do not dare that they are difficult.

SENECA

It is not easy to be a pioneer—but oh, it is fascinating! I would not trade one moment, even the worst moment, for all the riches in the world.

ELIZABETH BLACKWELL

FARMER'S MOON
THE GIBBOUS MOON IN TAURUS

During the Taurus Gibbous Moon, the Woodcutter plants the larger space that he has cleared for himself and realizes that this is a much greater endeavor than the simple plot of the Gardener. He now "possesses" a much bigger piece of land, enough to grow all his food needs, and perhaps those of a family and some extra to sell. His fences may go out farther than the eye can see from a single point . . . but it's not as simple as he thought it would be. The Woodcutter had the luxury of ignoring the interlocking ecosystem of Nature, which puts the Farmer in the position of having to create his own interlocking ecosystem from scratch . . . at least if he wants to be self-sufficient and make it all work.

On the old-fashioned self-sufficient farm—and this is the farm we're going to talk about here, as it's the archetypal and healthiest system—everything feeds each other. Livestock are fed grass and in turn they fertilize pastures, which will eventually be rotated into crops. Some fields are left fallow to recover and perhaps planted with "green manure" crops to be plowed under. Grain and vegetables are grown for human and animal, but all wastes are returned to the soil. Meat scraps are fed to the protective carnivores; bones are ground and returned to the soil or burned for warmth. Leftover human food goes into the bellies of animals and becomes more food; the whey skimmed from butter-making goes to the pigs and ducks, while vegetable scraps go to the goats. Bruised apples are pressed for cider; wormy apples become livestock feed. Composting is a holy act; no weed is merely thrown away. The woodlot is harvested carefully for wood in a way that takes no more than will grow again in a year, and ashes sweeten the soil and make soap when mixed with rendered fat. Nothing is ever wasted; if nothing else, it can rot.

Farming self-sufficiently, or even at least partly so, is a constant balancing act. It is no accident that Saturn, the ancient Roman god of farming, was shown as a dour old man hung with chains. Everything that a farmer does is a carefully considered risk, balancing one variable against another: Should I turn the sheep into the south pasture now, or is it still recovering? Can I send the ducks into my pea patch to eat those slugs, or will they eat the peas as well? How long can I go without breeding this cow and still have a decent milk supply? Where the Woodcutter wanted to be free of the system, the Farmer finds himself responsible for the entire thing. Such is the experience of good ownership.

He also finds that he is not released from the chains of Nature in the way that he hoped to be. The Farmer is dependent on climate, weather, and time of year in an almost imprisoning way. No matter how well he guesses and manages, there will always be that late or early frost, that horde of bugs, those coyotes killing new helpless lambs, those eight weeks of no rain or all rain, the illness that strikes his sheep, and the harvest that must be brought in now, today, and will not wait no matter how he may be feeling. He is a prisoner of the turning of the year . . . and yet this dependence brings him back to an appreciation of Nature, even as he may curse it sometimes. By taking responsibility, he moves again into a dance with Nature, this time at an even more hands-on level. He redeems the mistakes of the Woodcutter's Moon with a new relationship with the Earth. It may still be a bit adversarial, but he no longer pretends that he can ignore Nature and still get to the end of the day unscathed.

During the Farmer's Moon, we learn about being part of a balanced system that includes Nature and yet makes room for our own efforts. We learn about taking full responsibility for what we own, and all the work that taking care of it entails. We struggle more fully with the concept of ownership of land—or, at least, land *rights*—than we did on the Gardener's Moon. What does it mean to balance the needs of the land against the desires (and the Farmer would indeed call them needs) of human beings to live more than subsistence lives? We also learn about organizing a system, and, for the first time, dealing with profits. The question arises of whether to reinvest them or send them elsewhere in favor of personal cash. Where the Woodcutter sold off his wood without thinking about where the next batch would come from, on the Farmer's Moon we understand our limits and choose judiciously . . . or we fail disastrously.

People born under the Farmer's Moon want to see things grow, but unlike the Gardeners, they want to see *big* things grow. The urge to own land is strong among them, although they may sublimate it into business and imagine, on some abstract level, the company as their substitute farmland. While they may enjoy working with their hands, they are more comfortable in overseeing other people than the earlier Taurus Moons. They have learned patience, but they have also touched the good life and want their comforts as well. This is the first Taurus Moon where sensuous pleasures become a serious motivation, although they remain something to be enjoyed as a reward after one's labor.

Taurus Gibbous Moon people are fated to wrestle with the redemption of human effort in the face of damaged Nature. This may be as simple as realizing that one's body cannot perform like a machine in the service of money-making or as complicated as realizing one must whistle-blow on one's polluting company. For those born under the Farmer's Moon, environmentalism in all its forms may seem unimportant, but it is in fact their fate to strike a compromise with it. The Moon is a hidden force but a strong one, and nothing will go right for them emotionally unless they manifest the Farmer's struggle to live in balance with Nature and humanity in a real, physical way.

Quotes for the Farmer's Moon

What you give comes back in the same form. If you plant barley, don't expect to harvest wheat.

RUMI

The nation that destroys its soil destroys itself.

THEODORE ROOSEVELT

Whatever you cannot understand, you cannot possess.

JOHANN WOLFGANG VON GOETHE

I remember the evacuee children from towns and cities throwing stones at the farm animals. When we explained that if you did that you wouldn't have any milk, meat or eggs, they soon learned to respect the animals.

MARY WESLEY

Farming looks mighty easy when your plow is a pencil and you're a thousand miles from the corn field.

DWIGHT EISENHOWER

The thing about farming is it's so easy, half of it is learning to kill.

MICHAEL CAREY

Life on a farm is a school of patience; you can't hurry the crops or make an ox in two days.

HENRI ALAIN

There seem to be but three ways for a nation to acquire wealth. The first is by war, as the Romans did, in plundering their conquered neighbors. This is robbery. The second by commerce, which is generally cheating. The third by agriculture, the only honest way, wherein man receives a real increase of the seed thrown into the ground, in a kind of continual miracle, wrought by the hand of God in his favor, as a reward for his innocent life and his virtuous industry.

BENJAMIN FRANKLIN

> If a man owns land, the land owns him.
>
> RALPH WALDO EMERSON
>
> I had rather be on my farm than be emperor of the world.
>
> GEORGE WASHINGTON

MERCENARY'S MOON
THE GIBBOUS MOON IN GEMINI

As we move into the Gibbous Moon in Gemini, the focus changes. The Liar becomes a Mercenary, a duelist who will fight with anyone so long as there is pay. However, this period of time will teach the Gemini Moon a great deal. The Mercenary starts out with the flexible ethics of the Liar, but quickly discovers that untruths about one's abilities, in this job anyway, can be fatal. He learns about argument that is based on reality rather than fiction, and most important, he learns about discernment. In fact, *discernment* is the keyword of this phase.

In many spiritual and magical systems, the element of Air is associated with the symbol of a knife. This is because Air, which is also linked to the mental and intellectual capacities, analyzes things and cuts them apart. The mind and the tongue become precision instruments to deconstruct facts and knowledge, and everyone knows that words can slash. This is the place of the Mercenary Moon, where one needs to discern where the flick of the communicative blade must be wielded with precision to get the job done. No more imaginative sloppiness; the Mercenary hones his craft for effectiveness. His ethics are still flexible, but he is no longer out of control. He learns to rule the blade of words with discipline, rather than letting its flash and glitter rule him. Often, he learns it the hard way, recovering from a near-fatal slash from a more skillful opponent.

For Gemini, unlike Aries or Libra, the first step out of the morass of the Waxing Quarter Moon doesn't involve ethics or honor or compassion. That's because the Gemini Moon never started in a place of idealism; it started with "How far can I go here?" The question of "What's right to do?" will not be taken seriously until it is proven to be more effective, and to have superior goals, than what's wrong to do. The Mercenary learns that lies are not a good idea because in the long run, Lies Get You Killed. This is the time when the Gemini Moon learns about strategy and the long view versus immediate emotional gratification. "It's a bad idea" makes much more sense to him than "It's wrong."

The Mercenary also learns to stick to the point (of word or sword) and not go haring off on random escapades if he wants to finish his job. He also learns that if he wants to be hired, at least some part of his word must be seen as trustworthy; he must keep his agreements, without fail, or he starves. He learns about professional pride and the satisfaction of doing a job correctly. In other words, this phase is about Growing Up for the youthful Gemini Moon, and taking responsibility. The Mercenary ends his phase as a serious, grim-eyed professional who says little but pierces to the heart, a far cry from the frivolous children of the last phase.

On the Mercenary's Moon, we learn to properly edit our communication. While this may reek of censorship to some, anyone who has ever had to polish the rough draft of a paper knows how useful it is. Some things don't need to be said or are counterproductive to the goal . . . which is where you have to start. What's your goal with this piece of communication, be it an angry rant, an e-mail, a processing session with your lovers, a school paper, a book, a poem? Who is your audience? What's the best way to get your point across to that audience? Is there unnecessary fluff that can be pruned away? Be ruthless with yourself; that's the Mercenary's lesson.

People born under the Mercenary's Moon have the lifelong lesson of polishing their communication or being set up by the Universe to live with constant misunderstandings. This Moon often requires that the natives learn young to be mature in their communication, particularly their emotional dialogue. Their parents might have been intellectuals who expected them to use adult vocabulary and concepts at a young age, or psychologist types who expected clear emotional dialogue even from children. There may have been learning disabilities to overcome or particularly advanced schooling to adapt to. Their lives are characterized by continuing lessons in polishing and maturing their ability to communicate, especially with regard to expressing emotions. There may be a self-conscious precision to that communication that differs from their everyday casual mode of speech. They can be a terror in an argument, using their keen perceptions of the weaknesses of others to slash them and their stance to ribbons, but unlike the Evil Twins, it is done with a professional seriousness that knows facts are heavier weapons than exaggerations. While they can still do the Gemini banter, start conflict and you'll see them switch into life-or-death mode.

Quotes for the Mercenary's Moon

How come nobody wants to argue with me? Is it because I'm always so right?

JIM BOUTON

How many a dispute could have been deflated into a single paragraph if the disputants had dared to define their terms?

ARISTOTLE

Facts are ventriloquists' dummies. Sitting on a wise man's knee they're made to utter words of wisdom; elsewhere, they say nothing, or talk nonsense, or indulge in sheer diabolism.

ALDOUS HUXLEY

I am different from Washington; I have a higher, grander standard of principle. Washington could not lie. I *can* lie, but I won't.

MARK TWAIN

An intellectual is someone whose mind watches itself.

ALBERT CAMUS

The power of accurate observation is commonly called cynicism by those who have not got it.

GEORGE BERNARD SHAW

Whatever failures I have known, whatever errors I have committed, whatever follies I have witnessed in public and private life, have been the consequences of action without thought.

BERNARD BARUCH

How to think about a problem: The first step is to make the problem specific . . . ; The second step is to form theories freely of how to rid yourself of that burden . . . ; The third step is to develop in foresight the consequences of your proposals . . . ; The fourth and final step in thinking is to compare the consequences of your proposals to see which is best in the light of your scheme of life as a whole.

BRAND BLANSHARD

Most of what we say and do is not essential. If you can eliminate it, you'll have more time, and more tranquility. Ask yourself at every moment, "Is this necessary?"

MARCUS AURELIUS

The resolute determination of Self-realization is not formed in the minds of those who are attached to pleasure and power; and whose discernment is obscured by such activities.

BHAGAVAD GITA

LIFE-GIVER'S MOON
THE GIBBOUS MOON IN CANCER

As the Orphans of the Waxing Quarter Moon in Cancer mature into the Gibbous Moon, they come to one conclusion: the only way to regain what they have lost is to rebuild it again. The mourning work that they did during the Orphan Moon has cleansed them enough that they can now give with a whole heart, not as an open hole of need. They choose mates, marry, and begin the process of having children and building a new family. The Gibbous Moon pushes them to find their way out of the morass of pain, and this—for Cancer—is the way out. *I'll make my own family, so loved and cared for and well-protected and happy that this will never happen again.*

Being a Life-Giver means not just bringing forth, but sustaining that life as well. The archetypal Life-Givers, both male and female, see the act of procreating as sacred. While they long for it, their challenge is to refrain from making children (or letting their cats and dogs breed in order to have adorable puppies and kittens to love) when the resources do not exist to care for them. This is their biggest trap—diving into unrestrained creation out of their own great need and not considering the future. Another trap is making the eventual children into such talismans of redemption that they are reluctant to give them up to their own eventual futures. Parenting—and nurturing of any kind—is fraught with ambivalence for the Life-Giver, but nurturing is their great need. They plant gardens, not to work in the soil but to see life spring up. They raise animals, not for their utilitarian value but to have one more thing to love. They take in strays, because their image of the family circle is one that is flexible enough to open wide when necessary.

On the Life-Giver's Moon, we give our efforts to our family—however we conceive of that—to make cheer and bring joy. If that isn't an option, we donate our efforts to some family that needs help and aid. Donating Christmas presents or other toys to the proper organizations can be appropriate. So is giving aid to pregnant parents or to parents of newborns who really need a babysitter and a night off to refresh themselves. One magical group told me that they did a circle to bring fertility to a pair of their members to help them conceive a child. At the same time, it's good to think about our own attitudes toward children, families, giving birth, and nurturing.

People born under the Life-Giver's Moon will be intensely bound up with the need to create family. Most of them will probably want to do it the old-fashioned way—marriage and breeding—but some won't have that option, and they will either fall into depression or find another way. This can include adopting children, marrying into stepchildren, living with close friends as chosen family, creating polyamorous relationships and live-in tribes, developing alternative families, and so on. One way or another, their hearts will not be content unless their home is full of close-knit loving bonds. Breaking up a family is painful to them—as it is for any Cancer Moon person—but they are somewhat more resilient about it than people with the Weeping Moon (Waxing Quarter Moon in Cancer) or Widow's Moon (Waning Quarter Moon in Cancer), and their drive to create family will push them to do it over again, as many times as necessary. On some level, though, this Moon really wants to make biological children if at all possible. If they can't, something will always nag at them. I know of at least two Life-Giver's Moon men who didn't have that option, and in addition to adopting and parenting stepchildren, they provided significant amounts of sperm to donation centers.

They have a talent for "nesting" and making a comfortable home space. If Life-Giver's Moon people live in an ugly, bleak apartment, you can bet that it is a temporary situation from which they are getting ready to launch themselves into something more comfortable . . . or, possibly, they've given up and sunk into depression. The best thing for their heart is a snug and comfortable nest with hot cocoa and pancakes and at least one other beloved person (and ideally more) to share it with.

Quotes for the Life-Giver's Moon

When you have brought up kids, there are memories you store directly in your tear ducts.

ROBERT BRAULT

It would seem that something which means poverty, disorder and violence every single day should be avoided entirely, but the desire to beget children is a natural urge.

PHYLLIS DILLER

The guys who fear becoming fathers don't understand that fathering is not something perfect men do, but something that perfects the man. The end product of child raising is not the child but the parent.

FRANK PITTMAN

You can never go home again, but the truth is you can never leave home, so it's all right.

MAYA ANGELOU

Home is a name, a word, it is a strong one; stronger than magician ever spoke, or spirit ever answered to, in the strongest conjuration.

CHARLES DICKENS

She named the infant "Pearl," as being of great price—purchased with all she had.

NATHANIEL HAWTHORNE

Home is a place you grow up wanting to leave, and grow old wanting to get back to.

JOHN ED PEARCE

Cultural expectations shade and color the images that parents-to-be form. The baby product ads, showing a woman serenely holding her child, looking blissfully and mysteriously contented, or the television parents, wisely and humorously solving problems, influence parents-to-be.

ELLEN GALINSKY

Family love is messy, clinging, and of an annoying and repetitive pattern, like bad wallpaper.

FRIEDRICH NIETZSCHE

Feelings of worth can flourish only in an atmosphere where individual differences are appreciated, mistakes are tolerated, communication is open, and rules are flexible—the kind of atmosphere that is found in a nurturing family.

VIRGINIA SATIR

SINGER'S MOON
THE GIBBOUS MOON IN LEO

As the Leo Moon passes from the Waxing Quarter to the Gibbous phase, the Actor learns to sing and to write her own songs. She goes into hiding for a while to create, and she finds—to her surprise—that she misses the applause less. However, the gregarious Leo nature drives her out again, and she nakedly performs her soul-song up on a stage . . . and for the first time, people applaud who she really is, with nothing in the way. She is still a skilled performer, and still knows how to manipulate an audience, but now it is done entirely in the service of getting her soul-idea across to them, rather than being in the service of pleasing them.

Over time, she learns that the satisfaction of having one's own self applauded is joy enough to make up for the lost applause from those who are not pleased by the song. When they don't applaud, she shrugs, goes home, and throws herself back into the creative process. Her self-worth no longer depends on the audience's reaction. It has begun to depend on her own authenticity and her willingness to bare that to the world. The creative process fills her with joy, and she performs to audiences of shadows as she works.

This Moon still has pitfalls; it is a way out of the hollow despair of the Actor's Moon, but Leo is not entirely out of the woods. Leo has a strong ego, and the Leo Moon is an ego built on emotion. When the weight of human approval is lightened, and self-worth is built on authentic expression, ego can step in and decide that everyone should hear what I have to say, and value it, and if they don't it's because something's wrong with them and they're idiots with no taste. The Moon energy remembers the puppet-strings of the Actor's Moon, and this may be an unsurprising reaction in the other direction. The Singer needs to remember that if the song doesn't go over well, it might be that it was just the wrong time and place, not that there is some great failing among all the people who don't understand. The ego direction for the Singer can lead to "No one understands me because I am such a genius!" which can engender detachment from the audience. People can sense when you are contemptuous of them, even from a stage, and it tends to create a self-fulfilling prophecy. There's also that the shadows who always applaud can become more desirable than the real people who don't, a pitfall that would never occur to the Actor.

On the Singer's Moon, we do something creative that expresses our emotions and inner self and, ideally, perform it for an audience. If the idea of doing that is horrendous, or if it's not something that can be perfected and done in a day or so, try creating on the Singer's Moon of one year, and then take time to get ready and perform it on the Singer's Moon of the following year. There's no hurry—the Moon will always come back. It doesn't have to be a song; if you can't sing, do something else. Even just talking about something very important to you will work, if you do it sincerely and with an eye toward audience reception—although not so much that you dilute the message.

People born under the Singer's Moon have a strong need for creative self-expression. That's true for all the Leo Moons, but the joy for people of the Singer's Moon comes less from applause and more from having fulfilled a need to express their own souls to a group of people. Being their authentic selves where everyone can see is good for their hearts. All Leo Moons love to perform for their loved ones, who tend to become their audience whether they like it or not, but Singer's Moon people especially need that boost from their loved ones, since what they're doing is less saleable and more genuine, and thus makes them more vulnerable. Still, the loved ones who end up being the audience should continually make an effort to encourage the public performance of authenticity, even if that's just dressing up in unusual clothing and cheerfully going out to dinner.

Quotes for the Singer's Moon

Everyone has talent. What is rare is the courage to follow the talent to the dark place where it leads.

ERICA JONG

Yet we would die as some have done,
Beating a way for the rising sun.

ARNA BONTEMPS

I believe talent is like electricity. We don't understand electricity. We use it. You can plug into it and light up a lamp, keep a heart pump going, light a cathedral, or you can electrocute a person with it. Electricity will do all that.

MAYA ANGELOU

At moments of great enthusiasm it seems to me that no one in the world has ever made something this beautiful and important.

M. C. ESCHER

Talent is what you possess; genius is what possesses you.

MALCOLM COWLEY

To love is to admire with the heart; to admire is to love with the mind.

THÉOPHILE GAUTIER

In music one must think with the heart and feel with the brain.

GEORGE SZELL

Talent is God-given. Be humble. Fame is man-given. Be grateful. Conceit is self-given. Be careful.

JOHN WOODEN

Most men lead lives of quiet desperation and go to the grave with the song still in them.

HENRY DAVID THOREAU

A bird doesn't sing because it has an answer, it sings because it has a song.

LOU HOLTZ

HOUSEWIFE'S MOON
THE GIBBOUS MOON IN VIRGO

The Gibbous Moon in Virgo finds the Accountant of the Waxing Quarter Moon taking an entirely unexpected turn. Where once life revolved around numbers and criticism, and the pursuit of human company was entirely voluntary (if ideally necessary), here the Universe loses patience, takes the emotionally chaste Virgo Moon, and shoves her straight into a place where she is forced to balance both detail-oriented tasks and human interaction, often of the most difficult kind. The Housewife's Moon is also called the Stepmother's Moon, with all the connotations of the Stepmother's choice to be good or evil in her task. Virgo is not a natural mother of the sort that the Taurus and Cancer mother archetypes are; she is once removed, a caretaker who did not choose to be one, of people that she may have no instinctive feeling for.

The Virgo Moon Housewife desperately wants to live in a place of order, so she scrubs and organizes and toils, only to have her work undone in minutes by family members who do not appreciate her need for cleanliness and order. She values work, but the continual nature of housework makes her despair of ever having the satisfaction of a job well done, permanently. It also makes her resentful of the people who bring their untidiness into her world. If she gives up in despair and lets the filth pile up, she will fall into depression and fail. If she pastes a false smile on her face every day and tries to mimic the more feeling-based nurturing of the Mother Moons, the nervous energy of this Mercury-ruled sign will eventually disintegrate into an attack of neurosis. Those ways are a betrayal of her honest need for order and organization. On the other hand, if she falls into constant resentful carping and nagging of the people who fail to live up to her standards, she fails there as well. The Gibbous Moon is all about redemption of people's greatest internal sins, and usually the greatest sins are the ones that we are most inclined to try to cast as virtues regardless of their corrosive effect on our souls . . . because the redemption path involved is so difficult and intimidating.

The lesson of the Housewife is to learn, slowly and painfully, that people and relationships—even the messiest and most untidy of them— are equally as valuable as order and peace. Removing the human influence from one's life, even when that influence seems like nothing more than a big pain in the ass, is missing the point and the lesson. Social capital is invaluable, and sooner or later it becomes clear that if you want people to respect your boundaries, your setting of them must be not only firm but also respectful, even if you're not feeling like those particular people are worthy of much respect at the moment. Criticism must be phrased a certain way or you might as well be talking to yourself.

On the Housewife's Moon, we clean house—of course—but we also take into account the people living in our house and their needs in the matter. If you live alone, work on making some cleanliness and order in your neighborhood—not the community at large full of strangers, but the messy ambivalences of people who share a day-to-day living space of some sort with you, whether you or they like it or not. Again, keep their needs in mind as you go about creating order. Any project that degenerates into arguing or nagging during this time should be abandoned, and a new plan built. If you are a stepparent, this is a good time to focus on the joys and difficulties of that relationship.

People born under the Housewife's Moon will be continually faced, all their lives, with the choice of order versus messy human relationships, and if they do not learn to give them both equal value, their personal lives will not work well. If they revert to the Counting Moon's hermitude, the Universe will find some way to drive them out, some way to force them to depend on others. Those others may be legitimately unworthy, which is why it is important for people born to this Moon to actually go to the trouble of choosing worthy friends and loved ones. However, if they continually judge those loved ones unworthy because they are flawed and imperfect, they have failed again. The idea is to continue to value the people in one's life even when they are imperfect, and to get some objectivity about how their imperfections may be inflated by one's own troubles and irritation.

The Virgo Moon may be less emotional than some, but it is still a Moon. Its emotions tend to manifest in the nervous system and come out as irritation and frustration. Those born under the Housewife's Moon, of any gender, can bring great gifts to the world in their ability to make a space, a home, a workplace, a project, a community better organized and more peaceful, but only if they can hold onto their inner peace themselves, and not be overthrown by the inevitable entropy that is the price of being human among humans.

Quotes for the Housewife's Moon

Have nothing in your house that you do not know to be useful, or believe to be beautiful.

WILLIAM MORRIS

I long to accomplish a great and noble task, but it is my chief duty to accomplish small tasks as if they were great and noble.

HELEN KELLER

The reward of a thing well done is to have done it.

RALPH WALDO EMERSON

The question of common sense is always what is it good for?—a question which would abolish the rose and be answered triumphantly by the cabbage.

JAMES RUSSELL LOWELL

The society which scorns excellence in plumbing because plumbing is a humble activity, and tolerates shoddiness in philosophy because philosophy is an exalted activity, will have neither good plumbing nor good philosophy. Neither its pipes nor its theories will hold water.

JOHN W. GARDNER

A stepmother might have to rise above a little more than everyone else to make everything go smoothly and for everyone to feel comfortable. It's one of the nicest gifts they could give.

ELIZABETH HOWELL

Give me your spoiled, your unruly, your angry children yearning to break me.

KAREN PLOVERTY, THE STEPPARENT'S PLEDGE OF ALLEGIANCE

I will not be a resentful bitch. I will not be a resentful bitch. I will not be a resentful bitch.

KAREN PLOVERTY

Happiness is the natural flower of duty.

PHILLIPS BROOKS

I am thankful for a lawn that needs mowing, windows that need cleaning and gutters that need fixing because it means I have a home. I am thankful for the piles of laundry and ironing because it means my loved ones are nearby.

NANCIE J. CARMODY

LOVER'S MOON
THE GIBBOUS MOON IN LIBRA

As the Libra Moon moves from the Waxing Quarter to the Gibbous phase, the bitter Black Knight falls unexpectedly in love, and it saves his soul. After his uncomfortable sojourn on the side of justice, the Libra pendulum swings back toward the side of harmony as he discovers the Great Mystery that everyone has been talking about. As the White Knight, he was in love with an ideal from afar; as the Dancer he fell in love with whatever was beautiful. As the Lover, he is actually in an all-consuming relationship with a real human being, complete with flaws, arguments, mistakes, forgiveness, heart-wrenching passion, merging of hearts, and the sure knowledge that We Are a Couple. The back-and-forth of his inner pendulum stills for the time being, because he is one side and the Beloved is the other side. He realizes that all that back-and-forth was simply training him for this one moment, when he could be in this dance with the right person . . . the dance of I–Thou.

This is a strongly Venusian aspect of Libra, where the Love Goddess shines through clear and strong. It is also the moment of love-as-savior, the saving grace that brings the Libra Moon out of the morass of resentment that is the Adversary position. Love-as-savior is different from lover-as-savior; the latter is doomed, because the Beloved can only save if they are perfect, and no one is. It's love itself—the process, the emotion, the understanding, the sacred dance—that saves, because it sees past the conflicts, bridges the dualities, and brings every black-and-white picture into color. For the airy, in-the-head Libra, the idea that you can understand people better, and perhaps even forgive their flaws, by loving them . . . that's a world-shattering idea. Love is the lifeline that pulls him past his cold rage, and he throws himself into it.

Libra Moon love is not transpersonal love, where you spread it over a whole tribe or even world of people. It is not family love, nor parent-child love. It is one-on-one romantic love, complete with the chemicals rushing through your system, and the moment when you smell their hair and know that your body has imprinted on their pheromones. You can't be like that with everyone, but even being like that with one person can teach you how to go a little further with everyone else. Libra learns this lesson, connecting for the first time through the body and heart rather than merely the mind. He is the consummate lover, sincerely meaning every romantic gesture.

The danger is that he will fall so far into love that he loses himself. People, regardless of gender, can become so far subsumed into couplehood that they cease to exercise the parts of themselves that don't fit with their relationship, and they become less whole as a person. The Lover may project certain of his own traits onto the Beloved—"they can be that for me, so I don't have to"—or repress "unacceptable" traits (meaning ones that the Beloved finds inconvenient) in order to avoid conflict. Indeed, he goes from being the conflict-oriented Black Knight to being the conflict-avoidant Lover so quickly that it's shocking. To fulfill the Gibbous Moon promise, he needs to learn to balance couplehood with aloneness, I with Thou.

On the Lover's Moon, we think about romantic love. If you have someone to practice it with, go on a romantic date with that person. If you don't, facilitate the romance of others (if only by babysitting or buying them tickets). Do it in the spirit of making an offering to the Powers That Be to ask them to send over the right person for you.

Lover's Moon people really need to be half of a couple. That's a general need for the Libra Moon anyway, but Lover's Moon people really wither up if they can't do the dance of I–Thou. This means that some of them will offer themselves up too cheaply out of desperation or will stay too long with the wrong person. It's hard for them to be patient and not settle. Their heart really wants to be partnered, and without love they don't do very well in their lives. (That's an understatement, all right?) They tend to be conflict-avoidant and will do anything to keep the harmony going, up to and including hiding their actual feelings under loving gestures. Being alone while in a relationship is nearly as hard for them as being alone without one, but it's an art that they need to practice. A wise partner will encourage them to have their own life and reassure them that conflict will not mean disaster, but resolution.

Quotes for the Lover's Moon

Love does not consist in gazing at each other but in looking outward together in the same direction.

ANTOINE DE SAINT-EXUPÉRY

Love is an ideal thing, marriage a real thing; a confusion of the real with the ideal never goes unpunished.

JOHANN WOLFGANG VON GOETHE

There are four questions of value in life . . . What is sacred? Of what is the spirit made? What is worth living for, and what is worth dying for? The answer to each is the same. Only love.

DON JUAN DEMARCO

Free love? As if love is anything but free! Man has bought brains, but all the millions in the world have failed to buy love. Man has subdued bodies, but all the power on earth has been unable to subdue love. Man has conquered whole nations, but all his armies could not conquer love. Man has chained and fettered the spirit, but he has been utterly helpless before love. High on a throne, with all the splendor and pomp his gold can command, man is yet poor and desolate, if love passes him by. And if it stays, the poorest hovel is radiant with warmth, with life and color. Thus love has the magic power to make of a beggar a king. Yes, love is free; it can dwell in no other atmosphere.

EMMA GOLDMAN

Do you want me to tell you something really subversive? Love is everything it's cracked up to be. That's why people are so cynical about it. . . . It really is worth fighting for, being brave for, risking everything for. And the trouble is, if you don't risk everything, you risk even more.

ERICA JONG

Love works magic.
It is the final purpose
Of the world story,
The Amen of the universe.

NOVALIS

I wish that people who are conventionally supposed to love each other would say to each other, when they fight, "Please—a little less love, and a little more common decency."

KURT VONNEGUT

The worst part of life is waiting. The best part of life is having someone worth waiting for.

JESSICA BRUMLEY

Love is saying, "I feel differently," instead of "You're wrong."

GEORGE MOORE

Being deeply loved by someone gives you strength, while loving someone deeply gives you courage.

LAO TZU

CLOAKED ONE'S MOON
THE GIBBOUS MOON IN SCORPIO

At the turn of the last Moon, the Executioner has made his choice. He lays down his axe and walks away, his heart in turmoil, darkness raging within. He has tried to externalize his pain and it has failed, causing great suffering in others; he has tried to gain vengeance for the injustices done to him and only succeeded in being unjust to others. There is only one road out, and it leads downward. The Scorpio Moon walks into the darkness of his own soul and swears not to come out until the battle is won.

In ancient northern Europe, mystics and holy people practiced a technique of deep meditation and communion called "going under the cloak." In this custom, the mystics who sought to commune with the gods and divine the question to a crucially important problem—perhaps one that would determine the outcome for the future of an entire people—would roll themselves in a great cloak of dark wool to shut out the light and remain there for up to three days. During this time they would fast, be passed only a jug of water to drink and a container to relieve themselves, and exist entirely in their own sensory-deprived world. At the end of it, they would have the answer. Sometimes that answer was terrifying, but it was always true.

The Moon of the Cloaked One is similar to this practice. The Scorpio Moon goes inward, underground to the Underworld, down to the dark basement where all the monsters are kept who must be propitiated. Several Moons are associated with shadow work, but this one is fully dedicated to it. The complete understanding of one's own darknesses and the eventual acceptance of them are worthy and terrifying acts. This requires a courage that people born to the Scorpio Moon have, even if they don't know it yet.

The end result of shadow work, of talking to all those monsters, is that one must learn not only to accept them but to love them, exactly as they are, with no assumption that they will ever be healed. If you come to them with the assumption that you'll love them once they're healed, they spit in your face because you don't love them as they are. This is one of the hardest lessons for anyone to learn, especially for the monsters that aren't glamorous, that make us deeply ashamed of ourselves, that hurt the people we love. The Cloaked One must go down into the darkness and wrestle his demons to the ground and then find a way to love them. It is a long, hard, grueling task that is worth every moment of energy put into it.

This is a Moon of patience and courage. The Cloaked One needs to face every broken shard of pain, over and over again, until it is worn down and no longer hurts, until he can move beyond the pain entirely. He needs to rebuild himself from scratch as a whole person, going all the way back to the original Raging Child and soothing those long-ago scars.

On the Cloaked One's Moon, we go down into our own depths and deal with our monsters. It is a good time for therapy of any sort. This is not the time to compare your own monsters with other people's . . . just go down and face your own.

Those born under the Cloaked One's Moon will be dealing with their inner darkness and wounds as a lifelong quest. The longer they put them off, the worse they will be. Many Scorpio Moons are associated with abuse and trauma in the early years; this one is special in that it offers chances to heal this pain, over and over again. Cloaked One's Moon people are drawn down into their own darkness again and again, as seekers rather than victims. Once they have healed their wounds, they can be amazing healers of others, guides to the Underworld that lead people in and out of their own Underworlds. They understand brutality and horror, but they have the possibility of simply letting that knowledge make them unshockable in the quest to help others out of the same dark place.

Quotes for the Cloaked One's Moon

This is my death . . . and it will profit me to understand it.

ANNE SEXTON

Why should we honor only those who die on the field of battle? A man may show as reckless a courage in entering into the abyss of himself.

WILLIAM BUTLER YEATS

The best way out is always through.

ROBERT FROST

I dip my pen into the blackest ink, because I am not afraid of falling into my inkpot.

RALPH WALDO EMERSON

We should be careful to get out of an experience only the wisdom that is in it—and stop there, lest we be like the cat who sits on a hot stove-lid. She will never sit on a hot stove-lid again—and that is well, but also she will never sit down on a cold one any more.

MARK TWAIN

Deep into that darkness peering, long I stood there,
  wondering, fearing,
Doubting, dreaming dreams no mortal ever dared
  to dream before.

EDGAR ALLAN POE

Some people are afraid of what they might find if they try to analyze themselves too much, but you have to crawl into your wounds to discover where your fears are. Once the bleeding starts, the cleansing can begin.

TORI AMOS

Knowing your own darkness is the best method for dealing with the darknesses of other people.

CARL JUNG

Ever since I was a boy, I never was someone who was at ease with happiness. Too often I embrace introspection and self-doubt. I wish I could embrace the good things.

HUGH LAURIE

The longest journey is the journey inwards. Of him who has chosen his destiny, who has started upon his quest for the source of his being.

DAG HAMMARSKJÖLD

SCHOLAR'S MOON
THE GIBBOUS MOON IN SAGITTARIUS

Sagittarius rules higher learning as well as travel, and during the Gibbous Moon in Sagittarius the frustrated Seeker turns to the power of what has already been written down. Flinging himself into his studies, he looks for the truth among organized words and facts. His burning need to know sends him excavating through obscure and convoluted bodies of information, and he enjoys the process. The Scholar treats his facts and his long-crystallized historic opinions like the gems found by the Miner (Waxing Quarter Moon in Capricorn)—hoarding them, taking them out periodically and holding them up to the light, admiring them, defending them against calumny. They, rather than any human beings, are his children—adopted children, but it is certain that before long he will "birth" a few theories of his own to add to the family.

After the empty hands of the Seeker, the Scholar's path seems well-lit, well-trodden, and infinitely more useful, not to mention endlessly fascinating. The Scholar feels like he is actually getting somewhere and feels comfort with the tethers of tradition enclosing him. Like Aquarius, Sagittarius is doomed to struggle with the conflict of structured tradition versus independently striking out, only the battle is internal and spiritual rather than external and public. Here the Sagittarius Moon has swung back toward conservatism again, after all the endless hacking about on the road. That pendulum will go back and forth a few times more before it finds a balance. So will his ego, as one of the dangers at this point in the cycle is intellectual hubris, thinking that one knows it all when one has barely scratched the surface. From that unfortunate standpoint, all sorts of arguments and intellectual turf wars become possible. It is the Scholar's challenge to continue to keep an open mind no matter how in love he is with any one particular theory.

On the Scholar's Moon, we study what has been written in the past. The area of study doesn't matter so much as the attitude: one does it to absorb what is to be found, not necessarily to find one particular thing—

especially if that one thing is intended as a justification of some behavior. Let the quest come as it comes; if the road tangents off, take it like a Sagittarian and see where it goes. This is by definition a good time for research or academic writing if you're in school. A test taken on the Scholar's Moon will turn out well.

People born on the Scholar's Moon have a keen, perceptive intellect and an excellent facility for committing things to heart, although they may tend to limit themselves to areas of study that charge them emotionally. (This is a Moon position, after all, even though the emotional Moon has a little trouble with Sagittarius's abstract thinking.) They will, of course, have difficulty realizing to what extent their keenness on a subject is based on emotional appeal, and they will probably deny their vehemence as simply being a rational response. Like the Seeker, the Scholar has the foreshadowing echo of the future Hunter and his fanaticism (Waning Quarter Moon in Sagittarius), although it is still contained behind the happiness of learning.

Scholar's Moon people value their intellect more than anything else. Whether they're in academia or have never set foot in a college, their self-worth is usually based on their intellect, which means that they tend to denigrate any system or person's worth not based on that, as well as the various things that it might be based on. While this gives them a good base to stand on when it comes to dealing with the central Sagittarius Moon theme—the search for meaning—it can be problematic when dealing with devalued things like emotional relationships with human beings. Scholar's Moon people need to learn that family is more than just annoying people who interrupt their studies, but the ones who will someday benefit, if only indirectly, from the Sagittarians' research.

Quotes for the Scholar's Moon

The ink of the scholar is more sacred than the blood of the martyr.

MUHAMMAD

There are two ways to slide easily through life; to believe everything or to doubt everything. Both ways save us from thinking.

ALFRED KORZYBSKI

The scientists most esteemed by their colleagues are those who are both very original and committed to the abstract ideal of truth in the midst of clamoring demands of ego and ideology. They pass the acid test of promoting new knowledge even at the expense of losing credit for it.

EDWARD O. WILSON

The world's great men have not commonly been great scholars, nor the great scholars great men.

OLIVER WENDELL HOLMES, JR.

Learned men are cisterns of knowledge, not the fountainheads.

JAMES NORTHCOTE

Knowledge is of two kinds. We know a subject ourselves, or we know where we can find information upon it.

SAMUEL JOHNSON

Of all men's miseries the bitterest is this: to know so much and to have control over nothing.

HERODOTUS

It's what you learn after you know it all that counts.

JOHN WOODEN

In formal logic, a contradiction is the signal of a defeat, but in the evolution of real knowledge it marks the first steps in progress towards a victory.

ALFRED NORTH WHITEHEAD

All that you may achieve or discover you will regard as a fragment of a larger pattern of the truth which from the separate approaches every true scholar is striving to descry.

ABBOTT LOWELL

SMITH'S MOON
THE GIBBOUS MOON IN CAPRICORN

On the Gibbous Moon, we find the way out of the corner that the Waxing Quarter has backed us into. For the Miner, the way out is to bring the metal and jewels to the surface and, instead of merely selling them or showing them off, he is drawn by the urge to put them together into works of beauty and craft. He learns metalwork and becomes the Smith, and suddenly there is something more important than the opinions and respect of others—the self-respect that grows from mastering a craft, becoming competent in some kind of creation, bringing creative power into the world. What people think takes a back seat to the actual process of work, a process that is rooted deep in every Earth sign.

In ancient times, the smith was a central and very important member of the village. He got that way not because of his wealth or influence, but because his unique skills made him indispensable. His importance was such that he often had one of the few surnames in the village that stuck with his family, and thus Smith became an extremely common name. This is an important Capricorn point: to gain respect and the attendant security through being indispensable is an alternate goal that does not require great wealth and power. Since we are dealing with a Moon here, albeit ruled by strict Saturn, we are dealing with irrational emotions. Capricorn Moon people, like those with the Cancer Moon, want security and the knowledge that they will not be turned out of the community. Unlike the Cancer Moon people, they go about it by trying to be respected rather than depending on the vagaries of being loved, but there is still a root need for security. The Smith's position ensures that he will be an important and valued member of the community, and it provides the feeling of safety that Capricorn craves.

This is a Moon of learning about value, and values. As he handles the precious gems and works the metal into new shapes, the Smith learns more about the value of what he works with, in a way that the Miner could not see. He learns that there is no absolute value to the commodity, but that value varies wildly depending on what the community can afford, what it currently desires, how well the material is polished, whether it was made into a shape that appeals to the most people or to only specific people, and even on luck itself (a commodity that confuses Saturn-ruled Capricorn, who sees it as eminently unfair). The Smith prides himself on his competence and struggles with the issue of fair pay for fair skill—does he cut someone a break and cheat himself when that person is penniless and needs what he has to give, or does he hold to his principles and tell the needy one to find a way or do without? There's never an easy answer, and the Capricorn Moon wrestles with the thorny problem.

On the Smith's Moon, we work at a craft or skilled labor that directly benefits a group. We don't, however, donate our work. Instead, we concentrate on figuring out a fair price, one that the group can reasonably afford and at the same time one that will do honor to our efforts. Most commerce doesn't try to find that middle point. It tries to get whatever the market will bear, in the face of the market's trying to bear as little as possible. To find the right value for our craft means setting aside our need for security and perhaps thinking outside the box about what our labor is worth. Perhaps if there is no money, barter will do as well, but that requires even more negotiating and thinking about the value of people's efforts.

People born under the Smith's Moon have a need to perfect their craft and be seen as competent. If they don't have a craft to perfect, they will suffer emotionally for it. Learning skills that they can be proud of is the best medicine for them. They want security, and they are willing to learn to be indispensable in order to get it; community means a lot to them, but only if they are a central and respected member of it. If they are marginalized, they quickly become resentful . . . but they are still often reluctant to leave, hoping to prove themselves. They may struggle a good deal with their own value, perhaps resentful that the community will not pay well for their honest labor, perhaps overpricing or overvaluing themselves out of fear and greed, perhaps underpricing themselves out of despondency and fatalism. Taking pride in a job well done is what's best for their hearts, and as such they need honest assessment, not optimistic overestimation.

Quotes for the Smith's Moon

Happiness is like coke—something you get as a by-product in the process of making something else.

ALDOUS HUXLEY

A noble craft, but somehow a most melancholy! All noble things are touched with that.

HERMAN MELVILLE

Work while you have the light. You are responsible for the talent that has been entrusted to you.

HENRI FRÉDÉRIC AMIEL

What work I have done, I have done because it has been play. If it had been work I shouldn't have done it. Who was it who said, "Blessed is the man who has found his work"? Whoever it was he had the right idea in his mind. Mark you, he says his work—not somebody else's work. The work that is really a man's own work is play and not work at all. Cursed is the man who has found some other man's work and cannot lose it. When we talk about the great workers of the world we really mean the great players of the world. The fellows who groan and sweat under the weary load of toil that they bear never can hope to do anything great. How can they when their souls are in a ferment of revolt against the employment of their hands and brains? The product of slavery, intellectual or physical, can never be great.

MARK TWAIN

It is in the gift for employing all the vicissitudes of life to one's own advantage and to that of one's craft that a large part of genius consists.

GEORG C. LICHTENBERG

Work and rework, reach for the light, until you have it captured momentarily: the sprouting power in a seed.

JESSE COUGAR

The greatness of a craft consists firstly in how it brings comradeship to men.

ANTOINE DE SAINT-EXUPÉRY

Until you value yourself, you won't value your time. Until you value your time, you will not do anything with it.

M. SCOTT PECK

> A human being feels able and competent only so long as he is permitted to contribute as much as, or more, than he has contributed to him.
>
> ELBERT HUBBARD
>
> When pieces of bronze or gold or iron break, the metal-smith welds them together again in the fire, and the bond is established.
>
> SRI GURU GRANTH SAHIB

TRICKSTER'S MOON
THE GIBBOUS MOON IN AQUARIUS

As the crisis of the Rebel Moon passes, the Rebel realizes that the masses are easily swayed—and easily swayed back again, when the heat of the moment and all the screaming wears off. Few have his devotion to principles, and many are suspicious of the violence that rebellion brings. His most eloquent and sincere pleading for the depth of his cause is lost on them, because they start imagining mob rule and quickly vacate the public square. He needs to find a way to teach people about hard truths that doesn't frighten them away and doesn't get him ostracized. The scorched-earth policies are not working.

In the Gibbous Moon phase, the Aquarius Moon realizes that people respond well to humor, and he learns the magic of the Trickster. The Trickster is present in all cultures, and he lives in a special, enchanted place. Even in the most repressed and dangerous times, he appears like the court jester who was able to speak hard truths to the king that his courtiers dared not say, as long as he cloaked it in joking around. The Trickster makes people laugh, so he can say hard things and teach them subtle lessons. He also learns not to take himself too seriously and not to be afraid of being seen as a fool. This is where Aquarius, the opposite of image-conscious Leo, is able to let go and be ridiculous if it will get the point across to the masses. The Trickster does street theater rather than revolution and finds that it is just as revolutionary.

The dark side of this archetype is that sometimes Tricksters are penalized for their words. Sometimes denial is so thick that nothing will be heard, and it falls to Tricksters to speak the truth even when they know that they will not be heard, that they may well be killed for it. I once read a tale of a Native American tribe on the northwest coast who were being cheated of their furs by white traders who dazzled them with cheap trinkets. The female sacred trickster of the tribe dissuaded them from their greed by setting up a crude stall near the traders, where she loudly hawked dung, rocks, and sticks. The people turned sheepishly from their enthusiastic acquisition of cheap trinkets . . . and the traders killed the trickster. This punishment happens in myths, too. It's part of the deal: the safety that the Trickster counts on is paid for by being the one to take risks when even he will not be safe, and the truth must still be spoken. Why must it be spoken, even if the speaker will be silenced and nothing will change? Because someone in the future might hear the tale passed down, and understand, and make the change. People born on this Moon truly learn what it means to sacrifice for the future.

On the Trickster's Moon, we tell tales of trickery that worked, that brought justice when nothing else would, that got a lesson through a hard head. We do street theater, if that's in our repertoire. If nothing else, we attack a problem in an unusual way, brainstorming for something that's never been thought of before.

People born on the Trickster's Moon want to change the world, but when they try to do it grimly and seriously, they always end up clumsy. They are at their best when they can think up an original and slightly ridiculous way to get it done—the way that nobody expects and that only they can pull off. This is beyond thinking outside the box; it's thinking in a universe where there are no boxes. There is a faint echo of the Leo Clown's Moon in Trickster Moon people, at least when it comes to being the class clown, but where Leo does it to please the audience and get attention, Aquarius does it for the message . . . or they should. It's not their cosmic job to do it for applause. They need to risk the truthtelling, or it will all go wrong.

Trickster's Moon people may be attracted to "crazy wisdom gurus," and they are at their best when they're spreading their own whimsical message through venues where it will sink in subtly, without being noticed. They will also be the truthspeakers who sacrifice themselves, pointing out the emperor's nudity. If they're skilled, they'll manage to do this in a way that skates them by any repercussions . . . but if they can't skate by, they'll be driven to do it anyway, for the sake of Truth.

Quotes for the Trickster's Moon

There is no way to suppress change, the story says, not even in heaven; there is only a choice between a way of living that allows constant, if gradual, alterations and a way of living that combines great control and cataclysmic upheavals. Those who panic and bind the trickster choose the latter path. It would be better to learn to play with him, better especially to develop styles (cultural, spiritual, artistic) that allow for some commerce with accident, and some acceptance of the changes contingency will always engender.

LEWIS HYDE

Signs of the Bastard's holy presence tend to be unmistakable, to those who know Him. The screaming, the altercations, the people running in circles—all that was lacking was something bursting into flame.

LOIS MCMASTER BUJOLD

I shall continue to be an impossible person as long as those who are now possible remain possible.

MIKHAIL BAKUNIN

Many native traditions held clowns and tricksters as essential to any contact with the sacred. People could not pray until they had laughed, because laughter opens and frees from rigid preconception. Humans had to have tricksters within the most sacred ceremonies lest they forget the sacred comes through upset, reversal, surprise. The trickster in most native traditions is essential to creation, to birth.

BYRD GIBBENS

God is a comedian playing to an audience too afraid to laugh.

VOLTAIRE

There's always an easy solution to every human problem—neat, plausible, and wrong.

H. L. MENCKEN

In life you need either inspiration or desperation.

ANTHONY ROBBINS

"You say you're a Fool," Nita said. "Are you making a joke?"

"Always. But the jokes are always true."

DIANE DUANE, FROM *A WIZARD ABROAD*. THE CHARACTER NITA
SPEAKS TO AMADAUN (CELTIC FOR "DEADLY FOOL").

We have all seen how an appropriate and well-timed joke can sometimes influence even grim tyrants. . . . The most violent tyrants put up with their clowns and fools, though these often made them the butt of open insults.

DESIDERIUS ERASMUS

A king, in times long, long gone by,
Said to his lazy jester:
"If I were you and you were I
My moments merrily would fly—
Nor care nor grief to pester."
"The reason, Sire, that you would thrive,"
The fool said—"if you'll hear it—
Is that of all the fools alive
Who own you for their sovereign, I've
The most forgiving spirit."

OOGUM BEM, VIA AMBROSE BIERCE

POET'S MOON
THE GIBBOUS MOON IN PISCES

As the Waxing Quarter Moon gives way to the Gibbous Moon, the Martyr flees and hides in some dark place, unable to give any more . . . and to her surprise, the channel within herself that links to All That Is opens up, and poetry begins to flow through her. It is not her own energy, but that of the Universe, and she finds herself unable to resist its flow. Taking refuge in a dark attic with only the bare necessities to keep her alive, she opens herself fully to the creative process. The words of the Universe come through the pen in her tortured hand, but it is ecstasy. She does not care if anyone reads or appreciates her work, but when it leaves her sphere it inspires others.

There is still sacrifice going on—the Pisces Moon is intimately involved with sacrifice, always—but this time the sacrificing does not come between the Poet and the cosmic channel. Instead, the sacrifice is made for the cosmic channel itself, while the Poet still reaches out to give a gift to humanity, albeit from more of a distance. The Poet, like the Dreamer of the Pisces New Moon, turns away from direct giving to people in order to give to the Cosmos. (The dance, however, will soon turn back to people again.) As Pisces has trouble with boundaries, she may use her Art as a way to create space between herself and the needs of others, even as those who read her work find themselves drawn closer to her.

On the other hand, she does find that when she walls herself up to let the poetry come, eventually her creativity runs out, and it is only by leaving her garret and exposing herself to the world that she triggers real inspiration. Her need to create makes her live rawly, on the knife's edge, and she may look down contemptuously on the people who seem to have nothing that moves them so intensely, especially if they look down on her with contempt as well. It is not hard for her to imagine herself as some sort of superior cosmic aristocrat, but this is a profound error. Pisceans can be elevated only by first losing themselves, and to maintain that separation of contempt is to keep too much of the self separate. That's a hard and complicated lesson that it may take her a lifetime to understand.

On the Poet's Moon, we read the poetry that moves us, especially aloud in a group so that a variety of people can hear it. If you write poetry yourself, this is a good time to do it . . . and a good time to work on figuring out how to best open yourself to the Voice of the Universe. Do you work best after walking in Nature, or making love, or listening to music? Are you inspired by the works of others—or by silence? It's also a time to think about what you are willing to sacrifice for your own creative self-expression, or perhaps *why* you sacrifice it instead.

People born on the Poet's Moon have an ocean of images boiling inside them, and if the rest of their chart doesn't interfere (check the position of Mercury!) they have the power to bring those images out where the rest of the world can see them and be touched by them. For some, the job isn't so easy; they may have to fight the Neptune-ruled incoherence and vagueness that plagues and thwarts them. It's important that they give themselves permission to experiment and figure out how their creativity works best. Make the time to take that walk in Nature or get right up from the lover's bed and grab pencil and paper. Solitude may work wonders for them, which needs to be understood by their loved ones.

Poet's Moon people can be just as obsessive as any Scorpio Moon, but then suddenly they'll put their hand to their forehead and become limp and melodramatic. When the spirit moves them, they are afire with inspiration and find the strength to drive themselves, but then it's gone and they collapse like a puppet whose strings have been cut, unable to handle ordinary mundane tasks. They may also take refuge in a "nobody understands me" mindset to justify their lack of willingness to cope with ordinary life activities. A good partner will find the balance between being too supportive and enabling their listlessness, or nagging too much and clogging up their channel of Art.

Quotes for the Poet's Moon

All great poetry should produce the instantaneous conviction: This Is True.

JOHN KEATS

All art is a revolt against man's fate. Art is anti-destiny.

ANDRÉ MALRAUX

In a free democracy, the only justified aristocracy is that of the lonely creative bitterness, the artistically creative scars of the fight for the inner dimension against outer mechanization.

PETER VIERECK

Great talents are the most lovely and often the most dangerous fruits on the tree of humanity. They hang upon the most slender twigs that are easily snapped off.

CARL JUNG

The poem is where the intensity of one's mind finds expression. In the mind it is the pure force of intent; coming out in language, it is a poem. Emotions are stirred within, and take on form in words. If words alone are inadequate, we speak it out in sighs. If sighing is inadequate, we sing it. If singing it is inadequate, unconsciously our hands sway to it and our feet dance it out.

THE GREAT PREFACE OF THE BOOK OF SONGS,
ONE OF THE FIVE CLASSIC TEXTS OF CONFUCIANISM

The artist's talent sits uneasy as an object of public acclaim, having been so long an object of private despair.

ROBERT BRAULT

Poets do not go mad; but chess-players do. Mathematicians go mad, and cashiers; but creative artists very seldom.

G. K. CHESTERTON

The progress of an artist is a continual self-sacrifice, a continual extinction of personality.

T. S. ELIOT

You can tear a poem apart to see what makes it tick. . . . You're back with the mystery of having been moved by words. The best craftsmanship always leaves holes and gaps . . . so that something that is not in the poem can creep, crawl, flash or thunder in.

DYLAN THOMAS

Poetry is just the evidence of life. If your life is burning well, poetry is just the ash.

LEONARD COHEN

5

CONSUMMATION

THE FULL MOON

The heart has its reasons which reason does not understand.

BLAISE PASCAL

THE FULL MOON is a time of blossoming. All the personal work of the last four phases culminates in a Moon that is, perhaps, the most "archetypal" phase for that sign. The lunar energy flows through them unfettered, or fettered only by the element and sign of their Moon. Even an afflicted or unaspected Moon will have a good deal of influence if it's Full. The Moon "comes into its own," as it were, and shines brightly. If the Moon is strongly aspected in the chart, however, it is so powerful that it has a tendency to want to force the individual into being a sort of avatar of that Moon sign, a living archetype rather than a full human with depth. This may be, in a roundabout way, the connection with "lunacy."

People born under the Full Moon, I've noticed, have the best chance of all of becoming a master at being themselves, and of liking themselves. Being able to like oneself is something that anyone could and should strive for, but Full Moon people tend to have an easier time getting to that point than others. It's stepping outside themselves that's the harder part. The Full Moon "feels" like a climax, but it's not the end of the story. We like to think that stories end with the Big Kiss and that the "lived happily ever after" part is merely a footnote, but in real life the story is only half over, if that. The Moon understands this, perhaps better than the Sun. We need to remember that the waxing part of the Moon cycle is the personal part, and the soul needs to move out from its small circle of knowledge and find out, even if that knowledge is hard-won, how little it actually is in the greater scheme of things. The flower cannot remain at peak bloom forever.

The Full Moon begins with the opposition aspect, 180 degrees from the Sun. After this point, the Sun will be ahead of the Moon, and this phase ends when the Moon is

224 degrees past the Sun. The opposition that colors this phase is generally seen as a negative aspect, but its positive side is about distance and perspective. Two planets in opposition may disagree, but they also have the distance to have a clearer perspective on each other—clearer, for example, than the square aspects—and this may account for some of the "archetypal" quality that makes the energy of the Full Moon feel like something just a step more distant from fully human. There is something transpersonal about the emotions of a Full Moon person; it's not that they don't have them, but their emotional reactions do tend to be like something out of a story rather than the ordinary, cluttered, erratic Moon responses of the other seven phases. There can be a strangely "unreachable" quality about their hearts, which can be difficult for their loved ones to fathom. They may seem so wrapped up in fully being themselves that connecting to others may be a struggle on both sides.

WARRIOR'S MOON
THE FULL MOON IN ARIES

The Full Moon in Aries sees the daring Adventurer become the full-blown Warrior, who fights in honor for a good cause. The Warrior has come a long way from the Brigand who could not believe or trust in anything. His adventuring has shown him a wider world, and while he has seen its many trials and sorrows, he has also met brave souls trying their best to make it better. He decides that he is ready to become one of those brave souls, and he devotes himself to training for that job.

Training is the first part of the Warrior's path, and thus the Warrior's Moon. Fighting effectively is more than just running into the battle in blind wrath. The first demons that need to be subdued are the ones inside, and this is the lesson that the Warrior must learn before he can pick up a sword. There is the demon of Laziness; it's easier to skip over those little details or to ignore ambivalent truths in favor of writ-large, easy-to-understand sweeping generalizations, or to stay in bed that extra hour instead of getting up and running. There is the demon of Pettiness, which chisels away at honor with its bitter little voice telling the Warrior how much better he ought to be treated, or how he isn't really understood, or how he oughtn't to have to put up with all this hardship. There is the demon of Impatience—I want to be on the front lines *now,* never mind all this messing around with training and self-improvement! I'm sure that I could take the enemy now, no matter that he has ten years more experience and twice the allies! And, of course, there is the ever-present Mars demon of Wrath. This will be the hardest one of all for the Aries Warrior to wrestle down, and it is his greatest weakness . . . but any Warrior who can be goaded into rage can be herded blindly into a fatal trap. These, more than any more specific skill, are the lessons that the Warrior needs pounded into his head.

After the training, there is the battle. Here is where courage shows its flag. The Warrior must choose his cause carefully, because he needs to be able to believe in it no matter how badly things go; the courage of Aries is based in his ideals. If you can't believe that it is a worthy goal, the battle is lost before it is begun. After his first battle, the Warrior learns a potent truth: that if you have utter faith in the goal, it doesn't matter if you don't have complete faith in yourself to be the one to achieve it. Faith in the goal will pull you past your self-doubt.

On the Warrior's Moon, we fight for what we believe in. This is a lone battle, and it is especially effective if we are fighting with no approval from others, and perhaps even in spite of their disapproval (although deliberately inducing disapproval is missing the point). Such battles need to be fought as if there is no audience, just the Warrior and the enemy . . . and the innocents who must not be trampled, something that the Warrior often forgets. The Warrior's Moon is also a time of grappling with the aforementioned demons and learning patience. It may be that the best use of this Moon, if there are no external opportunities for fighting for a cause, is to choose one of those internal enemies to do battle with and dedicate the time to that lessoning.

People born under the Warrior's Moon need a cause that they can fight for with all of their heart—remember that the Moon is about emotions—and they must create room in their lives to make fighting for that cause into a spiritual quest. If they don't have a place to put their Warrior energy, it will spurt out in aggressive, harmful ways that can ruin their relationships. If the rest of the chart is particularly introverted, that energy can turn inward and create health problems, nervous breakdowns, and nightmares. A Warrior's Moon person who frequently dreams about being besieged by enemies and losing dramatically should take this as a warning: you need to be fighting real battles in real life, either with your own internal demons or with external injustices, and preferably both.

Warrior's Moon people also tend to be combative in their personal relationships, and ideally they choose a partner who they can consider a comrade in arms—someone who can push back when they push forward, but always in a loving way. A partner who is bearing the brunt of their combative instinct needs to set good boundaries and redirect their Warrior outward; there is plenty of injustice in the world that makes battles over the breakfast toast recede in importance.

Quotes for the Warrior's Moon

Cry in the dojo, laugh on the battlefield.

SAMURAI MAXIM

That which does not kill us, must have missed us.

MIOWARA TOMOKATA

In true budo there is no enemy or opponent. True budo is to become one with the universe, not train to become powerful or to throw down some opponent. Rather we train in hopes of being of some use, however small our role may be, in the task of bringing peace to mankind around the world.

MORIHEI UESHIBA

All problems become smaller if you don't dodge them, but confront them. Touch a thistle timidly, and it pricks you; grasp it boldly, and its spines crumble.

WILLIAM F. HALSEY

To fight and conquer in one hundred battles is not the highest skill. To subdue the enemy with no fight at all, that's the highest skill.

SUN TZU

It is easy to kill someone with a slash of a sword. It is hard to be impossible for others to cut down.

YAGYŪ MUNENORI

If the enemy thinks like the mountains, attack like the sea; and if he thinks like the sea, attack like the mountains.

MIYAMOTO MUSASHI

I dislike death, however, there are some things I dislike more than death. Therefore, there are times when I will not avoid danger.

MENCIUS

Courage is not the absence of fear, but rather the judgment that something else is more important than fear.

AMBROSE REDMOON

Victorious warriors win first and then go to war, while defeated warriors go to war first and then seek to win.

SUN TZU

EARTH MOTHER'S MOON
THE FULL MOON IN TAURUS

The Full Moon in Taurus blossoms into the figure of the Earth Mother, who echoes in many ways the Dryad of the long-ago New Moon. Where the Farmer was coming back toward the understanding of an ecosystem, the Earth Mother *is* the ecosystem, or at least is in complete harmony with it. Her generosity is unbounded. She births many children and has enough room for all of them. She feeds and clothes all who come to her and makes sure that their bodies are taken care of in as much comfort as can be mustered. She is practical and works hard, but never forgets the lives that are important.

If she has a fault, it is that she is more practical than empathetic, at least to her children and loved ones. They adore her and bless her for all that she gives them, and at the same time they curse her for not showing each of them the favoritism that they crave. She is not the Cancerian Sea Mother who moves out of feeling. She makes sure that all get their needs met if it's possible; if it's not, she expects the same stoic cooperation that she gives. If there is bounty left over—and she will work hard to make sure that there is—she will do her best to see that her selfish children get their desires met as well, but as soon as someone takes more than one share and robs another, she is there with a stern word and an immovable will. She goes from gentle field to stone and bedrock in a moment. They will give the toy back now, or suffer. They will eat their vegetables, or go hungry. It's not that she has no patience, it's that she has endless patience and is willing to outwait all her sullen and resentful loved ones, biding her time until they mature enough to understand the concept of doing what needs to be done.

The Taurus Full Moon is a not uncomfortable place to be, assuming that there are no major afflicting aspects. The Earth Mother knows who she is, what she's doing, what she wants, and (often enough) how to get there with slow, careful steps. She is generous but has good boundaries, knows how to give and how much to keep for herself. She will be accused of coldness when her comforting warmth gives way to stubborn practicality, and she will be accused of slowness when she sticks to her plodding path rather than embracing new feelings, but neither of these accusations really bother her much in the end, even if they're true.

On the Taurus Full Moon, we take care of our bodies and the bodily needs of others. Don't try to shift the focus to emotional needs—those are important, but the physical must come first or all else will suffer, a truth that the Taurus Moon understands. Are you eating healthy? Is there medical care that you need and aren't seeking? Are you getting enough sleep? (This is especially important to Taurus—if you spend the entire period simply catching up on your sleep, the Moon will approve.) Do you enjoy the feel of your clothing on your skin, or are you sacrificing comfort for stylishness? Are you getting enough hugs and regular body contact, or are you suffering from skin hunger? Are there small pains and annoyances in your physical surroundings that you endure every day that, with a little bit of practical organization or elbow grease, could be eliminated? The Taurus Full Moon asks these questions in a simple and straightforward manner, and we tend to blow them off . . . but to our peril. They are more important that we can imagine.

People born under the Taurus Full Moon are not easily thrown off course. It's one of the steadiest Moons of all, and it bestows an ability to look at the fluctuations of the heart in a practical and no-nonsense manner. These folks are not usually afraid of their emotions, and neither do they let them overwhelm their lives—which, since this aspect usually comes with a Scorpio Sun, is a very good thing. They pamper themselves and their loved ones, and have strong desires for wealth and comfort, but they don't usually go overboard with it like other Taurus Moons. Men with this Moon have a surprising talent for nurturing, in a down-to-earth, understated way. They'll give silent hugs and fix toys rather than chatter platitudes . . . and frankly the women are the same way. As this is a Full Moon, there is something archetypal and distant about their emotions, but they are honest and plain enough emotionally that it's not too much of a problem. People with this Moon only occasionally surprise with the cold practicality of a force of Mother Nature.

Quotes for the Earth Mother's Moon

Ecology has become the political substitute for the word "Mother."

JESSE UNRUH

A mother is a person who seeing there are only four pieces of pie for five people, promptly announces she never did care for pie.

TENNEVA JORDAN

My own recipe for world peace is a little bit of land for everyone.

GLADYS TABER

Sometimes, in a moral struggle, we discover the right thing to do—just as, on some cold day long ago, we discovered mittens pinned to our coat sleeve.

ROBERT BRAULT

You come to Nature with all of your theories, and she knocks them all flat.

AUGUSTE RENOIR

In our own beginnings, we are formed out of the body's interior landscape. For a short while, our mothers' bodies are the boundaries and personal geography which are all that we know of the world. . . . Once we no longer live beneath our mother's heart, it is the earth with which we form the same dependent relationship, relying . . . on its cycles and elements, helpless without its protective embrace.

LOUISE ERDRICH

War on nations changes maps. War on poverty maps change.

MUHAMMAD ALI

The lust for comfort, that stealthy thing that enters the house as a guest and then becomes a host and then a master.

JOSEPH CONRAD

A living planet is a much more complex metaphor for deity than just a bigger father with a bigger fist. If an omniscient, all-powerful Dad ignores your prayers, it's taken personally. Hear only silence long enough, and you start wondering about his power. His fairness. His very existence. But if a world mother doesn't reply, Her excuse is simple. She never claimed conceited omnipotence. She has countless others clinging to her apron strings, including myriad species unable to speak for themselves. To Her elder offspring She says: go raid the fridge. Go play outside. Go get a job. Or, better yet, lend me a hand. I have no time for idle whining.

DAVID BRIN

> *And would you gather turds*
> *for your grandmother's garden?*
> *Out with you then, dustpan and broom,*
> *she has seen the horse passing!*
> *Out you go, bold again*
> *As you promise always to be,*
> *Stick your tongue out at the neighbors*
> *That her flowers may grow.*
>
> WILLIAM CARLOS WILLIAMS, "A HISTORY OF LOVE"

STORYTELLER'S MOON
THE FULL MOON IN GEMINI

The Gemini Full Moon makes a great leap from the Mercenary, whose ends justified the means, to the Storyteller, who understands that the nature of the means determines the nature of the ends. The Storyteller contains within herself all the lies of the Evil Twins—and all their imagination as well. She also contains the Mercenary's hard-won excising and honing skills, as well as something else that is new to the intellectual Gemini: a concept of reality in words that does not derive from facts, but from feeling. She has, for the first time, touched the deeper Truth that is found in myth—the stories that never happened but are always True.

Fact, imagination, and myth. The Moon is a ball of rock that circles the Earth in a regulated and predictable way, occasionally getting between the Sun and its green planet and causing temporary darkness. The Moon is also a silver coin in the sky whose reflection I catch in my bowl of milk for good luck. The Moon is also the symbol of many gods and goddesses—Artemis, Mani, Arianrhod, Thoth, Yemaya, Tsuki-Yomi—and is astrologically the messenger of the heart, the inner parent, the inner child, all the wild and watery emotions. All of these are true, and for the real truth of the Moon to be told, they must all be taken equally into consideration. The Storyteller learns to do just this—not elevating fact, imagination, or myth, but combining them in the proper proportions. The story unfolds, and people listen, and they remember that Truth in ways that they never would have otherwise.

At her best, everything the Storyteller says is a story. Everything she sees becomes part of one. The difficulty comes in when, in order to truly live her path, everyone in her life gets cast as some sort of character in the internal screenplay. Since Storytellers don't just retell the same old thing over and over—they create new stories as well—it's hard for her to keep her hands off the personal journeys of her loved ones. She may subtly try to maneuver them into roles or actions that make their stories more what she wants them to be or that create the endings she hopes for. When they catch on (even if only vaguely) and dig in their heels, she is taken aback and a fight ensues. As long as they are characters in her stories, she's not really seeing to their full depths—and anyway, no one wants to be seen as a role or archetype rather than a whole person. In order to accept their independence from her story, she must accept that she has no real control over them.

On the Storyteller's Moon, we read and share good stories. It can be time dedicated to good books, or good movies, or sitting around telling tales of what you've experienced in your life. It is also a good time for writing fiction of any kind or writing about deeper truths such as myth and legend. This is the time to consider what part you play in your life, what archetypes you embody, and how much control you have over changing those roles.

People born under the Storyteller's Moon often have a gift for speaking things in ways that people hear and understand. This is different from the diplomacy of the Libran Ambassador (Disseminating Moon in Libra)—the Storyteller uses embellishment, drama, and sometimes outright falsehood to tell the underlying truth that no one else sees. It's a dangerous game, and they do have a tendency to get so caught up in the stories that they end up a fair distance from grubby everyday reality. In some cases, the stories may be an easement from a harsh reality; in others, they are a denial of it that will eventually become dangerous and impractical.

Storyteller's Moon people have Imaginations, capitalized, assuming that there are not too many stifling aspects to the Moon—and even then, the imagination will more likely be morbid rather than repressed. They may literally hear people speaking when they read, as if it was being read aloud to them, and strong images may accompany their thoughts. On the other hand, they may well be fairly detached from their own emotions. They may know how to talk about their feelings only by telling stories, which can irritate more straightforward people. They may also be so busy casting themselves in sacred tales that they miss out on creating original stories for themselves.

Quotes for the Storyteller's Moon

Poets say science takes away from the beauty of the stars—mere globs of gas atoms. Nothing is "mere." I too can see the stars on a desert night, and feel them. But do I see less or more? The vastness of the heavens stretches my imagination—stuck on this carousel my little eye can catch one-million-year-old light. A vast pattern—of which I am a part. . . . What is the pattern or the meaning or the why? It does not do harm to the mystery to know a little more about it. For far more marvelous is the truth than any artists of the past imagined it. Why do the poets of the present not speak of it? What men are poets who can speak of Jupiter if he were a man, but if he is an immense spinning sphere of methane and ammonia must be silent?

RICHARD FEYNMAN

Why do writers write? Because it isn't there.

THOMAS BERGER

Now I really make the little idea from clay, and I hold it in my hand. I can turn it, look at it from underneath, see it from one view, hold it against the sky, imagine it any size I like, and really be in control almost like God creating something.

HENRY MOORE

The best eloquence is that which gets things done.

DAVID LLOYD GEORGE

The destiny of the world is determined less by the battles that are lost and won than by the stories it loves and believes in.

HAROLD GODDARD

If stories come to you, care for them. And learn to give them away where they are needed. Sometimes a person needs a story more than food to stay alive.

BARRY LOPEZ

We are the first generation bombarded with so many stories from so many authorities, none of which are our own. The parable of the postmodern mind is the person surrounded by a media center: three television screens in front of them giving three sets of stories; fax machines bringing in other stories; newspapers providing still more stories. In a sense, we are saturated with stories; we're saturated with points of view. But the effect of being bombarded with all of these points of view is that we don't have a point of view and we don't have a story. We lose the continuity of our experiences; we become people who are written on from the outside.

SAM KEEN

If you keep telling the same sad small story, you will keep living the same sad small life.

JEAN HOUSTON

The master gave his teaching in parables and stories, which his disciples listened to with pleasure—and occasional frustration, for they longed for something deeper. The master was unmoved. To all their objections he would say, "You have yet to understand that the shortest distance between a human being and Truth is a story."

ANTHONY DE MELLO

Life itself is the most wonderful fairytale of all.

HANS CHRISTIAN ANDERSEN

I believe that imagination is stronger than knowledge—
That myth is more potent than history.
I believe that dreams are more powerful than facts—
That hope always triumphs over experience—
That laughter is the only cure for grief.
And I believe that love is stronger than death.

ROBERT FULGHUM, "THE STORYTELLER'S CREED"

SEA MOTHER'S MOON
THE FULL MOON IN CANCER

The Full Moon in Cancer is the most lunar of all the Moons. The energy shines through unfettered and luminous, and with all the attendant difficulties of an archetypal Moon. All Full Moons are somewhat archetypal, but Cancer is the most so. What do we know about the Moon? That it changes, constantly, but fairly predictably. That it cares not a whit for the Sun's grand progress and instead does its own little dance that refuses to fit in with comforting daylight time. That it pulls the tides back and forth, sometimes gently, sometimes violently, dashing them against the shore. That it is said to make people mad. That it runs the fertility cycle of women who do not live constantly in artificial lighting. That it lights the darkest times, but only with faint silvery light that makes people question the identity of those shadows in the night. That it is astrologically linked to feeling and imagery rather than logic and words. That it reflects the Sun's light as the Sun moves.

All these concepts are present in the Sea Mother's Moon. She is reflective of the Afro-Caribbean goddess Yemaya, who was raped by her grown and dangerous son but was unable to stop him out of maternal love. She is reflective of Artemis, who implacably shoots those who violate her privacy or come too close to her skirts. She is reflective of Mariamne, the Sea Mother who feeds all her young and all who fish her shores, but who must be placated by sailors lest she drown them in her storms. She is reflective of Hecate, who wanders dark crossroads with packs of hounds, blessing witches at their cauldrons. She is reflective of Mani, the Moon god who tends to stray from his path to rescue random abused children and take them with him, and must be kept on track by fierce wolves running through the sky. She is reflective of Arianrhod, Goddess of the Silver Wheel, who bore three children by three different spirits while claiming to be an untouched virgin. She is reflective of the nine daughters of the northern sea gods, mermaids more beautiful than the pearly waves with claws and fangs and bloody hands. She can be seen in the tricks of Thoth, who bought five days of moonlight in order to allow his dear friends, the gods of earth and sky, to meet, love, and bear children. And if this litany of images confuses you, imagine what having such a clear channel to the Moon does to the person bearing it? Not to mention the ones who love them.

The Sea Mother is not like the Earth Mother (Full Moon in Taurus), who faithfully hands out her nurturing on an as-needed basis, careful to play fair with her children. The Sea Mother fluctuates like the tides—motherly one moment and deadly the next. She is capricious and plays favorites; she grants mercy at her whim and condemns the next person merely because of her mood. She is all-giving yet sometimes withholds for no apparent reason. She is the place where water touches earth, creating the most nourishing places on the planet, but also eroding the ground and occasionally hitting it hard with a tsunami or two. It is impossible to understand her; the best we can do is to love her and stand in awe, and try very hard not to offend her.

On the Sea Mother's Moon, there is no one thing that we should do so much as go outside and salute the silver wheel in the sky. If the Moon is obscured due to weather, another possibility is to be near a body of water, particularly the ocean. Or, if that's not possible either, just stay home under a warm quilt and do what you feel.

People with the Sea Mother's Moon have a very strong and very changeable emotional nature. It can make them seem erratic, eccentric, drama-prone, nurturing, inconsiderate, wistful, unattainable, and many other seemingly inconsistent things. They may laugh and cry, rage and cherish, all in tune with some strange inner cycle that may have nothing at all to do with what's going on around them. They want to take care of other people, but they want other people to take care of them, too, and if they don't get enough of the latter by their own subjective measure, they stop doing the former. They are good to people when they feel like it, depending on whether they are well inclined toward that person at the moment, and that can change quickly. Unless there are other strong influences in the chart to make them sublimate their emotional responses, that is—and if that's the case, they'll be constantly sitting on a surging ocean of feeling that they are told isn't appropriate to acknowledge. Safety and security are important to them, because they know on some level that they are vulnerable, and they sometimes translate that into a physical instead of an emotional vulnerability. They can be needy and extroverted or happily introverted, chasing after their loved ones for attention or sitting curled up under their quilt, contentedly ignoring the world—or focusing their ocean wave of attention, like Leonard Cohen's *Suzanne,* on one bedazzled person who will remember it forever.

Quotes for the Sea Mother's Moon

The more complete one's life is, the more one's creative capacities are fulfilled, the less one fears death. People are not afraid of death per se, but of the incompleteness of their lives.

LISL MARBURG GOODMAN

Life is the fruit she longs to hand you,
Ripe on a plate.
And while you live,
Relentlessly she understands you.

PHYLLIS MCGINLEY

Home is the one place in all this world where hearts are sure of each other. It is the place of confidence. It is the place where we tear off that mask of guarded and suspicious coldness which the world forces us to wear in self-defense, and where we pour out the unreserved communications of full and confiding hearts. It is the spot where expressions of tenderness gush out without any sensation of awkwardness and without any dread of ridicule.

FREDERICK W. ROBERTSON

One of the hardest things in life is having words in your heart that you can't utter.

JAMES EARL JONES

Every creator painfully experiences the chasm between his inner vision and its ultimate expression.

ISAAC BASHEVIS SINGER

Before we are accustomed
to our bodies and minds
they are after them.
We nurture before we are
comfortable in our own skins.
Then, when we know
the joys of flesh
and wisdom shared
we are eager to meet
a world that has lost interest.

RUTH HARRIET JACOBS

I want a house that has got over all its troubles; I don't want to spend the rest of my life bringing up a young and inexperienced house.

JEROME K. JEROME

Suzanne takes you down to her place beside the river,
You can hear the boats go by, you can spend the
     night forever,
And you know that she's half crazy and that's why you
     want to be there . . .

LEONARD COHEN

Have you ever watched a crab on the shore crawling backward in search of the Atlantic Ocean, and missing? That's the way the mind of man operates.

H. L. MENCKEN

All rivers, even the most dazzling, those that catch the sun in their course, all rivers go down to the ocean and drown. And life awaits man as the sea awaits the river.

SIMONE SCHWARZ-BART

QUEEN'S MOON
THE FULL MOON IN LEO

As the Leo Moon passes into the Full Moon phase, the archetype focus changes. During the waxing period, the archetypes are Performers; now Leo comes into her own and moves into a period of being a Ruler. It is no accident that Leo rules both professions. In America, where we have no royalty to "perform" their sacred roles for us, we treat performers as if they were royalty. Both stem from the same place in our collective unconscious and in the spiritual "grooves" that we tap into in order to experience those archetypes more perfectly. Both specialize in getting people to do what Leo wants, and ideally in making people want to do it. The latter is the most important: any overbearing fool can order people around, but it takes someone with Leo energy to inspire people to want to do something of their own volition. At its best, Leo energy is inspiration as well as authority. Thus, the Singer is crowned and becomes a Queen.

The Queen is a mother to her people, but not a mother in the Cancer sense. She is warm, but approachable only so far. One keeps a respectable distance from the Queen, and she is very careful about who she lets herself be vulnerable to. She has a good deal of pride, and she tends to put her pride ahead of her willingness to let people come too close. This can mean that she finds herself lonely, and a lonely Leo Moon acts out in order to get more attention. When she has enough attention, she is an unending beacon of warmth and shining sunlight. People are drawn to her and inspired by her example to do things they never thought possible.

The other danger in this Moon is that the Queen may overreach herself. Unlike the King (Disseminating Moon in Leo), the Full Moon energy of the Queen spreads its light over her whole country, but no farther. If she extends herself beyond the limits of her reach, her light fades and she loses control of those at the edge of her kingdom. She is at her best ruling a smaller and more intimate kingdom where people come to her; at her best she combines the energy of the Leo bonfire and the Full Moon, drawing people into her circle.

On the Queen's Moon, we take charge of a situation. It's a day for leadership. If leadership isn't your thing, do something nice for a woman who is in a position of leadership and power in the outside world, and whom you respect. It's a way of showing appreciation for honorable and skilled leaders.

People born under the Queen's Moon want to be in charge. Many tend, however, to stick to being in charge of smaller situations, like the home or a small business. While some do end up in positions of power in large careers, the urge to rule comes from their hearts—it gives them emotional benefits—rather than from their self-identity. Both this Moon and the King's Moon generate the urge to rule, but not necessarily the ability; if people born to these phases are really serious about being in charge, they should get some training or mentoring so they can do it properly. Queen's Moon people may also play hot and cold, wanting people to come closer but then pushing them away through pride and the unwillingness to be vulnerable.

They also want plenty of appreciation. These are not wallflowers who will rule quietly from behind the scenes. Queen's Moon people, like the Queen who sits on her throne with courtiers buzzing around her, want to be noticed and acknowledged not only for their power, but for their competence. It's an ego boost, but it's also more than that—they rule from the heart rather than the head. This means that they know, on some level, that the part of rulership that is cold, hard decision-making will always be difficult for them, and they want to know that they're doing all right. The best gift that you can give them is to refrain from blowing sunshine up their asses, and to tell them honestly where they are strong and where they could do better. Do it in that order—lead with the compliment before you bring in the criticism, and it will go over better.

Quotes for the Queen's Moon

There is a natural aristocracy among men. The grounds of this are virtue and talent.

THOMAS JEFFERSON

We create a leader by locating one in the crowd who is standing up. We designate this victim as a "stand-up guy" by the simple expedient of sitting down around him.

ARTURO BINEWSKI

I hate careless flattery, the kind that exhausts you in your effort to believe it.

WILSON MIZNER

The attempt to combine wisdom and power has only rarely been successful, and then only for a short time.

ALBERT EINSTEIN

Disraeli cynically expressed the dilemma when he said: "I *must* follow the people. Am I not their leader?" He might have added, "I *must* lead the people. Am I not their servant?"

EDWARD L. BERNAYS

Leaders are the custodians of a nation's ideals, of the beliefs it cherishes, of its permanent hopes, of a faith which makes a nation out of a mere aggregation of individuals.

WALTER LIPPMANN

The brain says, "I am a ruler. The world is in those who rule."
The sea says, slumbering in its sleep, "All is mine."

KAHLIL GIBRAN

Men are especially intolerant of serving and being ruled by their equals.

BENEDICT SPINOZA

Power undirected by high purpose spells calamity, and high purpose by itself is utterly useless if the power to put it into effect is lacking.

THEODORE ROOSEVELT

There is a particular disdain with which Siamese cats regard you. Anyone who has walked in on the Queen cleaning her teeth will be familiar with the feeling.

DOUGLAS ADAMS

SPINNER'S MOON
THE FULL MOON IN VIRGO

The Full Moon in Virgo casts her as the first of the Fates, the Spinner who makes the thread of life for each person. Virgo's dance with and without human contact has finally brought her into a place of blossoming. She is the center of a great web, stretching out all around her, with its nodes being all the people with whom she is involved—and yet uninvolved. She cares for them, but never becomes subsumed by them. They turn to her for help and aid, and she gives it to them with care and attention, making sure that all get their due and that there is no favoritism.

The web is not just one of emotional contact. It is one of interlinked work and service. Work has always been the solace of the Virgo Moon, and Service is the miracle that she blossoms into, here on the Full Moon. She comes fully into the understanding of real service: that it does not calculate up the goodness of the served but gives usefully of its own accord; that it gives what is needed and not what the giver would like to give; that it is done humbly and with clear eyes that look to the future; that it is given with open hands and no grumbling in the heart; that it does not expect return or reward save the knowledge that a job was well done; that it need not be personal, but it must be done with some aspect of love.

The Spinner has come a long way from the Maiden who only wanted to be alone. She has learned the sacredness of the web of obligations. Today, it is fashionable to do everything you can to be obligated to no one, a situation that our ancestors would have found incredible. The network of obligations between people was what held you up when everything went down. You owed people, and people owed you, and this was wealth, not merely debt. Ten people working separately side by side do not get as much done as ten people working together, and this is the lesson that the solitary Virgo Moon has had to learn.

As the first of the Fates, she is associated with birth and life. While Virgo is still the virgin—she does not give birth to children on any of her lunar archetypes—the Spinner midwifes the children of others and takes them on as apprentices like the one that she once was, giving them a boost into their lives. In this way, she has many children, but lays claim to none of them. They look to her as a mentor, a classic Virgo relationship. In fact, this is the point where Virgo realizes that she is a master, like the ones who she served long ago in her Apprentice days . . . because people now come to her as she once went to them.

The Spinner's working net is built of ties created because people have observed her and trust her track record. She is in a position of influence with them, in a way that she could not be on the critical Counting Moon. Her term as the Housewife has taught her how to say words of self-improvement that actually get through to people. If there is a temptation to evil now, it is to manipulate people through the threads of her web in order to get them to improve. Occasionally she does fall prey to that temptation—it would be so good to see them achieve their potential, so she disbelieves the fact that they are not ready and pushes them into it—but she finds to her chagrin that their failure has become her failure. The strands keep them together, and pulling a strand must be well-timed and carried out with a light hand, or all suffer. It is the opposite of being alone, yet she still maintains a modicum of her mental privacy in the center of it all.

On the Spinner's Moon, we count up our web of obligations. Whom do we owe, and who owes us, and how do we feel about those obligations? Who will be there to catch us when we fall? We also look at our attitudes toward service and whether we render it with a whole heart. It's a good time to render service to others, especially to small organizations that are keeping people alive and functioning in their lives, or ones that are concerned with helping people become independent.

Those born on the Spinner's Moon need to be part of a working group in order to be happy. The apparently purposeless family is too vague; the cold atmosphere of a day-to-day job may not be intimate enough. They need an environment that combines useful work and friendly bonds, especially the bonds of mentor and student. They thrive on either side of a mentoring relationship. They are better than any other Virgo Moon at keeping the balance of intimacy and self-enclosedness that they require, and they are deeply drawn to service. In fact, their love may be entirely expressed through acts of service rather than words of romance. Duty is not a cold and frightening idea to them; it is a comforting thought. They do have more ambition than many Virgo Moons, and they like having influence over people. In less evolved cases, they may use it in a manipulative way, and learning to pull strings both effectively and ethically will be a major challenge for them.

Quotes for the Spinner's Moon

The difference between failure and success is the difference between doing a thing nearly right and doing it exactly right.

EDWARD SIMMONS

If I have been of service, if I have glimpsed more of the nature and essence of ultimate good, if I am inspired to reach wider horizons of thought and action, if I am at peace with myself, it has been a successful day.

ALEX NOBLE

One act of beneficence, one act of real usefulness, is worth all the abstract sentiment in the world.

ANN RADCLIFFE

It's important to know that words don't move mountains. Work, exacting work moves mountains.

DANILO DOLCI

If a man has important work, and enough leisure and income to enable him to do it properly, he is in possession of as much happiness as is good for any of the children of Adam.

R. H. TAWNEY

The secret of joy in work is contained in one word—excellence. To know how to do something well is to enjoy it. . . . I don't wait for moods. You accomplish nothing if you do that. Your mind must know it has got to get down to work.

PEARL S. BUCK

You, with your small mouth
and long tennis legs,
living with antiques
a husband and roses,
don't know what it is
to live alone on women's
tiny wages that buy
starches and roaches.
Uncordially
yours.

RUTH HARRIET JACOBS

To let oneself be bound by a duty from the moment you see it approaching is part of the integrity that alone justifies responsibility.

DAG HAMMARSKJÖLD

ARTIST'S MOON
THE FULL MOON IN LIBRA

In the Libra Full Moon, the emotions and appreciation of beauty of the Lover spring forth into the Artist. The experience of love has inspired Libra Moon people and thrown them into a paroxysm of creative fervor. The Muse has spoken, and the inner feelings are externalized onto paper, or on canvas, or in stone, or in music. The Full Moon is always a blossoming, and to some extent the purest and most archetypal form of that Moon sign, so the Artist is the ultimate expression of Venus filtered through intellectual Air.

In this phase the Libra Moon tips its scales once again toward aesthetics. Artists, whatever their Art, are primarily concerned with making an outlet for their creativity and secondarily with the impression that creative product makes on the audience. The rule of justice and law is a good ways down on the priority list, and the flow of Venusian feeling is the ruler of this phase. It isn't just about the creation of the Art; artistry becomes a lifestyle whereby everything is subordinate to the

Art, and these artists see Art everywhere. Some even take on a persona that is an extension of their Art, an elaborate basket to carry it in.

Still, art in the Libra sense is not solely a medium for the expression of beauty. It is also a means to justice, showing things as they ought to be striven for, and also the sorrow when circumstances are inharmonious. However, justice is still firmly given a back seat to appearance, because without that the Art will never get seen. No one ever became an Artist to change the world when there is no talent or drive for it. There are far easier and less tormenting ways to get things done. If they have turned to Art for their activism, it's because they would have turned to Art anyway.

Like those born under the Dancer's Moon, people with the Artist's Moon may fail by judging people and things on their aesthetic value rather than on another scale of worth, but the Artist has been the Lover already. She has the potential to fail further by treating love as a mere source of feeling to mine for the Work. The Artist needs to be careful not to cast other people as background or even subject without taking their needs into account. Instead, the idea is to see the beauty that is in them, uniquely theirs, and to bring it out into the open. Rather than using the plain woman as a model for painting mediocrity, it is a more rewarding path to bring out her inner beauty in a way that makes people turn and look again.

During the Artist's Moon, we look at artistry and learn to appreciate it with our intuition. It's a good time to start creative projects and an even better time to pick up creative projects that you put aside and forgot about or that lost inspiration halfway through. It's also a good time to go public with your art. If nothing else, go to a place where art is shown and look at it . . . and even better, buy some. Being an Artist doesn't pay well, and every small piece for sale is a plea for someone to please validate that Artist's brave and vulnerable path.

If someone born on the Artist's Moon doesn't do any kind of art or creative work, either that person should be doing it and isn't or there are serious afflicting aspects to the Moon. (Considering that the Sun often opposes the Moon during its Full phase, that's a good place to start. Sometimes the extroverted Aries Sun denigrates all that fluffy art nonsense and subjugates the more delicate Moon to the closet.) Usually these folks have the urge to create, sometimes to the point of letting it run rampant. It's better for them if they do, because people with a frustrated Artist's Moon will often lean too hard on the need for aesthetics to the point of judging everyone around them by their appearance or charm or their ability to fit into the Artwork that is their life.

Quotes for the Artist's Moon

Art is not a pastime but a priesthood.

JEAN COCTEAU

Art is a collaboration between God and the artist, and the less the artist does, the better.

ANDRÉ GIDE

The artist, like the God of the creation, remains within or behind or beyond or above his handiwork, invisible, refined out of existence, indifferent, paring his fingernails.

JAMES JOYCE

For the artist's life is, of necessity, full of conflicts, since two forces fight in him: the ordinary man with his justified claim for happiness, contentment, and guarantees for living on one hand, and the ruthless creative passion on the other, which under certain circumstances crushes all personal desires into the dust.

CARL JUNG

The truth is, as everyone knows, that the great artists of the world are never puritans, and seldom ever ordinarily respectable.

H. L. MENCKEN

That the whole of Art is inclined to lead to the bottomless pit is only too certain. But art, in spite of its connection with death and beauty, is still in a wonderful way associated with life, and finds in itself the antitoxin. . . . The artist, so it seems to me, is in reality the (ironical!) mediator between the realms of death and life.

THOMAS MANN

> The only things the creative artist can be opposed to are ugliness and injustice.
>
> LIAM O'FLAHERTY [HOW PERFECTLY LIBRAN!]

> We all know that Art is not Truth. Art is the lie that makes us realize the Truth—at least, the truth that is given to us to understand.
>
> PABLO PICASSO

> Every portrait that is painted with feeling is a portrait of the artist, not of the sitter.
>
> OSCAR WILDE

> The artist uses the talent he has, wishing he had more talent. The talent uses the artist it has, wishing it had more artist.
>
> ROBERT BRAULT

PRIESTESS'S MOON
THE FULL MOON IN SCORPIO

On the Scorpio Full Moon, we witness the moment when the Cloaked One, who has journeyed to the depths, suddenly discovers a great truth: that when you go deep enough, you emerge into a place that is far beyond you, and Powers await you there. She is touched by the Divine, and in her ecstasy she lifts her arms to the night sky and swears herself to the Powers that she has connected to. She becomes the Priestess, and all the dark secrets that she has studied have opened on the Mysteries, of which she is now the Keeper.

The Priestess is reminiscent of the High Priestess card in the Tarot, who holds the scroll of hidden knowledge and sits between two pillars, one black and one white. While the pillars have a Kabbalistic explanation, I have always been fond of the explanation that the High Priestess does not deny any knowledge or wisdom, regardless of whether others would consider it derived from darkness or light. She sits between them and links the lower worlds and the upper worlds, heaven and earth, spirit and flesh, and all the other dualities that people tend to create. Scorpio loves dualities as well. In fact, no one is quite as good as Scorpio at attempting to divide everything into piles of black and white, good and evil, with her and against her, something to be loved passionately and something to be hated passionately. The Priestess sits between the pillars because she has made a breakthrough that is one of the most difficult for Scorpio: understanding that there is no great gulf between one and another, no matter which great and terrible duality it may be. She has learned that really, it's all shades of gray, and no end is any better than the other, and where we sit is in the middle. In the middle, where there is no clean black and white, and that's just the way it is.

The Priestess has been down to the darkness and up again into the light. She has dragged herself down the road of deep introspection and learned that the best way out is with the aid of Deeper Powers. However, as with everyone who touches the numinous, she discovers that there is no guarantee that the Deeper Powers are necessarily always going to speak to her or come at her call. Thus she enters into the precarious longing of everyone with a personal relationship to the Universe, realizing painfully that sometimes her passions get in the way of hearing the call clearly . . . and yet her passions are a part of her that those Powers do not wish her to lose.

On the Priestess Moon, we walk in the moonlight, perhaps in a forest, or sit by the lake and meditate. We might also undertake to study the Mysteries, whatever that is for us. It is a time for spirituality; if you have no spiritual practice, look into that of others in order to understand them and their worldviews, and thus communicate better with them. If nothing else, go to Nature and be awed. I don't believe that anyone is above that.

People born on the Priestess Moon usually have a yearning either for the old, dark, ancient mysteries, or are drawn to Nature as the source of all things holy. Spirit calls them, although they may interpret that call in many ways. They may have an urge to teach, or at least to pass on what they have learned, but they need to be careful not to jump the gun on that process and offer knowledge before they fully understand something themselves. They are often self-appointed speakers for a particular cause, whether or not the other members of that cause feel that they are the appropriate choice to speak for them. At the same time, they struggle with the difficulty of being an imperfect channel for the higher understandings that they perceive, and grapple as well with their pride and ego over that issue.

The work of Priestess Moon people is to overcome the Scorpio urge to see everything in black and white. This will be a lifelong struggle, but the further they go with it, the more serene and self-possessed they become, and the more at peace they are with themselves and the rest of the world. It is only when they can find that middle ground of grayness and be comfortable with it that they can develop compassion for others and fully rid themselves of contempt.

Quotes for the Priestess's Moon

The personal life deeply lived always expands into truths beyond itself.

ANAÏS NIN

Superstition: Any practice or form of religion to which we are not accustomed.

VOLTAIRE

Those who dwell among the beauties and mysteries of the earth are never alone or weary of life.

RACHEL CARSON

There are more tears shed over answered prayers than unanswered ones.

SAINT TERESA OF AVILA

The unknown is an ocean. What is conscience? The compass of the unknown.

JOSEPH COOK

The next century's task will be to rediscover its gods.

ANDRÉ MALRAUX

The most beautiful thing we can experience is the mysterious. It is the source of all true art and science. He to whom this emotion is a stranger, who can no longer pause to wonder and stand rapt in awe, is as good as dead: his eyes are closed.

ALBERT EINSTEIN

Mysteries are not necessarily miracles.

JOHANN WOLFGANG VON GOETHE

Wherever we may come alive, that is the area in which we are spiritual.

DAVID STEINDL-RAST

Why must holy places be dark places?

I say the gods deal very unjustly with us. For they will neither (which would be the best of all) go away and leave us to live our own short days to ourselves, nor will they show themselves openly and tell us what they should have us do, For that too would be endurable. But to hint and hover, to draw us near in dreams and oracles, or in a waking vision that vanishes as soon as seen, to be dead silent when we question them and then glide back and whisper (words we cannot understand) in our ears when we most wish to be free of them and to show to one what they hide from another; what is all this but cat-and-mouse play, blindman's buff, and mere jugglery? Why must holy places be dark places?

C. S. LEWIS

PRIEST'S MOON
THE FULL MOON IN SAGITTARIUS

As the Sagittarius Moon moves from its Gibbous phase to the Full Moon, the Scholar finally finds what he has been seeking all this time. The Divine touches him, and he is blessed and opened up to the Powers of the Universe. Unlike the watery Priestess (Full Moon in Scorpio), however, the Priest is touched through the channel of the sacred texts and traditions that he has learned. In a haze of glory, he dedicates himself to the Truth that he has touched.

Sagittarius is the sign of religion. Not just solitary spirituality, but religion itself. The word *religion* is related to *re-linking,* as it is a set of beliefs that link people together. Religion is by definition a group activity, even when it is practiced alone, and it is the power of the group that defines what belongs and does not belong in that category of faith. Once the group has decided on it, the tradition is laid down and followed as closely as possible.

That can be a drawback if it becomes rigid, a barrier to the Divine energy rather than a channel . . . or it can become a stable and reliable set of symbols for a disparate group of people to use to commune together in a group. The difficulties and negotiation around those two possible outcomes has engendered more suffering than needs to be mentioned here. This, however, is part of the Sagittarius mystery, and tragedy.

The Full Moon in Sagittarius enacts the fullest and most archetypal manifestation of Sagittarius, and here we have to look at the picture of the centaur archer. Half man and half animal, half wise teacher (the Centaur, symbol for Sagittarius, is supposedly Chiron, mentor of heroes) and half child of Nature, Sagittarius is constantly pulled in two directions. One is the call of the body, the physical experience, the beauty of Nature, all the animal instincts and sensory happenings that were explored in the first few phases of this Moon cycle. The other half, the human half, both rationalizes mentally and thinks abstractly. The human side can read, can write down received knowledge and be illumined by it over and over, can think in intellectual absolutes and connect to the Universe through a higher channel than the body. But which should be most valued—the physical ecstasy or the intellectual ecstasy? The random experience of one or the relayed wisdom of the other? This is the Priest's dilemma. Pulled between the scholar and the shaman, between inspiration and tradition, he must find an answer not only for himself but for everyone who might follow him.

The Priest is a divine channel through whom inspired wisdom comes. He is also the archetype shown in the Tarot card of the Hierophant, benevolently upholding tradition while covertly striking down dissidence. The child of Nature might say, "I know it's so because I felt it in my body; it rang through me like a bell." The scholar might say, "I know it's true because I read it in the ancient words of the Wise One." Which is the Sagittarian's Truth? Is there, indeed a great Truth that encompasses both sets of knowledge, including their contradictions? If so, what does that mean for the Priest and his flock?

On the Priest's Moon, we think about the traditions and beliefs we hold—religious or otherwise—and whether we are able to objectively question them. If you think you don't have any traditions or beliefs, hunt up those friends everyone has (or should have) who are very different from you, but are somehow your friends anyway. Ask them what rigid beliefs you hold, and be prepared to think about the answer. If worst comes to worst, go to the Universe itself and pray or meditate (if that's something you do) for an answer. Make sure that you don't make the mistake of assuming that an answer, if you get one, applies to anyone but yourself.

People born on the Priest's Moon will spend their lives struggling with the boundary between inspiration and intellect, between reform and tradition, between doubt and faith. The point of the struggle is not to let one side win, however, or at least not to win too often. The point is to move continually back and forth between them, creating a balance, and eventually coming to a point where both are one, and nothing discovered on one side can make untrue the other.

In the meantime, since this is an emotional Moon, the danger will be to go with the side that is the most emotionally appealing. Priest's Moon people need to come to a humbling understanding about how much their own feelings influence their perception of the Truth, and the side they choose to find it on.

Quotes for the Priest's Moon

The greatest challenges facing both the arts and education are how to navigate the perilous course between adventure and discipline; how to respond to tradition without either rejecting it or becoming its slave.

ROBERT W. CORRIGAN

The Abbot ought always to remember what he is and what he is called, and to know that to whom much hath been entrusted, from him much will be required; and let him understand what a difficult and arduous task he assumeth in governing souls.

THE RULE OF SAINT BENEDICT

If someone asks you "Do you believe?" and you do not answer "In what?" then you have written a blank check on your brain, and it shall surely come back marked "insufficient funds."

ORSON SCOTT CARD

If we achieve satori and the satori shows, like a bit of dogshit stuck on the tip of our nose, that is not so good.

TAISEN DESHIMARU

Seek not to understand that you may believe, but believe that you may understand.

SAINT AUGUSTINE

A faith that cannot survive collision with the truth is not worth many regrets.

ARTHUR C. CLARKE

Science and technology revolutionize our lives, but memory, tradition and myth frame our response.

ARTHUR SCHLESINGER

Tradition is the illusion of permanence.

WOODY ALLEN

And all men are ready to pass judgment on the priest as if he was not a being clothed with flesh, or one who inherited a human nature.

SAINT JOHN CHRYSOSTOM

To know all things is not permitted.

HORACE

GRANDMOTHER'S MOON
THE FULL MOON IN CAPRICORN

The Full Moon in Capricorn is the Grandmother archetype, with all that implies. The Grandmother is the powerful Matriarch of the family, exerting her influence on all her descendants. She is the Eldress whose wisdom is respected by everyone, who people go to for advice. She is the comforting one who takes the child on her lap and tells him fine stories, and also the martinet who scolds him for his manners and despairs of young people understanding the true value of things. She is the embodiment of the Ancestors, who have a vested interest in seeing their descendants thrive.

In Norse mythology, there were beings called the *dísir,* who were propitiated and asked for aid. These were powerful women, former matriarchs of the clan, who after death took it upon themselves to guard and guide their direct descendants and safeguard their families. Their souls could be called upon for aid in family crises and prayed to for wisdom and advice when family members had gone astray. The Grandmother archetype here echoes the ancient *dís,* or the living woman who would one day become a *dís* to watch over her clan. Her interest is in protecting and caring for her family, but not just the young members of it. All members answer to her and to her wisdom. In contrast to Cancer mothering, her upbringing motto is more likely to be "I'm not raising children. I'm raising adults."

The Capricorn Grandmother is far more than just a cookie-giving, chair-rocking old woman; in fact one might consider that the reason we have that image so strongly associated with "grandma" is that women have been valued for only their nurturing ability, and infertile elder women have been devalued and denigrated for so long that we have trouble imagining them, at least on our first thought, as being as appropriate for the status of Elder Authority Figure as older men are. This Grandmother is a Ruler, just as much as the Leo Full Moon, but where the Queen is mother to an entire country of vastly diverging people, the Grandmother's sphere is closer to home. She is the ruler of her family, her clan, her tribe—no group so large that she does not know everyone by name, has held every child in her arms at birth, can recollect stories of their childhoods, and can recount their ancestors. Everyone she rules is related to her by blood, marriage, or adoption; they are all her descendants or at least the parents of her descendants. She cares, intensely, about the fortunes of these people she has seen be born and grow. Those outside of her clan are not so important to her, a trait that she shares with the Grandfather (Disseminating Moon in Capricorn), her partner and consort in the work of maintaining a clan.

You'll also notice that the other Moons reach their Elder status in the Balsamic phase, while Capricorn reaches hers early, on the Full Moon. Capricorn's ruler Saturn is the sign of old age, and any planet in

Capricorn is likely to feel "older" (and more rigid) than that same planet in any other sign. It is the destiny of every sign to reach a point of maturity; it is Capricorn's destiny to embody it. Blossoming, for Saturn, means becoming the Elder. The Capricorn Full Moon is the archetypal Elder in all her fullness.

On the Grandmother's Moon, we honor our family elders, living and dead. Blood family is the focus, although adopted family is fine too, so long as they accepted you wholly and raised you as their own. If you were adopted informally into a family as an adult, it counts so long as they acknowledge you openly as family. You can also honor, secondarily, the older people who mentored you and helped you mature.

People born on the Grandmother's Moon have a "born old" feel to them emotionally. They bear the heavy archetype of the Elder shadowing their Moon, and they may come across as very emotionally reserved and conscious of their dignity. That sense of personal dignity may get in the way of their full emotional expression, and a wise partner will understand that and not push them to be more expressive than is comfortable for them. They need time and patience to say important things like "I love you" or "You have hurt me." It isn't rejection that they fear—they can handle rejection stoically—but ridicule and loss of respect. Asking them to share their inner feelings should be done quietly and seriously, and only after you've made it clear that you respect them as competent people.

Grandmother's Moon people love to give advice and are happiest when they are respected as authorities by the people they consider family. If their own blood relatives think that they are ridiculous, they'll adopt friends or coworkers and give them advice about their lives. Family is sacred to them, even if they don't have good ones. They're generally clear when their own families are unworthy, but may stick it out anyway out of some sense of duty.

Quotes for the Grandmother's Moon

Grandmother, family-proud and so of house, with hob black-leaded, glistening like a raven's wings and brass like gold untarnished.

BRIAN HARRIS

It's not only children who grow. Parents do too. As much as we watch to see what our children do with their lives, they are watching us to see what we do with ours. I can't tell my children to reach for the sun. All I can do is reach for it, myself.

JOYCE MAYNARD

Good, honest, hardheaded character is a function of the home. If the proper seed is sown there and properly nourished for a few years, it will not be easy for that plant to be uprooted.

GEORGE A. DORSEY

What's done to children, they will do to society.

KARL MENNINGER

Every step of progress means a duty repudiated, and a scripture torn up.

GEORGE BERNARD SHAW

There is a kind of virtue that lies not in extraordinary actions, not in saving poor orphans from burning buildings, but in steadfastly working for a world where orphans are not poor and buildings comply with decent fire codes.

RANDY COHEN

Love is the expression of one's values, the greatest reward you can earn for the moral qualities you have achieved in your character and person, the emotional price paid by one man for the joy he receives from the virtues of another.

AYN RAND

My great-grandfather used to say to his wife, my great-grandmother, who in turn told her daughter, my grandmother, who repeated it to her daughter, my mother, who used to remind her daughter, my own sister, that to talk well and eloquently was a very great art, but that an equally great one was to know the right moment to stop.

WOLFGANG AMADEUS MOZART

Call it a clan, call it a network, call it a tribe, call it a family: Whatever you call it, whoever you are, you need one.

JANE HOWARD

And so our mothers and grandmothers have, more often than not anonymously, handed on the creative spark, the seed of the flower they themselves never hoped to see—or like a sealed letter they could not plainly read.

ALICE WALKER

FRIENDSHIP MOON
THE FULL MOON IN AQUARIUS

The Aquarius Full Moon blossoms with the highest octave of the Aquarius relationship experience: friendship. Aquarius is the most ruthlessly egalitarian of all the signs. All other relationships are built on power dynamics or are in danger of involving them: parents have power over children, bosses over employees, and rulers over subjects. Romantic partners either fall into an assumed power dynamic, step into an agreed-on one, or continually struggle for power. Families can be clannish and reject those who do not have the accident of being kin. Only friendship is egalitarian enough for Aquarius, spreading beyond the barriers of blood, law, and love, and every important relationship in the life of an adult Aquarius Moon person will have the dimension of friendship first and foremost.

On the Full Moon, the Friend comes into her own. She has suffered rejection from the family, from society, from those who did not understand. Only the love of friends sustained her all along, and she blossoms to this relationship in a way that she never has before. She realizes the importance of those bonds and takes the time to nurture them. In doing so, she also reaches out to others, to make new friends everywhere. It's a revelation to her: friendship can reach across the chasm of ideology. You may disagree with people, but if they are your friend, you can still care about them and have a few drinks together, without bringing up your differences. If you are their friend, the sort of person you are has a face to them and is much harder to demonize. Friendship can cut the legs out from under intolerance, one inch at a time. Finding common ground is a much more effective tool than emphasizing differences in getting people to open their lives to you and your ideas.

While we acknowledge the importance of friends in our culture, we also tend to place this bond further down the scale than other bonds, and we look askance at people who hold it in the highest esteem. As children, we are encouraged to ignore potential friends or dump existing ones if they don't fall into the right spectrum for our family and personal identity. As adults, friends get even shorter shrift. People who fall in love are expected to place their prospective partners first and blow off get-togethers with their friends if there's a chance at a romantic date. Married partners are supposed to put their spouses first and get rid of friends that the spouse dislikes, or at least never bring them home. Employers may transfer you and expect you to forget your network of buddies; new ones can always be made to replace them. If you move in order to be with a lover or to take care of elderly parents or to be around blood family, people nod; if you say that you're moving in order to be around your friends, they wince. It's assumed that those friends will have other relationships that will be far more important to them than you. Friendship is too slender a thread to base our life decisions on, we are told.

The Aquarius Moon feels differently. If the Friend has a fault, it is that she tends to spread herself too thin, making too many friends and forgetting to spend time with the closest ones. She may also be suspicious of the "best friend" category if she's too caught up in bringing peace by making friends with the whole world. She needs to accept that the fundamental difference in value between the close friend and the casual acquaintance is not unfair, and that close friends can be nurtured without guilt.

On the Friendship Moon, we hang out with our friends. You can sit around and talk about what friendship means to you and to society, but it's probably a lot more fun just to spend time with people you like and care about.

Those born on the Friendship Moon have a deep need for networks of social contact, from best friends who listen to your woes to common-interest buddies who share your fascinations. They will have a lot of them, if the Moon is not overly afflicted, and they will instinctively put their friends before other relationships. It will take a lot of social conditioning to force them to do otherwise. (This may be annoying to their dates and spouses, but the wise partner will understand that this isn't going to change.) At the very least, they will try to make friendships out of other relationships. Lovers will definitely need to be friends first, or it won't work. They may well want to live with their friends and would do well in communal situations. Social capital is more than just a theory to them—it really is their wealth. When they're down, it is that network of social capital that they turn to. They don't need face time to consider someone a friend, and they happily carry on multitudes of long-distance relationships. They do tend to spread themselves thin among friends, unless they're in trouble and leaning on one particular bond. Contacts who feel slighted by them may need to gently point this out in order to get the attention they need.

Quotes for the Friendship Moon

You do not know my aches, but you know your own and they are in the same places. This is what makes us a community. We have a lot of aches in common.

LAURA CREIGHTON

Friendships are fragile things, and require as much handling as any other fragile and precious thing.

RANDOLPH S. BOURNE

The truth that is suppressed by friends is the readiest weapon of the enemy.

ROBERT LOUIS STEVENSON

One's friends are that part of the human race with which one can be human.

GEORGE SANTAYANA

Each friend represents a world in us, a world possibly not born until they arrive, and it is only by this meeting that a new world is born.

ANAÏS NIN

Except in cases of necessity, which are rare, leave your friend to learn unpleasant things from his enemies; they are ready enough to tell them.

OLIVER WENDELL HOLMES SR.

The most beautiful discovery that true friends can make is that they can grow separately without growing apart.

ELIZABETH FOLEY

Every man should have a fair-sized cemetery in which to bury the faults of his friends.

HENRY BROOKS ADAMS

Anybody can sympathise with the sufferings of a friend, but it requires a very fine nature to sympathise with a friend's success.

OSCAR WILDE

I no doubt deserved my enemies, but I don't believe I deserved my friends.

WALT WHITMAN

HEALER'S MOON
THE FULL MOON IN PISCES

As the Pisces Moon blossoms into the Full Moon phase, he comes into his own as the Healer. This is the archetypal phase of the Pisces Moon, where Pisces learns to connect more fully to the energy of universal healing. Instead of simply being drained of life force by others, the Healer lifts his arms to greater Powers, and the energy comes through to sustain him.

Pisces and Virgo are the opposing points that revolve around the axis of service. While Virgo secretly believes that the best service is rendered impersonally, Pisces requires deeply personal service. At the same time, the Healer's karmic task is to create a dimension of service that is transpersonal, because personal effort costs as much as it gives. When one is giving of healing energy to a beloved few, it's easier to recoup one's energy than when one is giving out to the nameless masses, as the

Pisces Moon has already discovered in his sojourn as the Martyr.

Yet the Healer's job is just that: giving of healing to anyone who needs it, regardless of subjective worth. The surgeon in the emergency room does not turn away the crushed body just because it belongs to someone he doesn't particularly like. It's part of the deal. Being a Healer of any sort means expanding one's view to a larger audience, including complete strangers. Where the Poet (Gibbous Moon in Pisces) stays locked in his garret, sending the poems out the door to affect the world without his physical engagement (since, after all, creativity is hard enough without the attendant drain of having to deal with people on top of that), the Healer is up close and knee-deep in the woes of humanity. It's necessary for him to find that point of touching something greater than himself, something that gives him the strength to keep going and the energy to replenish.

He can't heal everyone, of course, and those he fails will blame him bitterly, which will cause him pain. It's important for him to remain humble in the face of that dilemma, accepting the inevitable uncertainty instead of embracing the certainty that he could have saved them had he only tried harder or done something different. That's the first step on the road to hubris, a place that the next phase will inexorably visit.

On the Healer's Moon, we find ways to bring healing to others. We might listen to a friend who needs to dump some anguish, or we might comfort someone in need. We could answer a hotline, or make someone medicinal herb tea, or give someone a massage who desperately needs it. The healing work can be physical, mental, emotional, or spiritual. A group that prays for others or sends out healing energy would find this Full Moon a good time to work. If nothing else, if you want to do something and have no skills or inclination at all in this area, you can fund and support those who do. Healers often need a little extra attention themselves to keep going, even if that's only a restaurant coupon mailed to their house.

Like all Pisces Moons, people born under the Healer's Moon are greatly moved by the suffering of others. The difference is the way that they react to it. Other Pisces Moon phases might protect themselves from the terrible pull by hiding or give of themselves until they are hardly there at all anymore. Healer's Moon people are actually fairly well equipped to find reasonable balance in how and when they give of themselves, and tend to be more skillful at (and drawn to) giving their services and attention to large groups of people rather than just helping out friends or family members.

The biggest drawback to this ability to transpersonally serve without being too personally drained is the drawback of all Full Moon types: becoming less emotionally personal in general. Healer's Moon people may anger their loved ones, who want to feel special in their eyes and may react badly to the idea that Healers are no less moved by strangers on the street than by their own family and friends. They may throw themselves into their work to the point that their personal life suffers, or is nonexistent . . . and it's far easier to justify the lack of a personal life when you're helping people than when you're merely sitting around fantasizing and avoiding reality. Also, Healer's Moon people aren't miracle workers, and they can burn out if they aren't careful. They tend to forget about taking care of themselves and others emotionally.

Quotes for the Healer's Moon

All healing is first a healing of the heart.

CARL TOWNSEND

We have to believe that even the briefest of human connections can heal. Otherwise, life is unbearable.

AGATE NESAULE

A lot of people say they want to get out of pain, and I'm sure that's true, but they aren't willing to make healing a high priority. They aren't willing to look inside to see the source of their pain in order to deal with it.

LINDSAY WAGNER

We are given to the cult of personality; when things go badly we look to some messiah to save us. If by chance we think we have found one, it will not be long before we destroy him.

CONSTANTINE KARAMANLIS

Healing is a matter of time, but it is sometimes also a matter of opportunity.

HIPPOCRATES

"Healing," Papa would tell me, "is not a science, but the intuitive art of wooing nature."

W. H. AUDEN

The first job of the spiritual healer is to discern whether a healing is even permissible.

J. J. DEWEY

There is something beautiful about all scars of whatever nature. A scar means the hurt is over, the wound is closed and healed, done with.

HARRY CREWS

The mind commands the body and it obeys. The mind orders itself and meets resistance.

SAINT AUGUSTINE

You don't have a soul. You are a Soul. You have a body.

C. S. LEWIS

6

THE GREATER GOOD

THE DISSEMINATING MOON

In the end, you belong not to yourself, but to the world.

ARI ULRICH

The world is not dangerous only because of those who do harm, but because of those who look at it without doing anything.

ALBERT EINSTEIN

ON THE DISSEMINATING MOON, the soul gets a wake-up call that brings it out of its self-absorbed cocoon. Up until now, the Moon phases have concentrated on self-knowledge and self-improvement, because you can't do anything huge until you've ironed out the sabotaging demons on the small scale. Now, however, the call begins. The blossomed figure of the Full Moon says, "I've found some sort of truth; perhaps it can help others?" or "I've learned this skill well; perhaps I can make a difference?" Whether it is a gospel to preach or a skill to pass on, for the first time other people—and not just loved ones, but the whole world of strangers—become vitally important to the soul's quest. The Disseminating Moon wants to send the energy of the last five phases out to everyone, and it becomes concerned with such things as Reputation, and Message, and How Do I Make People Pay Attention? Where the earlier phases had to learn to stand alone with strength, Disseminating Moon people must learn to work with many people in order to get their emotional needs met.

The Disseminating Moon begins at 224 degrees past the Sun and goes to 269 degrees. Like the Gibbous Moon before it, it contains the quincunx aspect, but it also contains the waning trine aspect. The irritational aspect of the quincunx nags them out of their self-absorption, and the trine helps them to relax. This is the most relaxed and confident phase, where people can take time to see the sights and rest on their laurels before the Waning Quarter looms overhead.

SOLDIER'S MOON
THE DISSEMINATING MOON IN ARIES

When the Aries Moon turns from Full to Disseminating, the Warrior goes in search of a cause that is larger than she herself can manage alone. She joins an army of other warriors and learns to fight in cooperation. This is not an easy lesson; Warriors tend to be individualists, and Aries always wants to be First. However, when the enemy is big enough, single warriors will be cut down no matter how brave. Some causes cannot be won without a team. The Soldier must learn to work in concert with other Soldiers, some of whom are better or worse than her, but many of whom are an even match. She must learn that comparing and ranking oneself within her team of peers is a useless and futile habit that takes away from her own performance and sows friction among the group. To function well together and get the job done, egos and insecurities need to be put aside, even when it rankles and irritates. The Disseminating Moon demands that the gains of the Full Moon be put into the service of broader humanity, and it's time for the Mars-ruled Moon to put aside personal desires and sign up.

The Soldier's Moon is a time of hammering rampant individualism into group cooperation. The first five Moon phases of Aries have been completely dedicated to internal values; Aries individuals may temporarily ally with others to get something they want, but a little friction sends them on their way again. After all, if you're Out Front, everyone else is Behind You, and you don't have to notice them if you don't want to. The Soldier, however, is forced to condense all her fire and energy into the group effort, and this is not easy for her. She must learn to see less skilled teammates not as a hindrance, but as comrades with whom she should share her skills to make the whole group better. She must also learn to see teammates who are better than her not as competition, but as a valuable individuals who will help them all to win. While the Warrior learns that the battlefield contains only himself, the enemy, and the innocents who must be protected, the Soldier learns that comrades are another class of being—people whose back you need to have so that they will have yours when the chips are down.

On the Soldier's Moon, we team up with others of like mind to fight for a mutual goal. The people on the team don't have to be people who you love, or even agree with on everything, but they need to be people who are on the same page with you about the goal in question. Even if the members of the team disagree passionately over other things, they need to be passionately in accord over what you all wish to achieve—and, hopefully, how to achieve it.

The Soldier's Moon encourages us to take the drive to be in the lead, to get ahead, to be special . . . and to detach that drive from our own ego. Instead, it should be aimed at the problem in question, with all our might, and no frittering away of our energies on the pettiness of who will get credit or be seen as heroic. There is also an emphasis on caring about one's teammates; help them out and bring them chicken soup or Chinese takeout when they're down, because the success of the team project depends on all hands being at their best. The Soldier's Moon reminds us that being invested in a team goal means being invested in the ones who will help you get there. Since this is also a time of discipline, it's good for practicing martial arts or some other regular physical exercise . . . but do it in a group, not alone.

People born under the Soldier's Moon need to pursue a quest and a goal just like those born under the Warrior's Moon, but they need to do it with other people. The lone quest may look tempting, but it's not their job this time around. They need to do their fighting as part of a group effort, even when the slowness of moving in a group seems to drive them mad. They also need to contend with the issues of being liked or disliked in that group, and they must try to ameliorate their emotional responses for the good of the team goal. Like the Warrior's Moon folk, giving up on the quest can result in poor health, nightmares, and constant low-grade wrath aimed at the wrong people.

Quotes for the Soldier's Moon

Do not pray for easy lives. Pray to be stronger men. Do not pray for tasks equal to your powers. Pray for powers equal to your tasks. Then the doing of your work shall be no miracle, but you shall be the miracle.

PHILLIPS BROOKS

The test of courage comes when we are in the minority; the test of tolerance comes when we are in the majority.

RALPH W. SOCKMAN

An idealist believes the short run doesn't count. A cynic believes the long run doesn't matter. A realist believes that what is done or left undone in the short run determines the long run.

SYDNEY J. HARRIS

Once you pledge, don't hedge.

NIKITA KHRUSHCHEV

What man actually needs is not a tensionless state but rather the striving and struggling for some goal worthy of him. What he needs is not the discharge of tension at any cost, but the call of a potential meaning waiting to be fulfilled by him.

VIKTOR FRANKL

Leadership is action, not position.

DONALD H. MCGANNON

It is easier to fight for principles than to live up to them.

ALFRED ADLER

Victory is reserved for those who are willing to pay its price.

SUN TZU

Unless you do your best, the day will come when, tired and hungry, you will halt just short of the goal you were ordered to reach, and by halting you will make useless the efforts and deaths of thousands.

GENERAL GEORGE S. PATTON

A boy doesn't have to go to war to be a hero; he can say he doesn't like pie when he sees there isn't enough to go around.

EDWARD W. HOWE

BUILDER'S MOON
THE DISSEMINATING MOON IN TAURUS

As the Full Moon moves into the Disseminating phase, Taurus moves outward from the circumscribed place of home and family and farm, into the realm of the outside world. Taurus wants to make things that last, that will be solid and standing hundreds of years in the future. He sees the people without roofs over their heads, remembers the Earth Mother's sturdy home, and wants to put roofs over the unhappy masses as well. He becomes the Builder, who works in wood and stone and concrete. He starts with houses and, eventually, moves upward into entire cities.

The Taurus story moves toward and away from involvement with Nature, and here the pendulum swings in the direction of civilization and the desires of people yet again. Making a city is a greater assault on the wilderness than the Woodcutter's little business ever was. On the other hand, the Builder's Moon is essentially creative. He's not merely whacking down trees to sell, he's putting up structures that have beauty and utility, that help people to survive. At the moment, the creativity outweighs the destruction. (That, however, will change soon.) The Builder is creative, but he is not the Artist (Full Moon in Libra). The latter is an Air sign and is fine with abstract creations that have no purpose other than being gazed upon. Taurus, although ruled by Venus, is an Earth sign and requires that creations be of practical use. Ideally, the Builder finds the perfect balance between beauty and utilitarian workmanship, creating tools and dwellings that will be used every day, that fit well in the hand, that give comfort and warmth to families, that will never break until they are worn out by a good long period of hard usage.

The Builder walks a fine line, however. Cities can be amazing things, or they can be boils on the ass of Gaea. Often they are both at once. If they are poorly designed, they pour their filth out onto the surrounding countryside and cover the Farmer's fields in wasteful concrete. They may attract too many people with their glitter, relegating the poorest of them to ugly slums and unemployment. Housing and caring for the masses starts in the Builder's heart as the passing energy of the Earth Mother. He wants to help, but it seems that no matter what he does, it isn't enough. There just aren't resources enough to help everyone who needs helping, and this pains and weighs upon him. If he is not careful, it can make him fatalistic enough that he abandons his plans of human aid and just builds monuments to his own creative urges. He can also forget himself and spread too far, undoing the necessary balance with the green spaces.

On the Builder's Moon, we pick up tools and make practical changes in our worlds. Even people who have never picked up a hammer should try putting up a nail for that picture they've been waiting for someone else to hang. If there's nothing to do around your house, call your friends and ask them—someone will likely have things that need fixing or even building from scratch. If even that turns up dry, try local organizations. Someone will want a coat of paint or a few shingles replaced, at the least. If you're really motivated, spend a couple of days working for Habitat for Humanity or a similar organization.

People born under the Builder's Moon find heartfelt joy in engineering things, making things, and making things better. That can include making people better, which can be a problem if they end up bossing around their loved ones in the name of improvement. While creativity draws them, they are suspicious of useless arts, preferring to make things that can be touched and used. Responsibility for their creations is strong in them—they don't like to be associated with shoddy work—and when they go wrong, that's one handle that can be used to pull them back. They love to surround themselves with fine things, and nearly all want to own their own home (but, as you can imagine, they have a picture in their head of what it will look like, down to the last nail). If they can't build physical things, they will build organizations, thinking ahead to the bodily needs of the masses. Their hearts often get caught between the pull to make new things and the pull to stay exactly the same, unchanging. That sometimes means that they have to distance themselves emotionally somewhat in order to force themselves to change; when they remain deeply involved, the urge for stasis overwhelms them.

Quotes for the Builder's Moon

The careful textbooks measure
So all who build beware
The load, the shock, the pressure
Material can bear,
So when the buckled girder
Lets down the grinding span,
The blame for loss or murder
Is laid upon the man.
Not on the steel, the man . . .

RUDYARD KIPLING

I believe that every right implies a responsibility, every opportunity an obligation, every possession a duty.

JOHN D. ROCKEFELLER

A city is a large community where people are lonesome together.

HERBERT PROCHNOW

Architecture begins where engineering ends.

WALTER GROPIUS

Faced with the choice between changing one's mind and proving that there is no need to do so, almost everyone gets busy on the proof.

JOHN KENNETH GALBRAITH

The wild places are where we began. When they end, so do we.

DAVID BROWER

The object of opening the mind, as of opening the mouth, is to shut it again on something solid.

G. K. CHESTERTON

Engineers like to solve problems. If there are no problems handily available, they will create their own problems.

SCOTT ADAMS

Among the many thousands of things that I have never been able to understand, one in particular stands out. That is the question of who was the first person who stood by a pile of sand and said, "You know, I bet if we took some of this and mixed it with a little potash and heated it, we could make a material that would be solid and yet transparent. We could call it glass." Call me obtuse, but you could stand me on a beach till the end of time and never would it occur to me to try to make it into windows.

BILL BRYSON

The ancient Romans had a tradition: whenever one of their engineers constructed an arch, as the capstone was hoisted into place, the engineer assumed accountability for his work in the most profound way possible: he stood under the arch.

MICHAEL ARMSTRONG

SCRIBE'S MOON
THE DISSEMINATING MOON IN GEMINI

The Disseminating Moon in Gemini moves the agenda of the Storyteller to fare outward in the world. The Scribe wants to prevent all those stories from being lost and wants a wider sphere of humanity to hear them—even the ones that are controversial, or hard to hear, or difficult to reproduce in written form. It is an art to take a living spoken story and recreate it on a printed page in a way that retains its vitality and subtler meaning; far too many tales when written down seem dry or garbled or uninspiring. This is the Scribe's task: to bring the spoken word into other media and send it to those who cannot come to the speaker.

This job is part writer, part researcher, part editor, part plagiarist, part publicist. The Scribe does far more than merely take dictation. She thoughtfully collects the work of others and compiles, translates, and interprets it in a way that will send the most information to the most people. Unlike the Scholar (Gibbous Moon in Sagittarius), who simply gathers information for the pure love of knowledge, the Scribe is concerned with access, as much access as possible. She wants more than a book that molders in the back of the library, to occasionally be cracked by a graduate student looking for thesis material. Gemini's love of advertising comes in handy here, as the Scribe's work is carefully designed to appeal to a wider audience and insert her ideas into the mass of skeptical minds.

The Gemini Moon's ongoing struggle with what is true and what is false continues on the Scribe's Moon, but on a subtler level. The pen that writes the information down, or that compiles and interprets the information of lesser-known writers, has a good deal of power to slant how that information is received by the readers. It takes staunchly objective and remarkably self-aware individuals to keep their own biases out of the work, including their desire to prove a point or send a particular message to the public. When the Scribe errs, it's usually on the side of wanting to prove one view—even a worthy view—so badly that she is willing to twist other people's hard-won information in a direction that they might not have intended and wouldn't approve. Sometimes she is so unaware of her own internal agenda that she honestly believes she is being objective when it's obvious she isn't.

On the Scribe's Moon, we read and compare the writing of different people, especially if they have different views on the same subject. It's a good time for a book discussion or for intelligent research, and an even better time to send ideas out to places where they can be read. Above all else, it's a good time to write . . . anything.

People born on the Scribe's Moon have a strong intellectual curiosity about a wide variety of subjects, and often have strong opinions about those subjects. They can be glib and articulate, especially in writing, and may actually express themselves better that way—I've met Scribe's Moon people who were reticent talkers in person but poured themselves eloquently into Internet posts. While they enjoy higher education, they are more goal-oriented about it than the Scholar's Moon folk; for them, a college degree lends their words credibility, and research is less about collecting knowledge for its own sake and more about collecting impressive references to prove their worth in the world. Dual majors and multiple degrees abound among the more academic of these folks, for similar reasons. The nonacademic ones may resort to quoting popular magazines or websites.

They are happiest when writing about something they love—this is a Moon sign, remember—and they may resort to all sorts of measures to get people to read their work. Above all, they want to be heard. Some may even resort to sensationalism if it means that they will be read. They should be encouraged to journal, and they need to learn to value writing that openly and honestly shows experiences through the lens of their own perceptions, rather than trying to pretend that those perceptions are not there.

Quotes for the Scribe's Moon

A book may be as great a thing as a battle.

BENJAMIN DISRAELI

Books won't stay banned. Ideas don't go to jail.

ALFRED WHITNEY GRISWOLD

There is no such thing as a moral or immoral book. Books are well-written or badly written; that is all.

OSCAR WILDE

Show me the books he loves and I shall know the man far better than through mortal friends.

ATTRIBUTED TO BOTH S. WEIR MITCHELL AND DAWN ADAMS

A book is the only place in which you can examine a fragile thought without breaking it, or explore an explosive idea without fear it will go off in your face. It is one of the few havens remaining where a man's mind can get both provocation and privacy.

EDWARD P. MORGAN

The writer is an engineer of the human soul.

JOSEPH STALIN

Do not talk to me of Archimedes' lever. He was an absent-minded person with a mathematical imagination. Mathematics commands my respect, but I have no use for engines. Give me the right word and the right accent and I will move the world.

JOSEPH CONRAD

> Books are here to show a man that those original thoughts of his aren't
> very original after all.
>
> ABRAHAM LINCOLN
>
> Fine words! I wonder where you stole them.
>
> JONATHAN SWIFT
>
> When a thing has been said and well said, have no scruple; take it and
> copy it. Give references? Why should you? Either your readers know where
> you have taken the passage and the precaution is needless, or they do not
> know and you humiliate them.
>
> ANATOLE FRANCE

SHIELD-FATHER'S MOON
THE DISSEMINATING MOON IN CANCER

The Sea Mother, for all her archetypal powers, is a vulnerable creature. She is often with child and cannot fight to protect herself. That is the job of her mate, the one who was once the Mother's Son. In the Disseminating Moon phase, the Cancer Moon steps through the door of the warm home and out into the world, to guard the shelter and protect his loved ones. It is a brave move for sensitive Cancer. He would far rather remain by the hearth under the wing of family, but he remembers how it all was destroyed, and he is determined never to see that again. Now that he has something to lose, he finds the backbone to defend it with all he has. It is the existence of the warm, welcoming hearth within that gives him the strength to do what he must.

The Cancer Moon is no warrior; he shudders to see Aries going off armored in search of violence and glory. It is a huge act of will and courage for him to venture again out into the world—to work the job and bring home the paycheck, but most especially to be the one who stands out in the cold while the children are all tucked in bed, grasping his stout stick and praying that the wolves and bandits do not materialize. In order to become the Shield-Father and protect the innocents, he must learn to shield himself, because he knows his emotional and fragile interior. Like the Crab that is his totem, he pulls on a hard shell. This can make him grumpy at the breakfast table, because he's been up all night protecting and is secretly and shamefacedly resentful of the very innocents he's been protecting and supporting. This phase of the Cancer Moon is, paradoxically, likely to be the most guarded one emotionally. His heart is as expressive as any other, but he doesn't give anyone easy access.

He may also go overboard on the protection. It's not unheard of for the Shield-Father to lock his loved ones up like precious jewels, preventing them from going out or growing up or learning anything that he deems might give them nightmares. While for some types that sort of thing might be done out of a need to control, in his case it's just fear—fear of the cruel world that hurt him before and might hurt others in the same way, and fear of his own ability to keep them safe if they're out of his sight. This causes many arguments when the offspring get itchy feet, especially if they are by nature Gypsies (New Moon in Sagittarius) or Rebels (Waxing Quarter Moon in Aquarius). He needs to learn to get beyond his fears, grit his teeth, and let them have a life of their own, complete with all possible mistakes. It's a hard lesson, and too many Shield-Fathers simply drive away and estrange the children who they spent their life on.

On the Shield-Father's Moon, we protect the innocent and stand between them and unnecessary pain. One good way to do this is, if you're a confident and articulate sort, is to offer to be an advocate for people who must face down intimidating bureaucracy—welfare mothers, for instance—and are terrified of it, and likely to let that terror keep them from getting their due. Another good task is to go with someone to do something that person finds difficult, and give moral support and a pep talk. It's also a good time to think about our own internal walls, the ones that we erect for self-protection, and check to see if they're really still needed . . . and if they are, determine whether they're in good working order and not full of holes.

People born under the Shield-Father's Moon are instinctively guard dogs who want to protect the innocent, although they'd secretly rather be curled up by the fire being petted. As parents, they are terribly overprotective, and sometimes that extends to lovers and friends as well, not to mention elderly parents. They are more sensitive than they let on under their sometimes crusty exterior. They may be drawn to careers where they look after people in some way, whether that's police or social work, or just parenting or being a busybody grandparent.

They don't trust easily, especially strangers, and they are suspicious of people who don't culturally resemble their precious family circle. Tolerance and appreciation of other lifestyles is often rough for them; their conservative attitude comes more from fear of the unknown than anything else. The way for them to get over their irrational fears of a certain type of person is for them to accept someone of that class into their family circle, which will take a long time and a lot of patience on the part of the stranger.

Quotes for the Shield-Father's Moon

Parents, however old they and we may grow to be, serve among other things to shield us from a sense of our doom. As long as they are around, we can avoid the fact of our mortality; we can still be innocent children.

JANE HOWARD

The desire for safety stands against every great and noble enterprise.

TACITUS

God be my judge that I hate fighting. If I be damned for anything, I shall be damned for keeping the two-edged sword of thought tight in the scabbard when it should be searching the bowels of fools and knaves.

SEÁN O'CASEY

It is not flesh and blood but the heart which makes us fathers and sons.

JOHANN SCHILLER

Our land is everything to us. . . . I will tell you one of the things we remember on our land. We remember that our grandfathers paid for it—with their lives.

JOHN WOODEN

I have often had occasion to observe, that a warm blundering man does more for the world than a frigid wise man.

RICHARD CECIL

A father is available to help his daughter balance both her love and her anger toward her mother, to moderate the inevitable emotional extremes in the intense mother-daughter equation. With Daddy's steadying influence daughters can learn to be comfortable with healthy anger, rather than feeling that they must be eternal good girls who must at all costs conceal it.

VICTORIA SECUNDA

He that hath wife and children hath given hostages to fortune.

FRANCIS BACON

For an impenetrable shield, stand inside yourself.

HENRY DAVID THOREAU

The superior man is the providence of the inferior. He is eyes for the blind, strength for the weak, and a shield for the defenseless. He stands erect by bending above the fallen. He rises by lifting others.

ROBERT GREEN INGERSOLL

KING'S MOON
THE DISSEMINATING MOON IN LEO

On the Disseminating Moon in Leo, the scepter passes from the Queen to the King. While I have chosen to differentiate the two archetypes by gender, gender is not their defining characteristic, and the Moon is no more "masculine" or "feminine" in either phase, Full or Disseminating. It does, however, have a slightly different focus in the King's Moon phase. Where the Queen concentrates on ruling her country as best she can, the King looks outward to alliances with other countries and explores ways to bring in prosperity from outside.

The King's Moon, like the Queen's Moon, is concerned with power, authority, and nobility. The King's job is to provide honest, capable, responsive leadership . . . but in addition to valuing the opinions of his subjects, the King also seeks the opinions of the rest of the world. The King plays on a bigger stage than the Queen, and he is more aware of scrutiny. In Celtic myth, the King represents the land, while the Queen represents the people; this suggests a stronger tie to land and territory than the Queen's Moon, which is more tied to tribe and nation. The King marks out the boundaries of the land, because he is more aware of the encroachers around it.

This Moon marks another step in the Leo struggle between the need for self-expression and the desire for applause. While the Queen dealt with this issue by limiting the scope of her rule and thus the number of people she needed to impress, the Disseminating Moon always turns outward to the greater world, and thus by definition must take into consideration how the greater public views the message. In Leo, the Moon must turn again, reluctantly, back to the Actor's dilemma. However, the King is in a much greater position of power than the Actor, and has more confidence in his ability to make people comply with his goals. If the Moon here is afflicted or the early years were particularly difficult, the King may go to great lengths to appear the perfect authority, up to and including becoming somewhat tyrannical. He may feed his ego at the expense of honesty or react out of proportion to any perceived slight. He may publicly build up his reputation while privately obsessing over and comparing himself with others in positions of power and influence. He may cave to public opinion out of a need to look benevolent and attractive, only to find himself the source of some other group's complaints. If he fails and reverts to unworthy behavior, his fall will be public and humiliating.

On the King's Moon, we continue our exploration of leadership, but now we work with other groups from within our own group. It's a time for leaders to make alliances and network with other organizations, and to articulate to outsiders the nature and mission of their own organization. Advertising is not the point; the King exemplifies his group's highest values and ideals, for outsiders to admire and insiders to emulate. He models the proper actions, rather than ordering others to behave nobly. If they choose to ignore his example, they wouldn't have followed his orders anyway.

People born under the King's Moon wrestle with leadership problems for much of their lives. If they shirk leadership—perhaps due to a shyer Sun or other planets—these situations will continue to appear until they take up the gauntlet, and make the requisite mistakes until they get good at it. If they accept this challenge right away, they will still make those mistakes. If they follow others, they will be the ones to hold those others to a standard of nobility . . . if they have figured out for themselves what that looks like; sometimes articulating what they want in a leader gives them insight as to how they could do it themselves.

King's Moon people need to learn to develop quiet self-confidence that balances taking the opinions of others into account just enough to be able to effectively communicate with them and be sure of their own worth and competence. They need to humbly ask their trusted friends to tell them when they are being tyrants, and take those criticisms seriously.

Quotes for the King's Moon

An aristocracy that shirks its leadership is done for. Its only excuse for existence is that it takes the lead.

ALFRED NORTH WHITEHEAD

In America, any boy can become President, and I suppose that's just one of the risks he takes.

ADLAI STEVENSON

The question, "Who ought to be the boss?" is like asking, "Who ought to be the tenor in the quartet?" Obviously, the man who can sing tenor.

HENRY FORD

It is essential for a prince to be on a friendly footing with his people, since otherwise he will have no recourse in adversity. . . . Let no one quote against me the old proverb, "He who builds on the people builds on sand," for that may be true of a private citizen who presumes on his favor with the people, and counts on being rescued by them when overpowered by his enemies or by the magistrates. But a prince who is a man of courage and is able to command, who knows how to preserve order in his state, need never regret having founded his security on the affection of the people.

NICCOLÒ MACHIAVELLI

The Emperor is one who upholds the right and the just through struggle and personal jeopardy.

F. D. GRAVES

There are four qualities essential to royal authority. First, the royal authority is sacred; second, it is parental; third, it is absolute; fourth, it is submitted to reason.

JACQUES-BÉNIGNE BOSSUET

O king ruling politically, rule your people also regally when the case requires, for not all cases can be embraced by the statutes and customs of your realm, and thus the remaining cases are left to your discretion; moreover, always rule all criminal matters at your will, and moderate or remit all penalties, so long as you can do this without harm to your subjects or offence against the customs and statutes of your realm. Equity, too, is left to your wisdom, lest the rigour of the words of the law, confounding its intention, injure the common good.

JOHN FORTESCUE

Back of every noble life are the principles that have fashioned it.

GEORGE HORACE LORIMER

No one can rule guiltlessly, and least of all those whom history compels to hurry.

EDGAR SNOW

But the King said, "Haven't I read somewhere
There is no act more kingly than to give?"
"Yes, but give character and not just food.
A King must give his people character . . .
Make them as happy as is good for them.
But that's a hard one, for I have to add:
Not without consultation with their wishes;
Which is the crevice that lets Progress in.
If we could only stop the Progress somewhere,
at a good point for pliant permanence . . .
But no, a woman has to be her age,
A nation has to take its course
Of Progress round and round in circles

From King to Mob to King to Mob to King
Until the eddy of it eddies out . . .
How hard it is to keep from being King
When it's in you and in the situation . . .

ROBERT FROST

WEAVER'S MOON
THE DISSEMINATING MOON IN VIRGO

During the Disseminating Moon in Virgo, the Spinner moves up in rank and skill to become the Weaver. Again, this is both a story about work and craft, and an echo of the legend of the Fates. The Weaver is the second Fate, who weaves the tapestry of life and determines the life story of each human being. As is appropriate for the Disseminating Moon, the Weaver works much more in public than the Spinner and offers his product to a wide audience. Where the Spinner is a master of creating raw material, the Weaver is a master craftsman who creates an actual finished product, something that delights the eye of the public and brightens their world. His woven designs become famous for their workmanship, quality, and originality.

The Weaver understands craftsmanship artistically, but in a way that is different from the Artist (Full Moon in Libra) or the Poet (Gibbous Moon in Pisces) or the other creative Moons. For the Weaver, craft is about perfection. Since he might well make the same thing twice or more, the idea is to get each version closer to the picture he has in his head. Each project is not so much an effort to create something new, like the Artist's work, as another chance at salvation, a humble attempt to creep that much closer to perfection, one careful hair further down the path. He studies plants to find new dyes; he experiments with mordants to get the sharpest red; he endures the stench of ammonia to find the best blue. He seeks out new breeds of sheep, new colors of lambs, new plant fibers, and mixes them together. He spends whole nights undoing his work because he realizes that the fourth line of the pattern should be changed about a foot back on the loom. The Weaver works in cloth, but he might also work in other materials—the instrument maker who crafts violin after violin to find the absolute clearest tone, the cabinet maker who spends all night sanding one piece of wood, the goldsmith who tries to construct the perfect setting for the precious gem. Being a taciturn Virgo Moon, he might not speak of it, but his work is the way that he gives glory to the gods.

The process is as important to him as the goal. This is something that people often lose sight of, especially if they are doing work that they do not love. Master craftspeople can lose themselves in a haze of Making, obsessively working out tiny flaws in a piece or spending hours on one small thing. Others may look askance, but the Weaver enjoys the process. It is the closest that he can come to the ecstatic state of Pisces. One thinks of Japanese monks raking perfect circles in sand, or European monks finding a state of patient worshipfulness while hoeing potatoes. The Weaver learns the secret: any repetitive labor can become a meditation, and any work you love can become a prayer.

On the Weaver's Moon, we do handcrafts or support others who do them. Another possibility is to take up some kind of work that you normally do, but strive for absolute perfection in it to see how close you can come. Try to find joy in the process and fulfillment in the final outcome.

People born on the Weaver's Moon really need to be doing work that makes them blissfully happy. The wrong career can make their whole lives dismal. They are generally willing to work hard to make their chosen career reasonably successful, but are less interested in doing well financially than in doing what they love. If the work supports itself and them with a basic standard of living, they are content. If they cannot work at what they love, they will make their work into an obsessive hobby that may threaten to push out everything else in their life.

A wise partner will let them have their work, and will take joy in their joyful labor. If the two can work together, so much the better. A wiser partner will convince their Weaver that polishing a relationship is also worthy and joyous work, and that will cultivate a Weaver who is willing to put in the time and effort to make the absolute best joining of two lives. But those partners should be careful what they ask for—the same dogged perseverance and drive for perfection will be expected of them as well.

Quotes for the Weaver's Moon

When I work, I work very fast, but preparing to work can take any length of time.

CY TWOMBLY

There is in every artist's studio a scrap heap of discarded works in which the artist's discipline prevailed against his imagination.

ROBERT BRAULT

The world is filled with willing people; some willing to work, the rest willing to let them.

ROBERT FROST

You have not done enough, you have never done enough, so long as it is still possible that you have something to contribute.

DAG HAMMARSKJÖLD

It is necessary to try to surpass one's self always: this occupation ought to last as long as life.

QUEEN CHRISTINA OF SWEDEN

Hold yourself responsible for a higher standard than anybody else expects of you. Never excuse yourself. Never pity yourself. Be a hard master to yourself—and be lenient to everybody else.

HENRY WARD BEECHER

Three Rules of Work: Out of clutter find simplicity; From discord find harmony; In the middle of difficulty lies opportunity.

ALBERT EINSTEIN

Nature uses only the longest threads to weave her patterns, so that each small piece of her fabric reveals the organization of the entire tapestry.

RICHARD FEYNMAN

> Concentrate all your thoughts upon the work at hand. The sun's rays do not burn until brought to a focus.
>
> ALEXANDER GRAHAM BELL
>
> Pray as though everything depended on God. Work as though everything depended on you.
>
> SAINT AUGUSTINE

AMBASSADOR'S MOON
THE DISSEMINATING MOON IN LIBRA

On the Libra Disseminating Moon, the Lover decides to spread the message of love and harmony to a wider audience, doing her part to make life easier for people. The Ambassador's Moon is a time of swinging from beauty and peace back toward justice, but the Ambassador, like the Lover, is still trying to find a balance. *If people would just listen to each other,* she reasons, *then there would be neither conflict nor disharmony. Perhaps I can help them to do just that!* She sets out to resolve the complaints of warring factions and bridge the gap between groups of people.

The Ambassador's strengths lie in her ability to see both sides of people's issues without being partisan, and to interpret their stances to each other. She can extrapolate what would be fair and unfair to each, and tries her best to come up with compromises. She can speak for those with awkward tongues and few social graces, and do a better job of pleasantly selling their point than they would be likely to do, especially when tempers are running high. Her downfall is that she is often unable to figure out for herself what her own opinions are. All that vacillation among different perspectives keeps her flexible, but often very indecisive. Either she doesn't have a firm opinion on something because she can't decide between two perfectly good but opposing ideas, or she has very firm opinions . . . that change regularly, depending on whose worldview she is sunk in at the moment. While this quality is useful for her job in bringing peace to the world, it can be hard on her personal life.

On the Ambassador's Moon we go out and make peace, and get people to listen to each other. This is a good time for educating groups of people about other groups or—even more appropriate—arranging for speakers from those groups to talk. It's good for any group effort where there has to be a concerted effort to get along and reach compromises. It seems like everyone is just a little more reasonable on the Libra Disseminating Moon. Make good use of that time.

People born under the Ambassador's Moon are peacemakers at heart, like the New Moon's White Knight, but they have not only the instinct for it but a natural knack. They learn quickly how to make people feel comfortable in a space or in a group. They can stop a quarrel with their very presence, interpret an unpopular opinion in a way that gets it accepted, and explain enemies to each other with such success that they find it hard to remain enemies. They are artists in their own way, only their art is made with people.

However, they may not be so good with conflict when the peacemaking has failed and there's no way around a messy argument. Ambassador's Moon people tend to gracefully retire when this happens. They are good at being gracious and they like etiquette, but they may not be so good at standing up for their boundaries when cornered. They can get overwhelmed by disharmony and get snappish or need to retreat when there's nothing but noise and ruckus. These folks like their partners to maneuver well in public; someone with low social skills makes them want to flee. They may judge people with awkward or rude social behavior as if they are practically criminals.

Ambassador's Moon people will throw great parties, as they live to bring people together. They are social animals, all the way, and they need family members who also love the idea of having china for fifty people in the house and actually using it regularly. If they can't have people over, they will go out somewhere they can mingle; they seem to draw energy from gregarious crowds. People like to see them coming, too.

Quotes for the Ambassador's Moon

An ambassador is an honest man sent to lie abroad for the good of his country.

SIR HENRY WOTTON

The real art of conversation is not only to say the right thing in the right place but to leave unsaid the wrong thing at the tempting moment.

DOROTHY NEVILL

Diplomacy is the art of saying "Nice doggie!" until you can find a rock.

WYNN CATLIN

I presented myself as the most amateur of diplomats. He (Nehru) proclaimed himself an amateur prime minister. I think that truth will not be a barrier to our association.

JOHN KENNETH GALBRAITH

Diplomacy is the art of fishing tranquilly in troubled waters.

J. CHRISTOPHER HEROLD

Don't ever slam a door; you might want to go back.

DON HEROLD

I cannot give you the formula for success, but I can give you the formula for failure, which is: Try to please everybody.

HERBERT BAYARD SWOPE

The prosperity of a country depends not on the abundance of its revenues, nor on the strength of its fortifications, nor on the beauty of its public buildings, but it consists in the number of its cultivated citizens, in its men of education, enlightenment and character.

MARTIN LUTHER

Whenever two people meet there are really six people present. There is each man as he sees himself, each man as the other person sees him, and each man as he really is.

WILLIAM JAMES

There can be no offense where none is taken.

JAPANESE PROVERB

WITCH'S MOON
THE DISSEMINATING MOON IN SCORPIO

The Priestess of the Scorpio Full Moon stays in her temple, and the people come to her. As the Disseminating Moon comes on, she looks outward from her protected space and sees the suffering of the people. On the Witch's Moon, the Scorpio story turns back to the darker (and in some cases, more practical) mysteries to help the ones who need it most. The Priestess becomes the Witch, living on the outskirts of the village, sought out for her healing knowledge and her more fearful powers. As the Moon wanes, her attention turns to the outside world rather than her own darknesses, and she finds that working directly with people does the most good.

Historically, the Witch began as the junior partner of the tribal shaman—herb-woman, cunning-man, hedgewalker, perhaps midwife and counselor. When the shamans died out, she carried on the scraps of knowledge—medical, magical, mental—and helped the people as best she could. As centralized state religion and medicine grew, she became a competitor for the hearts and minds of the multitudinous lower classes. It was easier and cheaper to go to the herb-wife for a remedy than to the more expensive leech-doctor, and if you needed it, she dispensed more than herbs. She gave out love potions, spells to know who had thieved from your house, and worse magics. People look down their noses, today, at the ethics of peasants who shopped for hexes and curses, but those people have little idea what it was like to live poor in Europe for a thousand years.

Documented accounts of witches nearly always revealed them to be members of the poorest and most oppressed classes, partly because it was much easier to torture and kill peasants for political reasons without repercussions, and partly because it was the powerless who needed negative magic the most. If the entire social system was set up in a way as to keep you in desperate poverty, rob you of your rights, and give you no recourse, then of course you'd find the power of a hex or curse attractive. After all, what else could you do? In crossing that line, the peasant found herself an outcast from the community, if only internally (if she kept it a secret) but sometimes externally (if she did it professionally). People avoided her out of fear—fear of her power, fear of social backlash—but they went to her when they were in trouble and had no other choice.

On the Witch's Moon, we confront what we would do—and how far we would go—if we were in a situation of powerlessness and oppression. If the option of magical power was open to us, how would we use it . . . especially if we, or someone or something we loved, was being threatened? How do we use small pieces of power every day? When do we speak a rumor? When do we say the word that will change someone's mind to blacker thoughts? When are we unkind to make a point or to make ourselves feel better? Is our daily "domestic" power always handled ethically and kindly? If not, how would we change ourselves to be more worthy of greater power? It's also a good time to look at how things that were once considered good have been demonized by society for evil purposes.

Those born under the Witch's Moon are more outwardly focused than people born on the Scorpio Waxing Quarter Moon, but they still carry the innate sense of vengeance that plagues the earlier Moons. Their sense of injustice is as keen as that of a Libra Moon, but they don't retaliate openly like the Libra opponent. Instead they work in small, subtle ways—insinuation, misdirection, the deliberate misplacing of a necessary form, the nail stuck in the car tire, the right rumor dropped at just the right time. They have a fine sense of viciousness and want to change things, but they don't like open confrontation, so it is all done quietly.

Witch's Moon people may feel more of a kinship with other outcasts than with the majority rule, but rather than the Aquarius "we are all different together," it is more of a "we are all wronged and must stick together to support ourselves against the evil of oppression." Teaching a lesson to the oppressors, regardless of the damage, is one of their favorite fantasies and probably has been since they were born. It's part of their life's work to learn how the education of one's enemies can be accomplished without beginning from a place of anger and pain, and how that is the more powerful tactic in the end.

Quotes for the Witch's Moon

I have gone out, a possessed witch,
haunting the black air, braver at night;
dreaming evil, I have done my hitch
over the plain houses, light by light:
lonely thing, twelve-fingered, out of mind.
A woman like that is not a woman, quite.
I have been her kind.

ANNE SEXTON

Do good by stealth, and blush to find it fame.

ALEXANDER POPE

The blackest chapter in the history of Witchcraft lies not in the malevolence of Witches but in the deliberate, gloating cruelty of their prosecutors.

THEDA KENYON

My mother says I must not pass,
Too near that glass;
She is afraid that I will see,
A little witch that looks like me;
With a red mouth to whisper low,
The very thing I should not know

SARAH MORGAN BRYANT PIATT

When, however, one reads of a witch being ducked, of a woman possessed by devils, of a wise woman selling herbs, or even a very remarkable man who had a mother, then I think we are on the track of a lost novelist, a suppressed poet . . . indeed, I would venture to guess that Anon, who wrote so many poems without signing them, was often a woman.

VIRGINIA WOOLF

Even in Hell the peasant will have to serve the landlord, for, while the landlord is boiling in a cauldron the peasant will have to put wood under it.

RUSSIAN PROVERB

And thou shalt be the first of witches known,
And thou shalt be the first of all in the world,
And thou shalt teach the art of poisoning,
Of poisoning those who are great lords of all;
Yes, thou shalt make them die in their palaces
And thou shalt bind the oppressor's soul with power.

CHARLES GODFREY LELAND

Now I say that with cruelty and oppression it is everybody's business to interfere when they see it.

ANNA SEWELL

We are the little folk, we,
Too little to love or to hate,
Leave us alone and you'll see
How fast we can drag down the state.

RUDYARD KIPLING

It has been rightly said that nothing is unimportant, nothing powerless in the universe; a single atom can dissolve everything, and save everything! What terror! There lies the eternal distinction between good and evil.

GÉRARD DE NERVAL

PHILOSOPHER'S MOON
THE DISSEMINATING MOON IN SAGITTARIUS

The Sagittarius Disseminating Moon sees the Priest become the Philosopher. As he ages, his religious fervor ceases to be satisfied with simple faith, and he wants to theorize about *why*. Why is a dangerous question to ask, and often people who can't find a good answer in the tenets of their faith do not go into a conversation with the Universe that is not bounded by what is already written down, but repudiate their faith altogether and seek a more human method of pondering things. This is the Philosopher's journey: the Priest became too dependent on the confines and trappings of his faith to explain everything, and the Philosopher turns away from faith as a result.

The Priest, ministering to a flock, serves the people, who also struggle with that faith, but his experience with the world is limited to that congregation. The Philosopher hopes to reach a wider audience, and he does that by writing and explaining his theory of living to everyone he finds. Where the Priest had moved away from the world of animal toward that of the gods, the Philosopher of the Disseminating Moon moves toward the human world, and this is the most human-centric of the Sagittarian Moons. He is not a hermit on a mountaintop; he wants intellectual congress with others of like mind, to trade ideas and stimulate each other to profound thoughts. He wants to be heard and to hear others. In a sense, he has come back to the Seeker's path, but he is calmer about it and is not upset by the idea that he may not find all truths before he is dead.

The Philosopher also loves people and experience, including the good things in life. His goal is to experience things not in a welter of hurry, gobbling down experiences like the early Sagittarian Moons, but to carefully savor and analyze each one. Quality of life dominates his consciousness. His downfall is what lurks on his horizon. When he forgets to keep an open and relaxed view of life his vision becomes smaller, and he remembers his resentments about the structured traditions that he walked away from. Then he becomes angry and lashes out at those who represent his past. This fault is continually correctable if he concentrates on the present and his love of learning, but sometimes old disappointments are hard to release.

On the Philosopher's Moon we read what other people have written about life, and we judge it. We also talk about our philosophy of life to others. This is a good time for a group discussion about a book that you have all read that offers to change people's ideas about the world. Don't let the discussion get out of hand, though; while anything can be said, make the group a sanctuary where no idea is penalized. In private, consider the ideas of people about whom you are ambivalent—perhaps their ideas are good but you find them personally reprehensible, or perhaps you approve of half their ideas and not the rest. Think about what sort of people they might be to make them feel the way they feel.

People born on the Philosopher's Moon are often born skeptics, but they are usually laid-back about it. Fanaticism lurks on their horizon, but does not usually possess them. They enjoy higher education and often continue learning for many years, formally or informally. They like to teach, and they like to give people advice. Their own views of the world are fairly static, but they are usually quite tolerant and open to at least considering other views.

Philosopher's Moon people love to be around other people; they are gregarious and may be the "smaller" life of the party—not the charismatic center, but the one in the corner with a group of people happily hanging on their words as they tell their tale. They are often counselors in a relaxed way, and help others to be more tolerant and not take themselves too seriously. If you want to be involved with someone born under this Moon, be interesting and willing to stay up until three in the morning talking about all manner of things.

Quotes for the Philosopher's Moon

The longer I live, the more obvious it is to me that the most sacred act of a man's life is to say and feel "I believe such-and-such to be true." All the greatest rewards and all the heaviest penalties of existence cling about that act.

THOMAS HENRY HUXLEY

You philosophize when you reflect critically upon what you are actually doing in the world. What you are doing is, of course, in the first place, living. And life involves passions, faiths, doubts and courage. The critical inquiry into what these things mean and imply is philosophy.

JOSIAH ROYCE

Philosophy's all right, when you have a house to think about it in.

ARLO GUTHRIE

I speak truth, not as much as I would, but as much as I dare, and I dare a little more as I grow older.

MICHEL DE MONTAIGNE

Let no man imagine that he has no influence. Whoever he may be, and wherever he may be placed, the man who thinks becomes a light and a power.

HENRY GEORGE

It is important that a philosopher remind himself now and then that he is a particle pontificating on infinity.

WILL AND ARIEL DURANT

Concerning the Gods: I am not able to know for a certainty whether they exist or not. For there are many things which prevent one from knowing, especially the obscurity of the subject, and the shortness of the life of Man.

PROTAGORAS

Homo sapiens, the only creature endowed with reason, is also the only creature to pin its existence on things unreasonable.

HENRI BERGSON

The philosopher has to be the bad conscience of his age.

FRIEDRICH NIETZSCHE

Three things cannot be hidden: The sun, the moon, and the truth.

GAUTAMA SIDDARTHA, BUDDHA

GRANDFATHER'S MOON
THE DISSEMINATING MOON IN CAPRICORN

The Full Moon in Capricorn gives way to the Disseminating Moon, and like the Leo's Queen's Moon that gives way to the Leo's King's Moon, Capricorn's Grandmother's Moon gives way to the Grandfather's Moon. The Grandmother's mate co-rules the family and clan, but where she looks to the wise governing of internal struggles, the Grandfather is concerned with the interaction of his tribe with the outside world. Like her, his focus is on kinship bonds, but he must also negotiate alliances with other people's kinship groups and decide who can be trusted with business transactions. He is the Patriarch of his clan, and he protects them not through skill at arms—that's the job of the Warriors—but through skill in dealings. He is vigilant and knows that being cheated in peacetime can be just as damaging as being attacked in wartime, and that one may lead to the other if things are not handled skillfully.

The Grandfather must be hard-working and shrewd to ensure that his people are not cheated. This means making hard decisions: Will our trade with this clan serve us, or should we be looking for markets elsewhere? What is this clan's reputation, and should we believe it? What is our own reputation with other groups, and how do we improve it or capitalize on it? How do we get the best we can without compromising our principles, at least where it can be seen and noted? Should we allow marriage with members of this other family, or will that bring a host of disreputable individuals into kinship bonds with us? Like the Grandmother, he is intensely partisan on a smaller scale than the Leo rulership, and his partisanship is tied to kinship bonds and the extended family. The Capricorn Moon, like the Cancer Moon, thinks in terms of family. If the scope of his "tribe" is people unrelated to him—like the CEO of a company—he establishes his boundaries of caring by conceiving of his company as one large family and treating his employees in a paternalistic way. As with the Grandmother Moon, this can be positive or negative.

The Grandfather is also aware, in the same way as the Ancestor (Balsamic Moon in Taurus), that he is building a legacy for his descendants. Both Taurus and Capricorn come to an awareness of building for permanence on the outward-looking Disseminating Moon, and they struggle with its repercussions later. Hard work is the Capricorn answer: labor doggedly, regardless of any joy in the toil. Duty to tribe and family requires it. On the positive side, an authority figure who works harder than anyone else is likely to be respected, and even loved, by those he sacrifices himself for. On the negative side, the Grandfather is falling into the trap of wanting to be respected for what he has sacrificed, which makes the obligated uncomfortable.

On the Grandfather's Moon, we take a hard look at what our family, kin, or clan—blood or chosen—needs in order to do better, and what work we are willing to do to achieve that goal. We also take a hard look at who we are willing to exclude because their presence would not give enough of a return to justify the work needed to sustain them . . . and we also look at the standards on which we base that decision. We should also take a hard look at our own reputations and that of our group, and at how this impacts our ability to function in the world. This is also a good Moon for doing work that may be uncomfortable but that one is duty-bound to carry out to ensure protection of one's people.

People born under the Grandfather's Moon like to be in positions of authority, and they are willing to wheel and deal with "outsiders" in order to protect their family. Actually, they have a hard time valuing anyone unless they are family, so if they value you, it's because they've mentally made you "family" in their minds. Reputation means a lot to them. It's said that Capricorn is cautious because he doesn't want to do anything he'll have to live down—not regret, live down—and this is especially true for Grandfather's Moon people.

These folks have a tendency to become workaholics and need to remember that the joy of family is why they started down this path in the first place, and if they get no joy, there's no point. They very much want to be seen as a respected authority, although their familial way of trying to achieve this tends to make them constant advice-factories. People who don't care about their reputations confuse them, and it appears somehow . . . unseemly to them. Asking them for advice about something, and actually taking it, warms their hearts.

Quotes for the Grandfather's Moon

It is harder to avoid censure than to gain applause, for this may be done by one great or wise action in an age; but to escape censure a man must pass his whole life without saying or doing one ill or foolish thing.

DAVID HUME

If you wish to know what a man is, place him in authority.

YUGOSLAV PROVERB

Some people like my advice so much that they frame it upon the wall instead of using it.

GORDON R. DICKSON

The problem with the rat race is that even if you win, you're still a rat.

LILY TOMLIN

My father taught me to work; he did not teach me to love it.

ABRAHAM LINCOLN

Hexagram of Great Power: Great power, when it befalls a person, is a true test of his character. What he says is heard, what he thinks is felt. He has the wherewithal to bring enlightenment and progress to his world or to lead it into chaos and evil. He can greatly further his inner development, or completely exhaust himself. Therefore the man possessing Great Power is concerned with Correctness. You would be wise to pause and be certain that your objectives are honorable. Take a cue from the past. Do not do anything that is not part of established policy. Unorthodox actions can lead to downfall during powerful times. Do not assume that your power indicates strength of character, or that it justifies all your opinions and attitudes. This is just another test.

I CHING

The great majority of people have a strong need for authority which they can admire, to which they can submit, and which dominates and sometimes even ill-treats them. We have learned from the psychology of the individual whence comes this need of the masses. It is the longing for the father that lives in each of us from his childhood days, for the same father whom the hero of legend boasts of having overcome.

SIGMUND FREUD

Men of integrity, by their very existence, rekindle the belief that as a people we can live above the level of moral squalor.

JOHN GARDNER

We must hold a man amenable to reason for the choice of his daily craft or profession. It is not an excuse any longer for his deeds that they are the custom of his trade. What business has he with an evil trade?

RALPH WALDO EMERSON

Without self-confidence we are as babes in the cradle. And how can we generate this imponderable quality, which is yet so invaluable, most quickly? By thinking that other people are inferior to oneself.

VIRGINIA WOOLF

APOSTLE'S MOON
THE DISSEMINATING MOON IN AQUARIUS

The Disseminating Moon takes the Aquarius figure onto the Disciple's Path. His time during the Friendship Moon has given him new hope, and he takes this doctrine of hope out into the world. Indeed, if the essence of this Moon can be summed up in one word, it would be hope. One remembers the Tarot card of the Star, whose meaning is hope and which bears a picture of a woman pouring out water from a jug, the Aquarius figure itself.

To have real hope for the future, not just ideas or plans or theories or even ideals, one has to have had the experience of being believed in by others. It is the hope in their eyes for your success that sends you forth with renewed energy, at least if you have an Aquarius Moon. Aquarius Moon people are often somehow ashamed and bothered by the fact that they need others to believe in them in order to fully embrace their missions, and they often act as if they wish it weren't so, as if they oughtn't to care so much about others. They do their individualist dance, daring groups to exile them and people to disapprove of them . . . and at least some of their motive is to prove to themselves that they don't need anyone. They can, of course, do without that look of hope and belief in someone else's eyes. They don't need the very people whose lives they are working to improve. They can love humanity and despise people and make it work just fine. Just watch them.

Except that they suddenly find themselves bogged down with so much cynicism that it all seems useless and futile. Many an Aquarian genius who has sworn to save the world has gotten sidetracked by bitterness. It's a humbling—and even humiliating—fact that to keep going, they need that infusion of hope. It is during this Moon that Aquarius confronts this dichotomy. He gets a huge dose of hope from his friends and compatriots, and it inspires him to go out into the world and spread his ideas. He's not alone, finally, and he becomes the Apostle. It may be that the ideas he's spreading aren't even his, but are those of someone he's discovered whose ideas he admires, who passed on a supply of hope to him. It doesn't matter whether he is the guru or follows the guru; what matters is that he now has a star to follow and to wish upon. As the Disseminating Moon pushes its energy outward, he greets the world with open hands, ready to inspire without the anger of the Rebel (Waxing Quarter in Aquarius) or the deception of the Trickster (Gibbous Moon in Aquarius). He is what he is, nothing more or less. The naked truth should be enough, he says.

On the Apostle's Moon, we think about what gives us hope. We wish on stars. If we have no hope, we go in search of it. If you don't know where to go, do you have friends? Maybe it's time to start there. If you don't have any human connections that can make you believe in the future, that right there says something about your choices. How do you feel about being bound to a web of people? Does it bother you? Would you prefer to be free of obligations? Do you want to be the rock, the island, or are you happily ensconced in a community that accepts you and gives you a glimpse of the joy of tomorrow?

People born on the Apostle's Moon need people, and need something to believe in. It's best for them if they can find those things wrapped up together, although life isn't always that convenient. They do tend to get wrapped up in a moving message and want to bring it to everyone they know; at its best this can be wonderful, but it can also manifest as naïveté and shock when people reject their message or as obnoxiousness in trying to get it across. They don't always understand that the medium is part of the message and that how they come across will affect whether people want to listen to the content. They need regular infusions of hope from their friends and peers, or they will become sad and bitter; an Apostle's Moon person who holes up like a hermit is someone who has lost hope and probably become lost.

Quotes for the Apostle's Moon

Believe nothing, O monks, merely because you have been told it, or because it is traditional, or because you yourselves have imagined it. Do not believe what your teacher tells you merely out of respect for the teacher. But whatsoever, after due examination and analysis, you find to be conducive to the good, the benefit, the welfare of all beings—that doctrine believe and cling to, and take it as your guide.

GAUTAMA SIDDARTHA, BUDDHA

Mourn not the dead . . .
But rather mourn the apathetic throng,
The cowed and meek
Who see the world's great anguish and its wrong,
And dare not speak.

RALPH CHAPLIN

Take from me the hope that I can change the future, and you will send me mad.

ISRAEL ZANGWILL

Treat the other man's faith gently; it is all he has to believe in.

HENRY HASKINS

Everyone thinks of changing the world, but no one thinks of changing himself.

LEO TOLSTOY

An idea that is not dangerous is unworthy of being called an idea at all.

ELBERT HUBBARD

Advice is like snow; the softer it falls, the longer it dwells upon, and the deeper it sinks into the mind.

SAMUEL TAYLOR COLERIDGE

The very least you can do in your life is figure out what you hope for. And the most you can do is live right inside that hope. Not admire it from a distance, but live right in it, under its roof.

ANONYMOUS

Throughout human history, the apostles of purity, those who have claimed to possess a total explanation, have wrought havoc among mere mixed-up human beings.

SALMAN RUSHDIE

Make no little plans; they have no magic to stir men's blood. . . . Make big plans. . . . Aim high in hope and work.

DANIEL H. BURNHAM

MOON OF THE ANGEL OF MERCY
THE DISSEMINATING MOON IN PISCES

They say that the most dangerous thing for any Pisces planet is to fall into a blitz of madness, or alcoholism, or drug addiction, or fantasy. However, there's another pole just as dangerous to them. Remember that there are two fishes facing each other in the Pisces symbol; this is a dual sign. We've learned of the first fish's flaw on the waxing half of the cycle. Now it's time to face the danger of the second fish: the messiah complex.

On the Disseminating Moon in Pisces, the Healer comes into that most damaging of faults—hubris—and assumes that her job is to heal the wounded and that they can be healed by her. She has had such success that it seems like a mandate from the Universe to go forth and heal all those who look as if they need it. This is one of the most complex and difficult Disseminating Moons, because it has the potential to do such amazing good and to create such a terrible downfall. The Angel of Mercy can be a bringer of good on the scale of a Mother Teresa, or she can create a fantasy in which she is the white-clad Angel come to save the pitiful people, and immerse herself in that fantasy to the point of ignoring their actual needs. Sometimes people aren't ready for healing yet, or you aren't the one to heal them. Sometimes they're not going to be healed, for a reason that is greater than your vision can understand. Sometimes you're going to make mistakes or outreach your competence. Sometimes you just have to step away and keep going. These are all hard lessons for an Angel of Mercy to go along with.

Suffering is part of the deal when you're an Angel of Mercy. It means being willing to suffer for the good of others, even to your own severe detriment . . . but sometimes suffering isn't what is called for, and unnecessary suffering is a sin against yourself. Making sacrifices can promote healing if done with no pride or expectations, but as soon as one takes the least little bit of pride in one's ability to suffer for a cause or feels superior to others who are unable to do this, it's the beginning of the end. The salvation of Pisces from the messiah complex is built on compassion. True compassion comes only from realizing that your soul is no better than that of anyone else. To be the Angel of Mercy, all-giving but not needing anything in exchange, the Pisces Moon must set herself above others, and thus taints her compassion. She cannot honestly see her own flaws, because that would shake her belief that she can fix everyone . . . and so she falls gently and lovingly into a morass of denial. The work of the Angel of Mercy can be undertaken only with complete humility.

On the Moon of the Angel of Mercy, we give selflessly of service to those who need it, to the point that we are able to humbly—and comfortably—give it. While this Moon involves sacrifice and suffering, it's best to use this phase as a time to discover where your front-line limits are with regard to such things. At what point do you become uncomfortable and begin to dislike the whole proceeding? At what point do you take pride in your ability to sacrifice and suffer? At what point does the service make you feel superior to anyone? As soon as you feel these things, stop. If that isn't far enough along for you—if, for example, you never make it off your couch—consider how you could get yourself to a point of being able to give cleanly and without special emotion toward any sacrifice that needs to be made.

People born under the Moon of the Angel of Mercy want to help people, but sometimes their need to help is less about the people they're aiding and more about needing to be needed, or it can be about casting themselves as the good guy in their own mental play. They want to be needed, because being needed gives them an anchor in the world of people and keeps them from slipping away into their own world. They are often drawn again and again to people who are troubled or damaged; if there's a wounded, screwed-up soul in the room, that person will be the one they instinctively approach. Then they wonder why their life is full of chaos. Like all the Pisces Moons, they need to set boundaries, but that's not going to happen for them unless they fully understand the reasons for their lack of boundaries.

Quotes for the Moon of the Angel of Mercy

To be willing to suffer in order to create is one thing; to realize that one's creation necessitates one's suffering, that suffering is one of the greatest of God's gifts, is almost to reach a mystical solution to the problem of evil.

J. W. N. SULLIVAN

Dispensing goodwill to mankind is a hazardous business at best.

YUKIO MISHIMA

When you strike a flowing river, no trace remains in the water.

O-SENSEI MORIHEI UESHIBA

Be loving, and you will never want for love; be humble, and you will never want for guiding.

DINAH CRAIK

Beginning today, treat everyone you meet as if they were going to be dead by midnight. Extend to them all the care, kindness, and understanding you can muster, and do it with no thought of any reward. Your life will never be the same again.

OG MANDINO

Prayer is not asking. It is a longing of the soul.

MAHATMA GANDHI

Having someone who understands is a great blessing for ourselves. Being someone who understands is a great blessing to others.

ANONYMOUS

Hell is yourself and the only redemption is when a person puts himself aside to feel deeply for another person.

TENNESSEE WILLIAMS

Imagine that you are creating a fabric of human destiny with the object of making men happy in the end . . . but that it was essential and inevitable to torture to death only one creature . . . and to found that edifice on its unavenged tears: would you consent to be the architect on those conditions? Tell me, and tell me the truth!

FYODOR DOSTOYEVSKY

7

THE WOUND ON THE OUTSIDE

THE WANING QUARTER MOON

I am I plus my circumstances.

JOSÉ ORTEGA Y GASSET

Experience is not what happens to a man; it is what a man does with what happens to him.

ALDOUS HUXLEY

THE WANING QUARTER MOON is again a time of crisis, but where the Waxing Quarter dealt with internal problems, the Waning Quarter—proceeding along the course set by the Disseminating Moon—is a betrayal from the outside. During the waning side of the Moon cycle, experiences evolve from the personal to those involving humanity (and eventually, on the Balsamic Moon, the Spirit). The Disseminating Moon encourages the heroes of these stories to take their hard-won wisdom to a wider audience . . . but sometimes that audience is not receptive. Sometimes they are even hostile and try to negate the heroes' wisdom and perhaps their very existence. In some ways it is a greater betrayal than that of the Waxing Quarter, because that betrayal came from within and could be challenged and changed with work and persistence. The Waning Quarter is about the external limit, the part that you cannot change because it is larger than you are.

The Waning Quarter is about people who never agree with your politics no matter how reasonably you explain them, lovers who never mature past their psychological problems no matter how much you try to save them, the hurricane that destroys the new building, the national economic crisis that crushes the new business, the child who becomes ill and puts the budding career on hold, the dictator who throws the retiring author in prison, and the cancer that strikes the body just as the best part of life has been achieved. The environment that produced this turmoil was never under the control of the heroes to change, and so their only recourse is to find a way to live with it, to modify their attitude and find hope in the rubble, to defy the forces that would collude to turn them into something evil, to survive. It is no accident that the first Waning Quarter Moon, in Aries, is the Survivor's Moon.

The Waning Quarter Moon begins with the square angle at 270 degrees past the Sun, or 90 degrees behind it; the ending comes at 314 degrees past the Sun or 46 degrees behind it. Like the Waxing Quarter Moon, it contains the square angle with all its struggle and discord. However, the sextile follows it up as the trine follows up the Waxing Quarter's square, softening the ground after the blow has been struck to the heart.

SURVIVOR'S MOON
THE WANING QUARTER MOON IN ARIES

The Waxing Quarter Moon in Aries finds the Soldier burned out after many years of battle, and coming home to put back together the pieces of his shattered body and mind. In the Waxing Quarter the Moon again reaches a crisis, but this time one that is external rather than due to his own internal problems. The continual years of war have stressed his courage and nerves to the breaking point, and he can no longer fight. He may be physically wounded, in a way that ruins him for whatever labor he might have taken up if he had not gone to war. The rest of his life will be spent with the pain of those wounds. He returns home, a shell-shocked creature who has given his entire self to battle, and no one cares. Even if he lives in a place where fallen soldiers are treated well, people do not understand the horror that he has seen. They expect him to get over it in due time, and not to spend hours cowering in the bushes, reliving his trauma. When he can't, they see him as weak, which is a deep insult. He boils with anger at them, the people who are supposed to support him, and at himself for not being strong enough to banish the shadows that torment him.

The Survivor's Moon is a time of anguish and healing of deep wounds. Up until now, the Aries mystique has been about finding bravery in the face of great odds, and feeling a kind of martial immortality, an untouchable confidence that allows the Aries Moon to succeed at all kinds of frightening things. Now it's not a matter of merely summoning enough courage to fling oneself at the task. It's a matter of learning how to summon the courage to do it without hope, without confidence, with a keen gut-understanding of one's mortality. It's about facing how broken you are and having the courage to seek healing. The Wounded Warrior can't truly accept healing until he admits how bad off he really is, and only when the healing commences can he see the true honor in being a Survivor.

On the Survivor's Moon, we confront our wounds. While the first round of wounds we must wallow in may be those inflicted on us by the people we care about and trust, there is also a second round of wounds behind that: anguish over the betrayal inflicted on us by Fate, or God, or the Universe, or Society. We confront our helplessness in the face of that pain—perhaps we fantasize that we might have been able to stop the abusive parents or lover, however irrational that might be, but even our fantasy fails at the onslaught of reality's pain. However, if we don't fully feel and inhabit our rage and pain and helplessness, even if only for a moment, we can't move past them into a healthier stage. This is the wrenchingly ambivalent gift of the Survivor's Moon, and it requires the greatest amount yet of that Aries gift, courage.

This is the most difficult Aries Moon of all to bear. People born on the Survivor's Moon often endure some kind of serious trauma in childhood, but unlike the Brigand's Moon people who externalize their anger and aggression onto others, Survivors internalize all that martial rage and let it eat them out from inside. Survivor's Moon people often seem emotionally withdrawn; it's the least "recognizable" of the Aries Moons . . . until finally something goads them into exploding. The explosion may feel to them like it came out of nowhere and vanishes again into nowhere— that dark place in their heart that they haven't fully explored.

Survivor's Moon people need to put a priority on finding healing for themselves and their wounds, and especially their anger. The Wounded Warrior within will not be satisfied until he is not only no longer in pain, but has regained his confidence and once again feels himself strong and powerful. It's not enough for a warrior to merely be able to walk; he has to be able to fight, and that's a lifetime's worth of work. Like all the Aries Moons, when they first gain confidence they may strike out at inappropriate opponents, and anger management training may be in order. Learning to trust will take even longer, and regaining faith in the Universe is the long haul after that. But in the end, they have the potential to be just as confident as any other Aries Moon, with more empathy earned from all those scars.

Quotes for the Survivor's Moon

If you are brave too often, people will come to expect it of you.

MIGNON MCLAUGHLIN

The only courage that matters is the kind that gets you from one moment to the next.

MIGNON MCLAUGHLIN

Through our own recovered innocence we discern the innocence of our neighbors.

HENRY DAVID THOREAU

Time heals what reason cannot.

SENECA

In times like these, it helps to recall that there have always been times like these.

PAUL HARVEY

Out of suffering have emerged the world's strongest souls; the most massive characters are seared with scars.

E. H. CHAPIN

It is a brave act of valor to condemn death, but where life is more terrible than death it is then the truest valor to dare to live.

SIR THOMAS BROWN

If you're going through hell, keep going.

SIR WINSTON CHURCHILL

> I don't want to be thought of as a survivor because you have to continue getting involved in difficult situations to show off that particular gift, and I'm not interested in doing that any more.
>
> CARRIE FISHER
>
> I am a frayed and nibbled survivor in a fallen world, and I am getting along. I am aging and eaten and have done my share of eating too. I am not washed and beautiful, in control of a shining world in which everything fits, but instead am wandering awed about on a splintered wreck I've come to care for, whose gnawed trees breathe a delicate air, whose bloodied and scarred creatures are my dearest companions, and whose beauty bats and shines not in its imperfections but overwhelmingly in spite of them.
>
> ANNIE DILLARD

MERCHANT'S MOON
THE WANING QUARTER MOON IN TAURUS

After the Builder has brought the Taurus Moon energy to the outside world, the Waning Quarter Moon arrives and another crisis ensues. It starts innocently enough; the Builder sees that he does not have enough financial resources to give all the aid he would like, and so he sets about acquiring more. It's meant to be for a good cause, but as often happens, before long the pursuit of wealth becomes its own goal. The Builder becomes the Merchant, who immerses himself in buying and selling. Money, and making more of it, is the center of his life. He lives in luxury and philosophically shrugs off the state of the poor folk. They'll have to help themselves. He gave already, after all. The state of Nature becomes entirely irrelevant; the Dryad of the New Moon is entirely forgotten. The woods and fields are for plundering, and today's bank balance is what counts the most.

The Merchant's Moon is dedicated to the spirit of Money. Money has its own spirit, which is neither good nor bad. Its nature depends entirely on how it is used. (For the best explanation of the spiritual aspects of money and how to manage them that I have ever read, look for *Root, Stone, and Bone: Honoring Andvari and the Vaettir of Money* by Fuensanta Arismendi and Galina Krasskova.) The Merchant can have a sacred relationship with Money—investing only in nonharmful and mindful businesses, buying things only from sellers and producers who do not create misery, giving generously—or he can go very badly with it. The strong likelihood is that he will do the latter. In fact, it's an archetypal part of the story that he must see what it is like, and how very tempting it is, to do it wrongly. (We have so many examples of this kind of thing that I'm not going to elaborate any further.) However, to throw off all his wealth and become a mendicant is not the answer either (although it might serve as a temporary refocuser). He cannot help but be the man with the resources. It is his task to figure out how to do that rightly, even in the face of the Taurus drive for comfort and security, and the Taurus fear of anything risky.

On the Merchant's Moon, we examine our relationship with money and resources. This is more than just the usual are-we-being-frugal-enough sort of search. It's the time to look at how we really feel about money and also how we feel about the place that money has in society. Is it possible to see money as a sacred thing? How would we have to treat it, and see it treated, in order to do that? During this time, keep a list of what you bought and find out, if possible, where it came from, who benefited most from its sale and production, how natural resources were treated through its manufacture and transport, and if there might have been a better alternative. Consider, also, its value and worth, how much joy and use you will get out of it, and how it will be disposed of when it is worn out or you are done with it.

People born under the Merchant's Moon are going to have an ambivalent relationship with money and resources, and the interaction of those two spirits. It might be their money and resources, it might be their money and the resources of the natural world, it might be their resources and someone else's money, and it might switch among these. It will be their challenge to forge a good relationship with wealth and then behave in the most moral and generous way possible. Since, as was mentioned, risk makes them nervous and many progressive and ethical propositions are smaller and more risky, this is a real challenge. Still, as this is the Taurus Moon most likely to pull away from the natural world and to drive a wedge of convenience between Nature and humanity, the native needs to push harder than normal to move things back toward a balance.

Merchant's Moon people also have a strong tendency to see people as well as items as possessions and as controllable through financial means. This needs to be carefully watched for, and loved ones who are made uncomfortable by this should be encouraged to set boundaries. While generosity is wonderful, Merchant's Moon people need to make sure that every gift they give actually has no strings attached, even an unspoken hope for the recipient's love, affection, or cooperation. Once they've got the lesson down, they can be a force for change in the world.

Quotes for the Merchant's Moon

If a man runs after money, he's money-mad; if he keeps it, he's a miser; if he spends it, he's a playboy; if he doesn't get it, he's a ne'er-do-well; if he doesn't try to get it, he lacks ambition. If he gets it without working for it, he's a parasite; and if he accumulates it after a lifetime of hard work, people call him a fool who never got anything out of life.

VIC OLIVER

What right have you to take the word "wealth," which originally meant "well-being," and degrade and narrow it by confining it to certain sorts of material objects measured by money?

JOHN RUSKIN

It's a kind of spiritual snobbery that makes people think that they can be happy without money.

ALBERT CAMUS

The wicked have a solid interest that the good never seem to possess. The good are grand for one great rally. Then they go home and work at their business. The cohesive power of public plunder remains on the job.

N. M. BUTLER

One cannot build life from refrigerators, politics, credit statements and crossword puzzles. That is impossible. Nor can one exist for any length of time without poetry, without color, without love.

ANTOINE DE SAINT-EXUPÉRY

Our true wealth is the good we do in this world. None of us has faith unless we desire for our neighbors what we desire for ourselves.

MUHAMMAD

The superior man knows what is right; the inferior man knows what will sell.

CONFUCIUS

Money is a good servant but a poor master.

PHINEAS T. BARNUM

It's possible to own too much. A man with one watch knows what time it is; a man with two watches is never quite sure.

LEE SEGALL

You have not lived a perfect day, even though you have earned your money, unless you have done something for someone who will never be able to repay you.

RUTH SMELTZER

MAGICIAN'S MOON
THE WANING QUARTER MOON IN GEMINI

On the Waning Quarter Moon in Gemini, the Scribe discovers strange and occult manuscripts in his research and proceeds to study them. After a short while, he excitedly decides that he will now be a Magician and control the forces of the Universe. He throws himself into his studies and creates bizarre experiments, some risky and many fairly unethical. After all, he tells himself, it's all in the name of knowledge. He convinces himself that this is following in the footsteps of the Storyteller, after all; isn't this magic the source of the power that rang through those stories?

It is, of course . . . but the problem is that the Magician has barely scratched the surface. His studies of magic are purely intellectual—this is an Air sign Moon—and he does not allow it to touch him deeply. To him, it's all a game, a strategy to be played out with fascinating toys. He is not in touch with All That Is, the Universal Powers that could tell him what is wise and what is not, and so all his "experiments" are shallow.

That doesn't mean that they can't do harm, however. The danger of the Magician's Moon is intellectual hubris, the kind of thinking that will eventually justify the use of magic to control others. It starts with controlling small spirits, because the Magician doesn't really see them as human enough to be "people," and it does not occur to him that other, larger forces might be watching and noticing his use of intelligent beings without their consent. Eventually he will turn toward human beings he finds stupid and cruel, and justify his actions as vengeance for all the people they've hurt. Eventually, again, he will expand his pool of test subjects to include anyone who annoys, disbelieves, or disrespects him. At that point, he is lost, and the crisis point of the Waning Quarter comes to haunt him. Since he has convinced himself that there is no such thing as a karmic return on his actions, he is unprepared when things go drastically wrong for him.

His original motivations were probably harmless enough, to be sure. He wanted to deliver this knowledge into many hands, and he wanted to help people. One is reminded of Gandalf's speech to Frodo in J. R. R. Tolkien's *The Lord of the Rings,* when Frodo offers the wizard the evil Ring and he refuses it, saying that it would reach him through his desire to help and eventually corrupt him. The Gemini Moon is quick and perceptive, and it isn't lost on the Magician that most people probably can't be trusted with such things. The hubris of this phase is that he doesn't count himself among those people, and also that he has forgotten the original tales of the Storyteller, many of which could have given him fair warning about the improper handling of magic and its consequences.

On the Magician's Moon, we think about censorship and about our attitudes toward people we think are too untrustworthy to have certain knowledge. Consider the matter of power and the power that lies in information—the true Gemini source of power. How do you control power with information, for good or ill? It's a good time to do magic, but be careful of your goals—are they themselves worthy?

People born under the Magician's Moon like to know how things work and enjoy taking them apart. That includes people and their motivations. They must continually fight against the urge to manipulate others; if the Moon is afflicted they might lose that fight more often than they care to admit. They also battle a general distrust of people—some of it well justified, but some simply a matter of their own damage. They tend to want secrecy and prefer to withhold information, for reasons of keeping power to themselves. It is very important that they absorb the lesson of Consequences for All Actions—also known in science-colloquial jargon as To Every Action There Is an Equal and Opposite Reaction.

It is also important that they learn compassion for others, a hard lesson for the airy Gemini. Like the Liar's Moon and Mercenary's Moon (Gemini's Waxing Quarter and Gibbous Moons, respectively), people born under the Magician's Moon are prone to going bad by splitting their hearts and minds with a huge gulf, then prioritizing the latter while burying the former in the basement. This creates a mental house divided against itself, with the revenant feelings moaning and banging on the walls until finally they break through and do something embarrassing. Working toward bringing their separate parts together will be the best magic they can do.

Quotes for the Magician's Moon

The greatest act of faith is when a man decides he is not God.

OLIVER WENDELL HOLMES, JR.

As far as the laws of mathematics refer to reality, they are not certain; and as far as they are certain, they do not refer to reality.

ALBERT EINSTEIN

Real wizards don't whine about how they paid their dues.

QUENTIN CRISP

The Universe is full of magical things patiently waiting for our wits to grow sharper.

EDEN PHILLPOTTS

We never stop investigating. We are never satisfied that we know enough to get by. Every question we answer leads on to another question. This has become the greatest survival trick of our species.

DESMOND MORRIS

The attempt to define all mystical, transcendental, and ecstatic experiences which do not fit in with the categories of consensus reality as psychotic is conceptually limiting and comes from a timidity which is not seemly for the honest, open-minded explorer.

JOHN CUNNINGHAM LILLY

There's a mighty big difference between good sound reasons and reasons that sound good.

BURTON HILLIS

All my life I've been harassed by questions: Why is something this way and not another? How do you account for that? This rage to understand, to fill in the blanks, only makes life more banal. If we could only find the courage to leave our destiny to chance, to accept the fundamental mystery of our lives, then we might be closer to the sort of happiness that comes with innocence.

LUIS BUÑUEL

The three chief virtues of a programmer are laziness, impatience, and hubris.

LARRY WALL

The antidote to hubris, to overweening pride, is irony, that capacity to discover and systematize ideas. Or, as Emerson insisted, the development of consciousness, consciousness, consciousness.

RALPH ELLISON

WIDOW'S MOON
THE WANING QUARTER MOON IN CANCER

Loss is inevitable, and no enchanted family circle lasts forever. The Waning Quarter Moon ushers in another time of crisis. This time the losses come again, but they are inflicted on the grieving adult, not the helpless child. This Cancer Moon introduces the Widow, whose beloved has been taken from her by death . . . the one thief that all the guarding in the world will not stop. At the same time, her children become adults and leave home to find their own way, as it should be. She finds herself alone again, solitary in front of a cold hearth. In a way, the betrayal is worse this time, because she worked so hard to create her perfect home after the early losses and succeeded, and yet even that great effort of love was blown away. In another way, though, it is better. The heart is not a weeping child anymore. There is still the warmth of all the memories and the knowledge that she did well. She faces becoming an elder of her small community, tempered with her pain.

First, however, she must grieve. This is not the child's helpless grieving, although it may start out that way. This is the kind of grieving that builds a monument to the loved one, or causes one to make one's remaining life into that monument, doing what that loved one would want done, seeing to their causes in the world. This is the kind of grief that built the Taj Mahal; wrote the *Sonnatorrek;* and inspired thousands of songs, paintings, poems, memoirs, charitable foundations, and other outpourings of love and memory.

It is also the kind of grief that made Queen Victoria put on black and never take it off, withdrawing from England's rulership and sleeping under a great painting of her dead husband every night, living in a cocoon of grief from which she never really recovered. The Widow's challenge is to find meaning again in life by any means possible—that does not include ceasing to live in reality. She needs to find what joy she can in other human contacts . . . which means continuing to make them. Not because they will replace what she has lost, but because they will bear her up. If she locks herself away in order to hold in her memories and insulate herself from the full impact of her loss, she will decay in her small, closed, empty home. It is only in opening it up to more fresh life that she can recapture her own vitality.

Death is not the only loss that makes one feel like a widow. Divorce is also a strong possibility, as is empty nest syndrome. Even the loss of children who go their own way on happy, supported wings is hard for a Cancer Moon parent, who usually has to use great self-control to open their hands and let the kids grow up. If the children left with arguments and hostility, which can happen when even well-meaning families have personality clashes and teens get stuck in the need to differentiate, it can be even more painful for the parent. The Widow may grieve for the child who left slamming the door and not looking back as severely as if that child had died, even though she may still feel that she was right in whatever actions she took that led to the argument. If the child returns as an adult to remake connections, she may or may not open the door again, depending on which is more profound for her: the desire to have family again or the grief that the departure caused her.

On the Widow's Moon, we mourn and grieve for our losses. We also give our aid to people who are lost and grieving, perhaps helping them with the everyday tasks that seem so hard for a grieving person to manage. If there was anyone who has passed that you don't feel you properly grieved for, this is the time to do it.

People born under the Widow's Moon seem to have a deep sorrow within them that may or may not be connected to what has actually happened in their lives. This sorrow makes them react to the everyday losses of life with more sensitivity and fragility than others, and to be more easily stopped in their tracks because of it. In this way they resemble the Orphan Moon people (Waxing Quarter Moon in Cancer), but the solution is somewhat different. Instead of simply working toward healing themselves, they must reach outward—this is a Waning Moon—to others in the world to give them warmth, and to the world in general to acknowledge and heal their wounds. Instead of keeping quiet, they should speak about their sorrow—or sing of it, or build something that might always be remembered and respected, and hopefully loved.

Quotes for the Widow's Moon

Solitude is being with oneself. Loneliness is being with no one.

HANNAH ARENDT

Sing out loud in the car even, or especially, if it embarrasses your children.

MARILYN PENLAND

Children begin by loving their parents; as they grow older they judge them; sometimes they forgive them.

OSCAR WILDE

A child enters your home and for the next twenty years makes so much noise you can hardly stand it. The child departs, leaving the house so silent you think you are going mad.

JOHN ANDREW HOLMES

You can turn your back on tomorrow and live yesterday,
or you can be happy for tomorrow because of yesterday.
You can remember her only that she is gone,
or you can cherish her memory and let it live on.
You can cry and close your mind,
be empty and turn your back.
Or you can do what she'd want:
smile, open your eyes, love and go on.

DAVID HARKINS

To spare oneself from grief at all cost can be achieved only at the price of total detachment, which excludes the ability to experience happiness.

ERICH FROMM

When a loved one is dying
go into the woods and cry . . .
The clumsy comfort of friends
and the strange running
or bargaining you will do
will only make a tighter vise
about your throbbing head and angry throat.
Go alone to beauty.
Mourn your aloneness and weep . . .
for the fragility of life
when the world shared is so beautiful.

RUTH HARRIET JACOBS

> I remember going shopping shortly after my husband left me. I kept walking around the market without putting anything in my cart. Suddenly, I realized I didn't even know what I liked to eat. For years, I had been buying what he liked and what the children liked and that is what I ate. I didn't even know my own tastes in food.
>
> RUTH HARRIET JACOBS

> It's so curious: one can resist tears and "behave" very well in the hardest hours of grief. But then someone makes you a friendly sign behind a window, or one notices that a flower that was in bud only yesterday has suddenly blossomed, or a letter slips from a drawer . . . and everything collapses.
>
> COLETTE

> The thorn from the bush one has planted, nourished and pruned pricks more deeply and draws more blood.
>
> MAYA ANGELOU

USURPER'S MOON
THE WANING QUARTER MOON IN LEO

The Waning Quarter Moon attacks Leo like a shark from out of the depths. This is the moment of the external betrayal, and the Leo Moon has built its entire reputation and happiness around outside approval. In one fell swoop, everything he has built falls down. The people rebel against him, rise up to tear him from his throne and cast him down, and put another in his place. The Usurper triumphs over the Fallen King, and he crawls away into the wilderness with his last faithful servant, wondering what will become of him. This Moon illustrates the story of the Fall from Hubris, which is retold so many times in human literature as a cautionary tale. Here, however, it is not so much cautionary as inevitable. Success can go only so high, and then there will be a fall. It is like the Wheel of Fortune as portrayed on the Tarot card—one figure rising and one falling, the king on his throne overhead and the beggar sitting beneath.

The ambiguity of this phase is that it is unclear whether the Leo Moon figure is the usurped or the usurper, or both. There is a sense of double betrayal—the emperor figure extending his realm and taking authority that is not his, and a rebellion that casts him down. Where the Queen was careful not to overreach her realm, the King took risks and spread his influence outward . . . but what expands must contract, and this Moon opens with the mistake of overextending oneself.

The betrayal is not just by some faceless power-hungry figure, and that is the real pain of it. One-on-one betrayal is the game of the Waxing Quarter; in the Waning Quarter the world strikes back. The Usurper would not be able to gain power without the aid and approval of the people. It is their loss, their turning away from the Fallen King and leaving him to his fate, that is the real wound. The love of the people has been his greatest tool and greatest reward, but the people are fickle . . . and even small mistakes, at the level of a king, lead to great resentments if they are not humbly corrected in good time. Ironically, the opposite number of the Leo Waning Quarter Moon is the Aquarius Waxing Quarter Moon, the Rebel who stands up and cries out against the king. He must reap what he has sown, and what he has sown is bitter indeed.

On the other hand, another name for this month is the Barleycorn Moon. There are legends, from the ancient times, that kings were once sacrificed after having ruled for a certain number of years. Certainly king-substitutes were chosen from among the best and brightest to sacrifice to the gods when danger loomed. This Moon illustrates the moment when the Leonine King becomes the Sacrificial King, and that tilts the story in a different direction—the King might not have been thrown down, but might have stepped forth willingly to be sacrificed for the bellies and lives of his people. His blood will mingle with the earth, and the crops will grow, and his death will give life. He becomes John Barleycorn, the Sun who falls, the golden grain that is cut down, the golden boar who becomes the feast. This is an equally true version of the story.

On the Usurper's Moon, we look at our failures. Some might have been the Usurper's failures—risking too much, overreaching ourselves, perhaps trampling on the hearts of others in our enthusiasm and arrogance. Some might have been the Fallen King's failures—giving in instead of fighting, letting fear and sadness drive us away. We forgive ourselves for these failures and resolve to face the day differently.

This is a Leo Moon without the confidence of the other Leo Moons. People born under the Usurper's Moon fear failure and were often belittled in childhood, letting others take their credit and spotlight. They are afraid that anything good that comes to them will be taken away, and they will not risk their meager comforts for anything bigger and better. They may live through their more successful partners or may simply keep their heads down and hide their ambition. The world, to them, is not a place where they will be allowed to succeed. Fatalism drags down their will, and they are filled with secret fears. This is the hardest of all the Leo Moons.

But deep inside of them lies the mystery of the Sacrificial King, and they must tap this mystery to find happiness. If they feel superfluous or unimportant, then they must transmute that feeling into a sense of having nothing to lose, of having a life to give. Instead of living as if life might take away everything at any moment, they should live as if they are certain it will be so . . . and so there is no reason for not seizing every moment as if it was going to be their last, loving with the passion of a man about to die. They are mirrored in the quiet man who one day steps forth into the line of fire to save the fallen child, just like that. Whether this Moon is the Usurper's Moon or the Barleycorn Moon for them will be very much their own choice.

Quotes for the Usurper's Moon

Can anyone love the man whom he fears, or the man by whom he believes himself to be feared? Yet tyrants are courted under a pretence of affection, but only for a season. For when by chance they have fallen from power, as they generally do, then it is known how poor they were in friends.

MARCUS TULLIUS CICERO

No man rises so high as he who knows not whither he is going.

OLIVER CROMWELL

My people and I have come to an agreement which satisfies us both. They are to say what they please, and I am to do what I please.

FREDERICK THE GREAT

When small men begin to cast big shadows, it means that the Sun is about to set.

LIN YUTANG

To give up pretensions is as blessed a relief as to get them ratified.

WILLIAM JAMES

Fortunately, there are still those among us who have a healthy irreverence towards power, even as we seek it.

WEIR REID

The wrong sort of people are always in power because they would not be in power if they were not the wrong sort of people.

JON WYNNE-TYSON

Wounds are for the desperate, blows are for the strong.
Balm and oil for weary hearts all cut and bruised with wrong.
I forgive thy treason—I redeem thy fall—
For Iron—Cold Iron—must be master of men all!

RUDYARD KIPLING

I have no ambition in this world but one, and that is to be a fireman. The position may, in the eyes of some, appear to be a lowly one; but we who know the work which the fireman has to do believe that his is a noble calling. Our proudest moment is to save lives. Under the impulse of such thoughts, the nobility of the occupation thrills us and stimulates us to deeds of daring, even of supreme sacrifice.

CHIEF EDWARD F. CROKER

The sacrifice which causes sorrow to the doer of the sacrifice is no sacrifice. Real sacrifice lightens the mind of the doer and gives him a sense of peace and joy. The Buddha gave up the pleasures of life because they had become painful to him.

MAHATMA GANDHI

FATE'S MOON
THE WANING QUARTER MOON IN VIRGO

On the Waning Quarter Moon in Virgo, the Weaver transforms to become the third Fate, the woman with the scissors who cuts the thread of those close to death. Of all three of the Virgo Fate Moons—Full, Disseminating, and Waning Quarter—this is the most "fated" of them. Those born on the Fate's Moon are forced to confront the difficult aspects of fate—that we all are left alone and die eventually.

The Virgo Moon story is one of turning from solitude to connection and back to solitude again. During the Housewife's Moon, the solitary Virgo is forced into making connections with others and learning to value them. Now the pendulum swings, and the Fate must serve others while slowly returning to solitude for herself. It often means that the service becomes more transpersonal—assisting large groups of people, or the public, instead of a close family or a chosen few.

The third Fate is the one who gets to say No, to draw the line and cut the cord and mark the boundary. After the hard-won lessons of saying Yes to people, that No is painful and difficult. By this time in the process, the Fate no longer merely criticizes imperfections but understands people enough to make allowances for their flaws . . . and she is lonely enough to want to reach out. Yet it seems that whenever she centers her life on others, things go wrong. She is forced to make difficult choices and defend her boundaries, and often cut the cord and retreat again into solitary meditation. Being the one to mark out death is not an easy job, and it makes her desperate for human validation and coldly withdrawn by turns.

Still, she is required to render service to others. That service consists of saying No, of setting boundaries, and perhaps of causing death. This is an important service that most people don't appreciate unless they are in bad need of it, so she receives a lot of hostility in spite of all her best efforts. Mercury-ruled Virgo is a nervous sign, and the strain of dealing with all her obligations drives the Fate to repeatedly hide on a mountaintop.

On the Fate's Moon, we set boundaries with those commitments that have been preventing us from getting the alone-time that we need. It is a good time for setting rules—with oneself and with others—and for a solitary time of meditation. This is the time when we go to the wilderness to find ourselves. It is also a good time for service that doesn't require us to get too involved, but to perform respectfully from an emotional distance. Caring for the ill or dying is a good option, but the task for this Moon is not to be the comforting counselor—that's someone else's job—but to gently and unobtrusively care for other needs.

People born under the Fate's Moon are driven to solitary introspection, often against their will. Instead of embracing it, they fear it and will surround themselves with others in order to distract against that urge. They allow others to take advantage of their need to serve, overrunning their boundaries and asking for more than they should be giving. Unlike other Moons, the Waning Quarter Virgo Moon is far more sensitive than she would like to be where encroachment is an issue. She wants to let them in, but ends up pushing them away. What she needs to do is to make adequate time for herself—and this may mean much more time than she thinks is necessary—and things will not go wrong so often with her relationships.

Many Fate's Moon people live alone or end up living alone. A lot of time is spent facing health issues and death, of loved ones or themselves. Work is important to them, and the best job is either a service job that does not get closely involved or some kind of solitary work. As with personal relationships, she will struggle with boundaries in any job that requires a lot of human contact, trying not to become too emotionally involved. This is not a Moon that is destined to learn about deep empathic melding with others, but one that involves developing healthy boundaries with others while learning to go back to the place of being one-in-oneself.

───────────── *Quotes for the Fate's Moon* ─────────────

How much there is in the world I do not want.

SOCRATES, UPON SEEING LUXURIES FOR SALE IN A MARKET

Service to others is the rent you pay for your room here on earth.

MUHAMMAD ALI

The greatest happiness you can have is knowing that you do not necessarily require happiness.

WILLIAM SAROYAN

It is possible to commit no mistakes, and still lose. That is not weakness, that is life.

JEAN-LUC PICARD

Experience enables you to recognize a mistake when you make it again.

FRANKLIN P. JONES

I confess that mankind has a free will, but it is to milk kine, to build houses, etc., and no further.

MARTIN LUTHER

It is not necessary to hope in order to undertake, nor to succeed in order to persevere.

CHARLES THE BOLD

I have a secret passion for mercy, but justice is what keeps happening to people.

ROSS MACDONALD

I have offended God and mankind because my work didn't reach the quality it should have.

LEONARDO DA VINCI

Twice I have set my heart upon a sharing,
Twice have imagined a real human home,
Having forgotten how some fiercer caring
Demands this naked solitude for loam.

MAY SARTON

JUDGE'S MOON
THE WANING QUARTER MOON IN LIBRA

The Ambassador is promoted to the position of Judge, and suddenly the Libra Moon has all the authority to challenge wrongdoers that he wanted back when he was the Waxing Quarter's Black Knight—but this time with the might of social approval behind it. Justice is his to bestow, and repercussions are his to assign. It is a great responsibility, and a great temptation.

On the Waning Quarter Moon, the betrayal of the Waxing Quarter comes again, only this time on a larger external scale that involves many people. The Judge's failing is that, in his desire to balance the scales and right wrongdoing, he becomes rigid and unmerciful, giving no leeway to anyone who comes before him. If they are accused, they are probably guilty, and he takes great satisfaction in sending them away to prison or execution. He speaks of fairness, and to him it is fairness; his earlier rage at those who didn't share his principles, long buried, rises again with terrible force.

You would think that everything that Libra has learned during the time of being the Lover and the Ambassador would prevent this development, but people are human and the astrological stories describe human behavioral trends. The Judge makes many fair decisions, but also many that are strongly affected by his emotions (remember that this is the Moon, not the Sun, and it can never be wholly objective), as well as many that follow the letter of the law but not the spirit, or that follow the letter when there is no good that can come of it, and mercy might be the better option. Mercy is something that he is rarely interested in, because in his view mercy keeps people from receiving what they justly deserve. He also has the bad habits of bringing his work home and turning on his loved ones the gaze that shows his disapproval of their imperfections.

Being judgmental, especially after many years of having to helplessly watch people hurt each other, is a hard habit to break. We all have our moments, no matter how compassionate we try to be, of playing judge and jury to our temptingly convictable fellow humans. It's not fair to say that the Judge is simply evil and cruel; he honestly wants the world to be better, and since the worst element has been given to him to deal with, he shoulders the burden and does the best he can through the veil of his understanding. If he has an ugly secret, it is that he nurses a private addiction for that dangerous drug vengeance. Publicly, he will justify his sentences by saying that it is a good thing when someone bad is prevented from doing more bad things . . . but privately he struggles with that guilty pleasure.

On the Judge's Moon, we consider what we really think about people and all the ways we judge them. We also think about what we believe to be fair and how much of that is influenced by our feelings. The point is not to deny the latter, but to be aware of them; Moon work is all about being calmly aware of your emotions before you, well, judge them to be in need of changing or locking up.

People born under the Judge's Moon have fairly solidified opinions of people and how the world should be, and they are neither shy to express those opinions nor slow to dispense retribution when it is given to them to do so. However, they are not immoral or wanton in their cruelty; they have strong, unbending principles and will hold to them steadily . . . until they decide to change them, and then they will adhere to the new code as if it had never changed. (It's not that they can't change; they just have trouble admitting to change.) They will not go after vengeance if getting it would put them outside of their code, but they will use every tool that they have within those boundaries. They can get into bitter arguments with friends or family members that last for years, and hold grudges nearly as well as a Scorpio. On the good side, if you do happen to live well within the boundaries of their code, they will be unflinchingly loyal to you and go to the wall for your well-being should something bad or unfair happen to you. If you can prove to them that their behavior toward you is unfair, they will silently change it.

Quotes for the Judge's Moon

When you prevent me from doing anything I want to do, that is persecution, but when I prevent you from doing anything you want to do, that is law, order, and morals.

GEORGE BERNARD SHAW

To declare that in the administration of the criminal law the end justifies the means—to declare that the government may commit crimes in order to secure the conviction of a private criminal—would bring terrible retribution. Against that pernicious doctrine this Court must resolutely set its face.

LOUIS D. BRANDEIS

I am the inferior of any man whose rights I trample underfoot.

HORACE GREELEY

Remember particularly that you cannot be a judge of anyone. For no one can judge a criminal until he recognizes that he is just such a criminal as the man standing before him, and that he is perhaps more than all men to blame for that crime. When he understands that, he will be able to be a judge.

FYODOR DOSTOYEVSKI

Each morning puts a man on trial and each evening passes judgment.

ROY L. SMITH

If you think that you can think about a thing that is inextricably attached to something else, without thinking of the thing it is attached to, then you have a legal mind.

THOMAS REED POWELL

Law is merely the expression of the will of the strongest for the time being.

BROOKS ADAMS

Those who uphold the law must be wiser and calmer than those who seek to repudiate it.

JOHN LINDSAY

Not to decide is to decide.

HARVEY COX

Authority intoxicates,
And makes mere sots of magistrates.
The fumes of it invade the brain,
And make men giddy, proud, and vain.

SAMUEL BUTLER

MADWOMAN'S MOON
THE WANING QUARTER MOON IN SCORPIO

The Waning Quarter Moon in Scorpio ushers in a new crisis, this one triggered and determined by the outside world. After the Witch's attempts to help her flock at all costs, one can almost see the terrible betrayal coming. The Witch is captured, persecuted, perhaps tortured by those whose evil she threw herself against. While she does not lose her life, the strain is too much for her. She cracks and becomes the Madwoman, running half-naked through the countryside, screaming and babbling. The demons that she thought she had defeated during the waxing part of the Moon cycle come back to haunt her, now that her Plutonian will is broken. The darkness that was once her friend devours her. All the parts of herself that were less than stable, but that she kept anyway for her own irrational lunar reasons, shatter and leave her broken in the rain.

Up until now, Scorpio's battles have been fought alone. The solitary Scorpion has toughed it out in the darkness, conjuring up the demons and conquering them, learning the mysteries and keeping their secrets, communing in the lonely temple with the Universe, and pitting herself in a one-Moon battle against overwhelming odds. In spite of all her strength and willpower, the outside menace is stronger. She despairs and thinks that there is no way out, because up until now it has not occurred to her that one possible solution could be to depend on others . . . but this is about to change. This is the Moon phase where Scorpio realizes that she can't do this alone. While it is up to her to get her demons under control, she will need to depend on others to survive during her battles, or she will just get sucked back under.

It is a humiliating moment for the suspicious, untrusting Scorpio Moon, but one accompanied by a flash of inspiration: the betrayal came from outside, and the solution will come from there as well. The people who were helped by the Witch may have been powerless to prevent her capture and breaking, but they gently bring her in from the rain, cleanse and clothe her, and take care of her while she battles herself back to mental health. They have seen her worth, and they will risk themselves to keep her safe until she recovers. In the midst of terrible torment, it is an unexpected blessing, a ray of light in the darkness, an unforeseen gift. If she wants sanity, she needs to follow that ray of light. The perspective of others—of minds that may not be as learned or experienced, but that are sturdy and have a better grip on reality—will be the lifeline to bring her back.

On the Madwoman's Moon, we examine our own sanity and how other people see our sanity. This may be a different question for people who have actually struggled with sanity, but even the most stable can ask: What would happen if I believed something that no one else could see, and it was important for their own safety that they know about it, and they would think that I was mad if I told them? What would I do? For that matter, was there ever a time in my childhood when I told the grownups something, and they told me to hush up because it wasn't possible . . . and I still think it was true? Dare to dance on the edge of that uncertainty.

People born under the Madwoman's Moon aren't necessarily any crazier than anyone else, but they fear that they are. The best thing that a loved one can do for them is to be the person with the stable outside perspective who gently offers the simple reality alternative, over and over. They are as suspicious as any other Scorpio Moon, and will have a hard time accepting, but it's still the right gift even when it's spurned.

Madwoman's Moon people not only have strong, intense emotions, they also have strong and intense imagery that wells up in them. Expressing their emotions through that imagery can disturb people with pleasanter mental apartments, and they can easily be misunderstood. At the same time, one of the lessons for Madwoman's Moon people is to learn to reach out to trusted sources and depend on them for regular sanity checks. Isolating themselves is the worst thing they can do, even when they fear that those who don't understand will penalize and possibly harm them. They need to learn the difference between who they can trust with their insides and who they can't, and to value the former group as the greatest treasure in their lives.

Quotes for the Madwoman's Moon

For practical purposes we have agreed that sanity consists in sharing the hallucinations of our neighbors.

EVELYN UNDERHILL

To read of emotions that reflect our own is the only proof we have we are not mad.

KENDALL HAILEY

I have no problem dealing with reality, but as a lifestyle I find it too confining.

LILY TOMLIN

What sane person could live in this world and not be crazy?

URSULA K. LE GUIN

Intellectual despair results in neither weakness nor dreams, but in violence. It is only a matter of knowing how to give vent to one's rage; whether one only wants to wander like madmen around prisons, or whether one wants to overturn them.

GEORGES BATAILLE

In the past men created witches; now they create mental patients.

THOMAS S. SZASZ

I have a huge, active imagination, [and] I think I'm really scared of being alone; because if I'm left to my own devices, I'll just turn into a madwoman.

CLAIRE DANES

Wandering between two worlds, one dead,
The other powerless to be born.

MATTHEW ARNOLD

I am interested in madness. I believe it is the biggest thing in the human race, and the most constant. How do you take away from a man his madness without also taking away his identity?

WILLIAM SAROYAN

"But I don't want to go among mad people," Alice remarked.

"Oh, you can't help that," said the Cat. "We're all mad here. I'm mad. You're mad."

"How do you know I'm mad?" said Alice.

"You must be," said the Cat. "or you wouldn't have come here."

LEWIS CARROLL

HUNTER'S MOON
THE WANING QUARTER MOON IN SAGITTARIUS

As the Sagittarius Moon moves into the Waning Quarter period, the benign Philosopher gives way to the Hunter. The Waning Quarter involves an external crisis provoked by the actions of others that one cannot control, and this Moon finds Sagittarius and all his fine truths, all the knowledge that he strove for during the early Moon phases, in conflict with the opinions of others. They may question, they may scorn, they may reject entirely. The rejection is especially sharp when it comes from others who supposedly shared his beliefs up until the moment they began to question. It is especially difficult because the Sagittarius Moon desperately wants to be seen as Right. It's an old saying about the Fire signs: Aries wants to be First, Leo wants to be Big and In Charge, and Sagittarius wants to be Right. In the light of the Waning Quarter Moon, his need to be Right is so strong that he is willing to hunt down and kill anyone who disagrees with him.

This is a different reaction from, say, that of the Aquarius Heretic (Waning Quarter), who finds himself rejected because of his beliefs. In the Aquarius cycle, the Heretic is bound up emotionally with the group's response, and the more intellectual Aquarius is less likely to demand that his knowledge be seen as Spiritual Truth That Everyone Should Follow. The more fiery Sagittarius is a little less objective and a lot more prone to enthusiastically jumping on the bandwagon of Complete Faith, especially when it comes to something religious (this is the sign of religion) or something that he can treat as his own religion in the same way that other people treat theirs. He is much more willing to decide that he is the

Spiritual Authority and that the others are not a majority with the right to throw him out, but an infestation to be stamped out by himself and those who are still true to his way of seeing things.

A lot of things have been said about the famous Sagittarian inability to commit, which is embodied by the Waxing Quarter Moon phase in this sign (the Seeker). The Seeker reflects the "horse" side of the centaur, always running off to find new and greener pastures. What no one knows is that there is more to that fear, gnawing in the belly of every strongly Sagittarian individual, than just the terror of the enclosing walls with no way to escape. There's also a fear of the other possibility, the other pole of Sagittarian negativity . . . the human failing as opposed to the horse's failing in the centaur metaphor. When Sagittarius commits, finally, of his own free will, it will be because he has found some real Truth that moves him . . . and he will defend that Truth with a single-minded fervor that seems more like it should belong to a Scorpio, except that it is backed with a flame burning clear and true. The natural phenomenon most associated with Sagittarius is lightning, and it can strike like a flaming arrow when the Hunter decides to hunt out evil in all its forms. Fanaticism can be an ugly thing, and Sagittarius knows this instinctively even as he twists away from committing, knows on some level how susceptible he is to it, especially when it comes to the emotional, irrational Moon.

Hunters, in all mythic cycles, are implacable. The Greek lunar huntress Artemis slays any man who gets too close to her; when Actaeon stumbled across her naked and bathing, she turned him into a stag and had him torn apart by his own hounds. The wintry Norse hunter goddess Skadi hung a serpent over the enchained Loki's head to constantly drip venom on him, out of anger for a past slight. The Celtic Herne grimly chases evildoers through the forest on the Wild Hunt, even into their own bedrooms. In order to kill, and to be focused for a long period on killing one being, there needs to be a justification. The earliest justification, of course, is "My people must eat, or they will starve." This can slowly turn into "My people must be protected from this evil or they will be harmed," or "I think this being might do harm to me or mine—including my beliefs—and therefore it is better to kill it now."

The Hunter is without mercy, and the only way out of his implacable trap is to develop some. This doesn't necessarily mean that he needs to find his worldview to be wrong, unless it specifically speaks against tolerance of others. He does need to understand that people are on different paths and see different truths, and those truths came reasonably from their own experiences. He needs to realize the hubris in thinking that he will necessarily be the one to change them, especially if he cannot bring himself to understand them. He also needs to grasp that no one ever changed his mind because of someone else's angry or disapproving words, at least not to any real depth or for any length of time.

On the Hunter's Moon, we think about fanaticism all over the world and all throughout history, including the beliefs that we ourselves will not brook any challenge to. Even if you think you don't have any, you do. For example: Are you monogamous? How would you feel about a worldview where monogamy was not important, and people could have sex with anyone who was willing, and it was expected that partners would not be jealous or insecure or have any objections? For another example: Do you believe that children should be having sex before the age of legal majority? What if society changed and made that ordinary and accepted? I'm sure that these topics can provide plenty of debate on all sides, but the point isn't debate—it's to challenge yourself and your beliefs, and to watch the reaction of the Hunter within. Whatever it is, it will be edifying.

People born on the Hunter's Moon have a strong need for unswerving spiritual beliefs, and an even stronger need to validate those beliefs by being around other people who share them. They have a hard time with tolerance—the Sagittarian Moon dance is about Truth, and really it's a dance toward and away from the Truth of others. Being Right is so important to people born under the Waning Quarter Sagittarian Moon that it can swallow up all their relationships; they may be able to tolerate around them only those people who believe they are Right.

The Universe, of course, will keep giving them opportunities to challenge their need to be Right and to make others see their rightness, and if they are wise they'll meet those challenges with humility and patience. There is no place for implacability in love. Love passes through all boundaries, when you let it. This can be seen in the strength of those Hunters who have taken the qualities of tolerance, compassion, and non-judgmental outlook as their religion. It's amazing what the Right Truth can do for a soul.

Quotes for the Hunter's Moon

Freedom is only the distance between the hunter and his prey.

ZHENKAI ZHAO

Rather than love, than money, than fame, give me truth.

HENRY DAVID THOREAU

There is perhaps no phenomenon which contains so much destructive feeling as moral indignation, which permits envy or hate to be acted out under the guise of virtue.

ERICH FROMM

Fanaticism consists of redoubling your efforts when you have forgotten your aim.

GEORGE SANTAYANA

A fanatic is a man that does what he thinks that the Lord would do if He knew the facts of the case.

FINLEY PETER DUNNE

If you are afraid of being lonely, don't try to be right.

JULES RENARD

Where so many hours have been spent in convincing myself that I am right, is there not some reason to fear I may be wrong?

JANE AUSTEN

The worst vice of a fanatic is his sincerity.

OSCAR WILDE

The downright fanatic is nearer to the heart of things than the cool and slippery disputant.

E. H. CHAPIN

> *This wild swan of a world is no hunter's game.*
> *Better bullets than yours would miss the white breast,*
> *Better mirrors than yours would crack in the flame.*
>
> ROBINSON JEFFERS

MISER'S MOON
THE WANING QUARTER MOON IN CAPRICORN

In the Waning Quarter of the Capricorn Moon, the Patriarch (or Grandfather) has been supporting his family and slaving for their needs for a long time, and he becomes obsessed with collecting enough money to do the job. However, the more money he collects, the more he expects them to appreciate him and take his advice, and when they do not, he is reluctant to spend it on them. Like Pisces, Capricorn will slave and sacrifice for a long time for those he loves. Unlike Pisces, who does it out of a sense of self-abnegation, Capricorn does it out of duty. As such, he expects those loved ones to hold up their end of the bargain, which means doing their duty with as much doggedness as he does his. Part of that duty, more often than not as far as he is concerned, is treating him as an authority and showing him constant respect. When he doesn't get that respect in the way he desires, he becomes resentful and feels that they have let him down.

Then he withholds money and resources, because that's where his values are invested. On some level, he believes—or fears—that earning money and creating resources is all he's good for, the only thing that makes him worthy, and so he withholds it from the ungrateful wretches who won't give him the respect that he feels he deserves. Thus the kindly Grandfather becomes the hoarding Miser who tries to manipulate people with his wealth.

Greed is never a simple emotion. It's almost always caused by some pathological feeling of neediness; greed and need are the opposite sides of the same coin. When Cancer hoards, it's to make himself feel emotionally secure. When Taurus hoards, it's out of obsessive love for her possessions.

When Capricorn hoards, it's partly because the size of the hoard indicates, to him, the size of his accomplishment. It's also because resources are useful tools for manipulating people, if you're into that sort of thing, which far too many people are. On the Waning Quarter, the Miser's personal needs collide with those of other people, and he reacts by retreating into the darkness of the Miner (Waxing Quarter), or even the Forgotten One (New Moon).

On the Miser's Moon, we face up to our conflicting attitudes toward money and wealth. What does wealth mean to us, beyond the ability to pay our rent? It's a rare one of us that has an untroubled relationship with it, regardless of the amount of it we may personally have. It's also a good time to give something to charity, even if it's only a small amount—and observe our feelings on the matter. Does it panic us because we feel we don't have enough to spare? Does it make us want to be acknowledged for our generosity, and resentful if no one seems to care? How can we give cleanly, with no expectations or ulterior motives?

People born under the Miser's Moon may have grown up in families with unhealthy attitudes toward money. Perhaps they were poor and there was never enough, and money became the slave driver who made them suffer in order to barely survive, and it was hard to be "seen" as poor. Perhaps they were poor and finally became well off, and clung to money and conspicuous spending as a way to impress people and look higher class. Perhaps there was plenty of money, but it was used as a way to replace or buy love and affection. Perhaps providing for one's family, even at the cost of one's soul, was seen as the only real way to show love. Perhaps the size of their paycheck was simply the only measure of their success as a human being in the world, and no other quality really mattered. Whatever happened, wealth was bound up with self-esteem and reputation and respect and the right to affect the behavior of others. It can take decades to untangle the ambivalent effects of the Money God, especially when she is married to the Respect God in one's mind.

Miser's Moon people need to let go of all their negative attitudes about both money and social respect, or the quest for it will eventually grind them down into a bad place. As long as they are ruled by it, they can't escape it. There's a saying that has always symbolized the best of Capricorn to me: To have is riches, to be able to do without is power. Miser's Moon people need to learn that lesson more than anything else if they are to take back power over their own lives.

Quotes for the Miser's Moon

He does not possess wealth; it possesses him.

BENJAMIN FRANKLIN

The history of the world is the record of man in quest for his daily bread and butter.

HENDRIK VAN LOON

Success—the "bitch-goddess Success," in William James' terms—demands strange sacrifices from those who worship her.

ALDOUS HUXLEY

I have no faith, very little hope, and as much charity as I can afford.

THOMAS HENRY HUXLEY

The miser is in as much want of what he has as of what he has not.

PUBLILIUS SYRUS

A miser is a guy who lives within his income. He's also called a magician.

ANONYMOUS FROM THE ALLISTON HERALD

O man bowed down with labor,
O woman young yet old,
O heart oppressed in the toiling breast
And crushed by the power of gold . . .

ELLA WHEELER WILCOX

It is pretty hard to tell what does bring happiness; poverty and wealth have both failed.

KIN HUBBARD

You had better settle for work.
Love is for the blond, the lithe,
the lucky, the others.
You are a workhorse
pulling weights piling weights
putting weights upon yourself.
Learn to love your work
or talk a good line.
Maybe someone will
pat you
pet you
"nice horsy."

RUTH HARRIET JACOBS

If money is your hope for independence then you will never have it. The only real security that a man can have in this world is a reserve of knowledge, experience, and ability.

HENRY FORD

HERETIC'S MOON
THE WANING QUARTER MOON IN AQUARIUS

On the Waning Quarter Moon in Aquarius, the Apostle's message is rejected by the people he tries to communicate it to, and they brand him a Heretic. This is a different sort of crisis than the Rebel Moon's troubles (Waxing Quarter). The Rebel wanted to win, but still had a fine disregard for the opinions of others. He had not yet experienced true belonging, and it was easy for him to throw away what he didn't really have. The Heretic has been part of that accepting group—or so he thought—and this makes it even more painful when he is cast out yet again. He has also experienced the joy of bringing his message to others and seeing their eyes light up, gathering them into his domain to become part of his horizons. To be outcast in the face of all that is terrifyingly painful. Unlike the Rebel, he has something valuable to lose, and he loses it.

Yet it is a necessary part of the cycle of belonging and unbelonging.

The Aquarius Moon must never find himself in a place where he must suppress his own truth in order to belong to the group. When one casts a wider net, the group becomes larger and more diverse, and it's increasingly likely that violent disagreement and complete misunderstanding will ensue. When the group is large, stratified, and has its own culture, and anything can be said . . . then the Aquarius Moon is driven to speak the truth even if it means blowing up his home among them that was so painfully won. He must become the Heretic, because someone has to do it.

The word *heretic* comes from a Greek root meaning *free choice*. In order to have free choice, one must paradoxically be able to give up anything or the choice isn't real. The path of the Heretic is to bring his truth to the people he values, to be rejected, and to find the strength to walk away. There is always another group, another family of like minds, another place to call home . . . and if there isn't, there is the strength to be alone with one's convictions. While it is painful, the Aquarius Moon's natural sense of distance helps with the walking-out process.

On the Heretic's Moon, we look at any opinions we have that would get us thrown out of certain groups. (There are always some, because people are all so different.) What opinions do we have that we'd be complete outcasts for rather than compromise? Which ones would we keep to ourselves to avoid conflict? If you're actually involved in a situation like this, the Heretic's Moon is the right time to walk in and state the truth at last . . . but don't expect to keep your place in that group. It's possible, but not likely. If you're not ready to confront anyone, use this Moon time to confront your own fears about being cast out and your own willingness to compromise for the sake of herd comfort.

People born on the Heretic's Moon are continually at odds with any group they're in. Like other Aquarius Moons, they speak their truth whether it's wanted or not, but they also question everyone else's truth as well. Questioning any group on principle is a good thing, but Heretic's Moon people have a tendency to expect that they will be cast out and that all authority will be unreasonable. Those assumptions tend to color all their dealings with authority and create a self-fulfilling prophecy.

Heretic's Moon people also need to confront the fact that this is stemming from their Moon, their point of emotion, and they are probably not all that objective about either their own subjective truth or their perception of other people's response to it. For that matter, they aren't all that objective about other people's truths, either. Learning to recognize and cull the parts that are more about their own fears than the reality of another person's world is a lesson that they'll struggle with for a long time, but when they get there, they'll find that being the Heretic is a lot easier.

Quotes for the Heretic's Moon

Risk! Risk anything! Care no more for the opinions of others, for those voices. Do the hardest thing on earth for you. Face the truth.

KATHERINE MANSFIELD

Here I stand, I cannot do otherwise.

MARTIN LUTHER

What luck for the rulers that men do not think.

ADOLF HITLER

It doesn't seem to me that this fantastically marvelous universe, this tremendous range of time and space and different kinds of animals, and all the different planets, and all these atoms with all their motions, and so on, all this complicated thing can merely be a stage so that God can watch human beings struggle for good and evil—which is the view that religion has. The stage is too big for the drama.

RICHARD FEYNMAN

The reasonable man adapts himself to the world; the unreasonable one persists in trying to adapt the world to himself. Therefore all progress depends on the unreasonable man.

GEORGE BERNARD SHAW

For you are not to suppose, brethren, that heresies could be produced through any little souls. None save great men have been the authors of heresies.

SAINT AUGUSTINE

> It is frequently a misfortune to have very brilliant men in charge of affairs, as they expect too much from ordinary men.
>
> THUCYDIDES

> If the individual heretic gets hold of some essential truth, or sees some error in the system being practiced, he commits so many marginal errors himself that he is worn out before he can establish his point.
>
> EZRA POUND

> It doesn't pay well to fight for what we believe in.
>
> LILLIAN HELLMAN

> To try to fashion something from suffering, to relish our triumphs, and to endure defeats without resentment: all that is compatible with the faith of a heretic.
>
> WALTER KAUFMANN

MOON OF LOST SOULS
THE WANING QUARTER MOON IN PISCES

The Disseminating Moon passes into the Waning Quarter Moon, once again a time of difficulty and trouble. The Angel of Mercy has pushed herself too far and has lost herself once again. The people she has served have moved on and forgotten her, or died under her hands no matter how hard she has tried to save them, or rejected her mercy in a rage . . . or they needed so much from her that she has bled herself dry for them. Even after all her work, they still come, trailing in like lepers, broken by the world.

The Pisces Moon would love to forget the world, as we have touched on many times in this book. During the Disseminating Moon, however, the Angel of Mercy swore to keep her connection to the world and to never stop caring. There is a price to be paid for this, and now, as a Lost Soul, she pays it. Every crack of the world's brutality is written on the faces of the people she tries to help, and as she is now irrevocably bound to the world, she can only face it day after grueling day. Her empathy is in overdrive; she suffers with every person who suffers, and cannot distance herself. She is wracked and wrung over and over by each new case of suffering until she is a ghost of herself, and still the torment goes on . . . because the world can always provide us with another case of pain, if we are forever on the front lines of affliction.

The Lost Soul tries to close herself off, but the pain seeps through. She tries to escape into her fantasy world, but finds that it too has become a mirror of the fog outside. Worst of all, she is consistently wronged by those who mock her fragility or take advantage of her, and she finds little support in the world, although she herself supports so many. Her salvation lies in seeking out hope. There may not be much hope in her life, but there is still hope in the world, and she needs to find it. There are still people stronger than the Lost Soul who fight, and she needs to watch them succeed and know that she is not alone in the world. It is the light cast by the shadow of great hearts that will save the Lost Soul.

This is one of the times when Pisces' willingness to be a follower is a good thing. The Lost Soul cannot make it work on her own. More than just friends and lovers, more than just people to hold her close when things go wrong, she needs to be around and working with people who she can admire and look up to, whose luminous, indomitable spirits she can bask in. She needs people whose dedication to the work of the world gives her hope.

The Moon of Lost Souls is a gray and hollow time. It is a time of seeing clearly the worst of the world, all the bad things that humanity does to itself, and empathizing with that pain even when it hurts. On this Moon, we stretch our pity and see how far we can go before our defense mechanisms kick in. We stare down into the Universal Sorrow and see if it breaks us.

Those born under the Moon of Lost Souls are endowed with such a strong sense of empathy that they are constantly bombarded by suffering. Some try to close themselves off from it out of self-defense, which locks them in a different sort of gray world. Some are drawn again and again to suffering, desperate to help, unable to turns their backs. Some simply go about in a haze of gray despair from taking it all in. Something seems to be wrong with their emotional filters; someone in the room might begin to weep and they will be weeping along with that person in no time. It is important for them to learn to psychically shield themselves, for their own safety and sanity.

It is also important for them to find small joys to absorb, ideally in the form of good and positive deeds done by others, to counteract the sorrows that they see. This needs to be a full-time quest for them, chasing hope in equal measure with the despair that hounds them. The despair will come whether they want it or not; finding hope needs to be an active process. It may seem impossible at first, but each small bit of hope that they seek and find will be another dose of medicine for the grayness that threatens to drag them under.

Quotes for the Moon of Lost Souls

More persons, on the whole, are humbugged by believing nothing than by believing too much.

PHINEAS T. BARNUM

Ring the bells that still can ring
Forget your perfect offering
There is a crack in everything
That's how the light gets in.

LEONARD COHEN

We are healed of suffering only by experiencing it to the full.

MARCEL PROUST

An era can be said to end when its basic illusions are exhausted.

ARTHUR MILLER

Life beats down and crushes the soul and art reminds you that you have one.

STELLA ADLER

What a wonderful life I've had! I only wish I'd realized it sooner.

COLETTE

We are the hollow men
We are the stuffed men
Leaning together.

T. S. ELIOT

The deepest personal defeat suffered by human beings is constituted by the difference between what one was capable of becoming and what one has in fact become.

ASHLEY MONTAGU

Seeking to forget makes exile all the longer; the secret of redemption lies in remembering.

RICHARD VON WEIZSÄCKER

We are threatened with suffering from three directions: from our own body, which is doomed to decay and dissolution and which cannot even do without pain and anxiety as warning signals; from the external world, which may rage against us with overwhelming and merciless forces of destruction; and finally from our relations to other men. The suffering which comes from this last source is perhaps more painful than any other.

SIGMUND FREUD

8
INTO THE EMBERS
THE BALSAMIC MOON

There will come a time when you believe everything is finished. That will be the beginning.

LOUIS L'AMOUR

I wanted a perfect ending. Now I've learned, the hard way, that some poems don't rhyme, and some stories don't have a clear beginning, middle, and end. Life is about not knowing, having to change, taking the moment and making the best of it, without knowing what's going to happen next. Delicious Ambiguity.

GILDA RADNER

THE BALSAMIC MOON is the Waning Crescent, the phase before the Moon sinks into darkness and regenerates in the New Moon. It is a time of rest and retirement; the "old" Moon has lived through the whole story, absorbed its lessons, and made peace with the world. In this stage, the heart turns to the transpersonal rather than the personal, to spirituality rather than to simple human relationships. There is a quality of "I've been there and done that" to people with Balsamic Moons. They tend to be more emotionally self-sufficient and comfortable with themselves than those with "younger" Moons. Ideally, they should be letting their personal Moon paths lead them toward a higher communion with the Universe, rather than getting bogged down in the drama of everyday life.

Balsamic Moon people may seem somewhat emotionally unadventurous; even the more impulsive signs are calmer and more toned down in this phase. They don't have the drive and zest for new feelings of the waxing signs; they may seem emotionally conservative and unwilling to risk themselves for an unknown. They may have a feeling link with the swell of humanity and be unconsciously wary of creating disturbances there.

The Balsamic Moon starts at 315 degrees past the Sun, or 45 degrees behind it, and continues until the next New Moon begins. It contains no major aspects; like the New Moon, its lunar energy is undisturbed by major upheavals. The Balsamic Moon person walks calmly into the unknown as if coming home.

VETERAN'S MOON
THE BALSAMIC MOON IN ARIES

The Balsamic Moon in Aries brings us to the last figure in the Aries story, the seasoned and grizzled warrior who is retired from the fight and healed from the wounds of the Survivor. She no longer feels the need to get back out on the front lines, although she will do so if it is necessary and there is no one else with her experience and wisdom. She has no illusions about the dangers of fighting for a cause you believe in, but at the same time she has regained some of the hope and idealism that the Survivor had lost. She is nowhere near as much of an idealist as the earlier Aries Moons, but she has her own inner hope that sustains her.

The Veteran is admired by the youngsters, and her main job is to give them as much of her hard-earned knowledge as possible; the rest they must learn from experience. She sees them as younger versions of herself, back from the days before her martial fire was tempered, and she desperately wants to teach them what she wishes had been impressed upon her, before she made all those mistakes. On the other hand, she is painfully aware, in retrospect, of how her own impulsiveness and idealism prevented the wisdom of her own elders from entering. She knows that they will listen to her only so much, and she knows that some truths must be experienced to be understood; her words are not an adequate preparation even if they were entirely well received. It is a rare battle plan that survives first contact with the enemy.

This is a Moon for strategy and tactics, for planning the attack rather than battling on the front lines. It is also a Moon for remembering the whole point of fighting. In her retirement, the Veteran spends time with the loved ones she did not have time for before, and she comes into a deeper understanding of who she was protecting and why they were valuable. She becomes one of the home guard of last resort rather than the army on the offensive, and knows on a deeper level why this is just as valuable as the front line that was so important to her before.

On the Veteran's Moon, we go to people who are beginning a hard process we've already experienced, and we teach them what we know about how to do it right. This knowledge must be wanted and freely given; unwanted advice or wisdom with a high price tag doesn't save the most lives. We also work in our community to protect our own, without considering whether or not they deserve it.

Veteran's Moon people are fighters who are reluctant to fight unless it is absolutely necessary. This is an Aries Moon that doesn't always jump in first without looking, and these folks have the most tempered emotional responses of all the Aries Moons (although they can still blow up a few things when they're pissed). They love to give advice, and they love to tell stories about what they've done; each trip to the customer service counter becomes an epic battle in the retelling. They have a good instinct about where to go to heal their own emotional wounds, and those of others.

One shadow of Veterans is a tendency, once the battle is safely behind them, to glorify the struggle in a way that glosses over its pains and wounds, something that the Waning Quarter's Survivor would not have done. Similarly, seeing the past or the fight through rose-colored glasses hazed over by years of forgetting is an uncomfortable tendency of people with the Veteran's Moon. Such tales are most prone to pop out when talking to less experienced people, giving them inspiration for fighting a battle themselves. On some unconscious level, this is more than just not wanting to remember pain. It is a buried fear that if you don't make the battle look attractive enough, the future generations will not be willing to fight for what is right. Veteran's Moon people have to accept that they can't control the decisions of others when it comes to honor, courage, commitment, or that person's inevitable fate.

Quotes for the Veteran's Moon

Another such "victory" and we are undone.

PYRRHUS

The riders of a race do not stop when they reach the goal. There is a little finishing canter before coming to a standstill. There is time to hear the kind voices of friends and to say to oneself, "The work is done."

OLIVER WENDELL HOLMES JR.

They kick you when you're down, but if you don't get down they can't kick you.

HEIDI LEITER, HIGH-SCHOOL STUDENT

WHO TOOK HER GIRLFRIEND TO THE PROM

Think like a man of action, act like a man of thought.

HENRI BERGSON

I am now seasoned enough to have learned that the hardest thing about any political campaign is how to win without proving that you are unworthy of winning.

ADLAI STEVENSON

He who is prudent and lies in wait for an enemy who is not, will be victorious.

SUN TZU

From quiet homes and first beginning,
Out to the undiscovered ends,
There's nothing worth the wear of winning
But laughter and the love of friends.

HILAIRE BELLOC

If you have a strong enough "why," you can bear almost any "how."

FRIEDRICH NIETZSCHE

Victory is won not in miles but in inches. Win a little now, hold your ground, and later, win a little more.

LOUIS L'AMOUR

Do, or do not. There is no "try."

YODA

ANCESTOR'S MOON
THE BALSAMIC MOON IN TAURUS

The Ancestor Moon, the Balsamic Moon in Taurus, is also called the Inheritance Moon. Here Taurus has created a legacy for all who come after her. It may be a legacy of amassed money and property; it may be a legacy of traditions and rules for behavior; it may be a legacy of qualities of character; it may be all of these. The Ancestor is aware that they are going to become an Ancestor, a forebear who is remembered and wants to be so, and the last part of the Taurus cycle is concerned with the future and the legacy of goodwill. This may mean that the values of the Merchant are turned around, as Taurus realizes that accrued interest will do no good after death. Ancestors hold dear what can be left to the future, not what is hoarded in the present.

The Native Americans speak of borrowing the Earth from our children rather than inheriting it from our ancestors, and this is the main realization of the Ancestor Moon. The redemption of the crisis of the Merchant Moon engenders a kind of desperate rush, which for Taurus is a very uncomfortable feeling. The Balsamic Moon is a time of summing up the story. Taurus looks around at all that has been done since the Dryad stepped out of her tree, and realizes that much of that needs to be undone, and even more remains to be finished. She throws herself into the business of creating her legacy and making sure that it will be passed on, and also that it will be something worthy of being passed on. This means a sorting-out of the useful and beautiful from the once necessary but now defunct.

On the Ancestor Moon, we look at the gifts we inherited from those people who struggled and survived that we might live. If you are adopted and don't know your biological ancestors, your adoptive ancestors count as well, as they struggled to ensure the creation of the people who loved and raised you, and thus made certain your own survival. We can also look at ancestors of the mind and spirit, people whose works and deeds reverberate in us and inspire us. It's also important to look honestly at the evils that have been passed down, with a thoughtful understanding of the era and beliefs and human fears that produced those evils.

People born under the Ancestor Moon are drawn to the world of the past, either finding strong comfort in family traditions or trying ancient or archaic customs they read about and deem attractive. Some may be strongly moved to preserve traditions, languages, or artifacts of the past for future generations. Their goals in saving and transmitting money, property, or customs are not necessarily streamlined or discriminating; the bad is saved possessively with the good, and passed on with it.

They are keenly aware of their inheritances, including the unpleasant parts. People born to this Moon hold on to what they are given in childhood, for better or worse, and when it is necessary to give up negative opinions or patterns, they find it excruciating even if they will be better off afterward. It is hard for them to be rejected by their families, and those with dysfunctional immediate family may delve into ancestral traditions in order to be connected with their bloodline a little further back, where people are safely dead and cannot reject one. Indeed, if an Ancestor Moon native rebels against the family, it will likely be in the name of keeping discarded ancestral traditions. The great lesson of this Moon is to discern which of our inheritances are worth keeping and which are not, and which look good but will bear a price tag that our descendants will be ill equipped, or otherwise reluctant, to bear. Taurus individuals are often motivated by sheer possessiveness, not necessarily sentimentality, so when the time comes to discard something no longer useful, if they can get their paws to unclench, they can usually toss it away. It's just a matter of reminding them of their values, and sometimes getting them to reexamine those values and discard any that no longer bear fruit.

Quotes for the Ancestor's Moon

We are all omnibuses in which our ancestors ride, and every now and then one of them sticks his head out and embarrasses us.

OLIVER WENDELL HOLMES SR.

If they try to rush me, I always say, "I've only got one other speed, and it's slower."

GLENN FORD

We pay for the mistakes of our ancestors, and it seems only fair that they should leave us the money to pay with.

DON MARQUIS

Confound these ancestors. They've stolen our best ideas!

BEN JONSON

We all grow up with the weight of history on us. Our ancestors dwell in the attics of our brains as they do in the spiraling chains of knowledge hidden in every cell of our bodies.

SHIRLEY ABBOTT

I think nobody owns the land until their dead are in it.

JOAN DIDION

If you cannot get rid of the family skeleton, you might as well make it dance.

GEORGE BERNARD SHAW

I almost believe we are all of us ghosts! It is not only what we have inherited from our father and mother that haunts us. It is all sorts of old, dead ideas, all kinds of old, dead, beliefs, and so forth. They have no life, yet they cleave to us, and we cannot shake ourselves free of them.

HENRIK IBSEN

Tradition means giving votes to the most obscure of all classes, our ancestors. It is the democracy of the dead. Tradition refuses to submit to that arrogant oligarchy who merely happens to be walking around.

G. K. CHESTERTON

The old that is strong does not wither; deep roots are not touched by the frost.

J. R. R. TOLKIEN

TEACHER'S MOON
THE BALSAMIC MOON IN GEMINI

As the Gemini Moon moves into the Balsamic stage, the elder Gemini surveys her life. She has acquired a great deal of knowledge over her many phases . . . including information on how to use that knowledge, and how not to. She also has a fine way with words and an ability to use them to reach people's hearts. She has learned all manner of lessons in how to manipulate people, but also understands when it's not a good thing to do. She decides that her destiny is to teach others what she knows, so that her knowledge will not die with her. Always youthful at heart, she dedicates herself to educating youth, or perhaps anyone who is still flexible enough to want to learn.

The Teacher's Moon is the culmination of the Gemini Moon cycle, and it illustrates the end of Gemini's forward-and-backward dance with truth. The Balsamic Moon is about paring down, discarding the fluff and bother of the previous Moons, and in the Teacher's case she must decide which knowledge she has gathered is worth passing on, and to whom. In a sense, this reflects a wiser use of the Magician's secrecy. Instead of assuming that almost everyone is too stupid to understand certain things, she learns to key her teaching style to individual students, assessing their strengths and giving them the knowledge that will best help them to grow into their own paths, with each path being different but no less valuable than any other.

Teachers can have a spiritual bent as well and may assemble disciples rather than students. If she goes down this path, it will be because she has learned her lessons well from the Magician's lack of faith in anything bigger than his own will, and she has learned, finally—for this does not come easily to intellectual Gemini—to understand the connection of Spirit, and the sacred underpinnings of Causality. This path carries some risk, because teachers can make the well-meaning mistake of being sure that they know what is best for a student. The Teacher's task is to make change in the world through others, and this is why it is a perilous undertaking as well as a deeply sacred one. Even if she only teaches people how to knit or do algebra or speak a second language, it is still a spiritual act for her—the transmission of civilization from one generation to another.

She must also never forget her own days of being the incorrigible child who was bright enough but resistant to sitting still and listening. If she becomes staid and boring and out of touch with her students, she loses her ability to reach them. This means that she must also be willing to learn new things frequently to keep herself sharp.

On the Teacher's Moon, we get together and teach each other things or take a class of some sort. It's also a good time to assist someone in teaching, in honor of that person's work, or do a favor for a teacher you respect. Distance or online learning, though, doesn't connect with the essence of the Moon—meeting with a Teacher in person is what you are looking for. It's better to ask your aunt to show you how to crochet than to simply study on your own with distant aid—that's what more solitary Moons are for.

People born under the Teacher's Moon love to pass on their knowledge, but it has to be something that reaches them emotionally. If they aren't moved by the information itself, they can be moved by the satisfaction of dispensing it and seeing people absorb it. They love the mentor-student relationship, and their hearts are fed by it; if you want to make them happy, just ask them to teach you something and enter into that relationship, if only for a few minutes. For them, this is a relationship just as intimate, in many ways, as a parent-child relationship—parenting of the mind rather than the heart.

Teacher's Moon natives, like people born to other Gemini Moons, are fairly intellectual rather than emotional, but if you ask them to talk in parables, or write, or point to characters in stories, or even make metaphors with equations, they are much better at telling you how they feel. They revere books and knowledge, and if you want to understand them, you will as well. They are usually happy to learn, but they gauge whether they have properly learned anything in their lives by how well they could teach it if they had to.

Quotes for the Teacher's Moon

The object of education is to prepare the young to educate themselves throughout their lives.

ROBERT MAYNARD HUTCHINS

Socrates gave no diplomas or degrees, and would have subjected any disciple who demanded one to a disconcerting catechism on the nature of true knowledge.

G. M. TREVELYAN

Education: A debt due from present to future generations.

GEORGE PEABODY

"The best thing for being sad," replied Merlin, beginning to puff and blow, "is to learn something. That's the only thing that never fails . . ."

T. H. WHITE

Great minds are to make others great. Their superiority is to be used, not to break the multitude to intellectual vassaldom, not to establish over them a spiritual tyranny, but to rouse them from lethargy and to aid them to judge for themselves.

WILLIAM ELLERY

One mark of a great educator is the ability to lead students out to new places where even the educator has never been.

THOMAS GROOME

In teaching you cannot see the fruit of a day's work. It is invisible and remains so, maybe for twenty years.

JACQUES BARZUN

A good teacher is one who makes himself progressively unnecessary.

THOMAS CARRUTHERS

Education is the transmission of civilization.

WILL DURANT

To teach is to learn twice over.

JOSEPH JOUBERT

MOON OF THE KEEPER OF MEMORIES
THE BALSAMIC MOON IN CANCER

The Cancer Moon moves into the Balsamic phase, and the Widow becomes the Keeper of Memories. In an ideal society, this role is that of the wise elder whose job is to remember things, that the knowledge might not be lost. For this role, all memories are useful. What someone said or did in a crisis might be the much-needed key for someone many decades younger. "Has this ever happened before, Grandmother?" the young ones ask. "Who did it happen to, and what did he do? How did that work out?" The Keeper of Memories pulls out her mental scrapbook and gives them the best she has.

She has this ability in part because she lives much of her life in the past, and in some cases a softer-edged and more romantic past where everything was happier and people didn't make the terrible mistakes they do today. The strong pull of memory makes the past more real to her than the present, even if it's only her wishful view of the past. If she is wise and not too wounded by the events of her life, she will keep the memories that might actually be useful to others in fairly clear glass, not romanticizing or demonizing them. Being someone who can be depended upon to pull the correct picture out of the scrapbook and tell the right story about where the treasure is hidden is what separates the sacred Keeper of Memories from the batty old woman to whose rambles no one listens.

The danger of the Moon of the Keeper of Memories is getting stuck in a past that never was and insisting that it is of more value than the present. When the present is painful, the past can be a solace. When the past is painful too, the Keeper of Memories may decide that it deserves a rewrite, especially when the point is to hold it up as some kind of ideal against which the present utterly fails. To be willing to keep the pain in the pictures means that she must be willing to admit that there was a point to all the pain, that it wasn't just something that everyone would have been far better off without . . . and if she is still nursing resentments, she will not be able to come to that point.

Forgiveness is a major aspect of this Moon. Forgiveness is more than just letting the memory fade until there isn't much to it anymore. For Moon signs whose emotions do not get carved so deep, this may work as a long-term replacement for forgiveness, but true forgiveness is not a passive act. It is actively forgiving someone, letting yourself feel the willed act of opening the clenched fists and letting the resentment go, feeling the salt wind blow clean across those empty palms. Active forgiveness is what really purifies the memories and allows pain to be given its full respect, thus giving respect also to the strength that survived that pain.

On the Moon of the Keeper of Memories, we get out the scrapbooks and look at the old pictures. We watch the movies that we first saw at crucial stages of our lives, and we talk about what we remember. If possible, it's a good time to compare memories with other people who were actually there, because you can help keep the story sharp and relatively unaffected by any one person's perspective.

People born under the Moon of the Keeper of Memories have a strong tendency to romanticize the past. This can be their own personal past—no one was as wonderful as their mother, their father never beat anyone regardless of what all their siblings said, and their spouse was the first person that they ever fell in love with. If their personal past is too raw to idealize, they may turn instead to a past that happened before they were born, romanticizing a historical way of being made rosy by selective accounts and comparing it wistfully to gritty modern life. They complain about how much better it would be if people were like they must have been in this long-ago time when everything was a different . . . refusing to believe that human beings haven't changed that much at heart and were always capable of injustice and terrible wounding. The problem with this is that their real lives are now, in the present, and they must not lose sight of that. It is a good thing to be a bridge between the ideals of two eras, but to do that effectively, both sides of the bridge must be equally valued.

Quotes for the Moon of the Keeper of Memories

I remember those happy days, and often wish I could speak into the ears of the dead the gratitude which was due to them in life and so ill-returned.

GWYN THOMAS

Why abandon a belief simply because it ceases to be true? Cling to it long enough, and it will turn true again, for so it goes. Most of the change we think we see in life is due to truths being in and out of favor.

ROBERT FROST

I live in that solitude which is painful in youth, but delicious in the years of maturity.

ALBERT EINSTEIN

A memory is what is left when something happens and does not completely unhappen.

EDWARD DE BONO

How pleasant it is for a father to sit at his child's board. It is like an aged man reclining under the shadow of an oak which he has planted.

WALTER SCOTT

Family faces are magic mirrors. Looking at people who belong to us, we see the past, present, and future.

GAIL LUMET BUCKLEY

Everything has been said before, but since nobody listens we have to keep going back and beginning all over again.

ANDRÉ GIDE

Memory is a crazy woman who hoards colored rags and throws away food.

AUSTIN O'MALLEY

The Past: Our cradle, not our prison; there is danger as well as appeal in its glamour. The past is for inspiration, not imitation, for continuation, not repetition.

ISRAEL ZANGWILL

Forgiving does not erase the bitter past. A healed memory is not a deleted memory. Instead, forgiving what we cannot forget creates a new way to remember. We change the memory of our past into a hope for our future.

LEWIS B. SMEDES

BARD'S MOON
THE BALSAMIC MOON IN LEO

On the Leo Balsamic Moon, the deposed King goes back to his roots as the performer, but this time he has the experience of ruling and being in power behind him. He has made his mistakes and is willing to go forth and speak in a sacred voice, telling even rulers how to rule and putting a check on tyranny. The Bard's weapon is his words, which can create a cutting satire to ruin people's reputations and make them disrespected laughingstocks all over the countryside. Those same words can defend someone unjustly accused and make a hero's epic tale ring for all time.

In ancient Europe, a King could not be a Bard, and a Bard could not be a King. This was because only a King could judge a Bard, and only a Bard could judge a King. In a later and less free era, the place of the Bard was taken by the jester, who echoes the Clown, the earlier Leo incarnation. The Bard was deemed too dangerous to less secure Kings, and he was taken out of the equation . . . a deed that became deadly in the end. When the Leo Bard cannot act as check and balance to the Leo King, the situation is turned over to the Aquarius opposition, who will have all Kings down as fast as possible. Thus the Bard's job is crucial to the King, even if the King dislikes it occasionally (or often).

The Bard must stand up and stare at the people who sit where he once sat, who have everything that he has lost, and yet not one word uttered from his mouth can come from a place of resentment or envy, or everything he says will be tainted and thus go unheard. The great rule of being a Bard is that everything you say, every weapon you level at authority or shoot into the great crowd of the people, must be spoken from a clean place. If you speak from anger, it must be well-justified anger for clear injustice. If you speak from a desire to help, it must be given with no ulterior motives. Any words that come from devious ambition or resentment or contempt will be scorned. Perfect motivation protects the Bard, allows him to walk in and out of court and say what he will, without censure from any honorable monarch.

Of course, many tales tell of arrogant Bards who forgot these rules and allowed their egos to overwhelm their sacred duties . . . and most of them came to bad ends. Arrogance is the Leo curse no matter what phase, and here in the Balsamic Moon, it is the last curse that still remains. The Bard is pretty much entirely over the need for applause. He knows his own worth and does not need it proved again and again by the crowd. He knows that if he wants to be loved, he can inspire that. What he needs to inspire now is positive change, in the greatest number of people possible.

On the Bard's Moon, we speak or write our opinions, or read aloud the eloquent and persuasive opinions of writers we respect. It is acceptable to debate during this time, so long as people are careful to speak from their highest selves and not their bitter shadows. If you cannot speak publicly with other people, at least read eloquent and inspirational political writing and think deeply about how it moves you.

People born on the Bard's Moon have a gift for persuasion and public speaking (and, often, politics). If they don't do pursue these avenues, it's because they lack confidence or are still too wounded to speak from a clean place, and on some level they know that. Their lesson is to scrutinize their motivations and make sure that their words are honorable. Like many other Leo Moons, they love to perform, but for them it is less for reassurance and more for the joy of performing, of knowing that one has made an impact on the Universe. As such, their works tend to center on changing people and society. They may have an ambivalent and divided attitude toward authority—both scorning it and desiring it dearly, even if they are loud about the former and quiet about the latter. A wise partner will encourage them to assume authority when possible, but will also remind them about principles and honor, especially when they get to criticizing others in authority.

Quotes for the Bard's Moon

A thing is not necessarily true because badly uttered, nor false because spoken magnificently.

SAINT AUGUSTINE

Remember, Information is not Knowledge; Knowledge is not Wisdom; Wisdom is not Truth; Truth is not Beauty; Beauty is not Love; Love is not Music; Music is the best.

FRANK ZAPPA

O great creator of being, grant us one more hour to perform our art and perfect our lives.

JIM MORRISON

A celebrity is a person who works hard all his life to become well-known, and then wears dark glasses to avoid being recognized.

FRED ALLEN

If you would not be forgotten after you are dead, either write things worth reading or do things worth writing.

BENJAMIN FRANKLIN

I put all my genius into my life; I put only my talent into my works.

OSCAR WILDE

My life has been one great big joke,
a dance that's walked,
a song that's spoke,
I laugh so hard I almost choke
when I think about myself.

MAYA ANGELOU

Nothing is so unbelievable that oratory cannot make it acceptable.

MARCUS TULLIUS CICERO

When Demosthenes was asked what were the three most important aspects of oratory, he answered, "Action, Action, Action."

PLUTARCH

MONK'S MOON
THE BALSAMIC MOON IN VIRGO

The Balsamic Moon in Virgo concludes the dance of the Virgo Moon. Virgo has turned toward and away from human connection many times in the dance, and now he ends by becoming a Monk and shutting himself away from people. He is no solitary anchorite, though; he lives in a community of people who likewise value silence, work, service, discipline, and contemplation. He can have the level of connection that he wishes, up to and including spending days praying alone in his cell, or he can connect with like minds over the same great work. In a sense it is similar to his time as an Apprentice, but the Monk is no beginning youth. He has found inner peace and an internal haven from the chaos he fears. Now, at the end of his life, he seeks a place where he can be solitary and yet part of something, disciplined and yet free to contemplate, of service and yet not deeply involved, away from the rush and bustle of the world yet not entirely away from humanity and its beautiful, frustrating, awe-inspiring connections.

It is said that monasticism never works when it is about running away from something, only when it is a purposeful movement toward something. Even with all his life experience, the Monk does not simply fall effortlessly into mindfulness. He still has to work at it, but Virgo is happy to work as long as there is an achievable goal in sight. He still has his bad, cranky days and hates having his peace disturbed, but he is less thrown off balance by the interruptions and more able to keep his own inner peace and speak from there.

The big challenge with this Moon is deciding where it is best to put one's energies. While the Monk archetype is usually found in a religious context, it can also be followed to one extent or another in other lifestyles that emphasize peace, discipline, and service. However, the Moon is only one part of the individual's chart, and there may be other parts that might feel constricted in a more classical situation, so the place where people with this Moon fit may need to be specially constructed.

This period of the Virgo Moon's story is a long lesson in mindfulness. Virgo is naturally detail-oriented, and mindfulness is something that this sign is actually good at, if he can keep himself from being distracted by the chaos that threatens to overwhelm him. The rulership of Mercury gives a certain level of nervous speed and noise to the Virgo Moon, which makes him irritable and critical. The keywords to maintaining mindfulness in the face of the Mercurial nerves are *slowness* and *silence*. When things become chaotic, the Monk needs to remember to slow everything down, make everything quiet (earplugs may be useful for this), and focus entirely on the next thing that must be done, then the next thing, and so on.

On the Monk's Moon, we go alone to contemplate. If others wish to do this with us, we can go in a group, but the group needs to focus on its goal rather than turning the day into a social situation. Being solitary together is an experience that most modern people do not understand. Another possibility is to do some service work together, or some household cleaning, but try to do it as a spiritual exercise. Repetitive work is especially good for this.

People born on the Monk's Moon have a strong emotional need for a quiet, peaceful, and highly structured life. Like many of the other Virgo Moons, if they apply themselves, they have a gift for making any kind of labor into a spiritual process. However, they also have the knack of extending this to their entire life if they work at it. They tend to be hermits, or if they're not they may constantly wish that they could be. They do best if there is some form of structured spirituality in their lives that they can hang a regular discipline on, although it need not be a common or traditional one.

Monk's Moon people like to create their own space, and it is usually quiet and aesthetically spare. Others may find themselves slipping into that space to find a few moments of peace and quiet, which Monk's Moon people are a vortex of, if they're at their best. If they don't have the peaceful structure that they crave as a major focus in their life, they need a lot of privacy in order to fit the inner monastery in between the cracks of the rest of their fast-paced existence.

Quotes for the Monk's Moon

Let us suppose the message of a so-called contemplative to a so-called man of the world to be something like this: My dear Brother, first of all, I apologize for addressing you when you have not addressed me and have not really asked me anything. And I apologize for being behind a high wall which you do not understand. The high wall is to you a problem, and perhaps it is also a problem to me. Perhaps you ask me why I stay behind it, out of obedience? Perhaps you are no longer satisfied with the reply that if I stay behind this wall I have quiet, recollection, tranquility of heart. It is true that when I came to this monastery where I am, I came in revolt against the meaningless confusion of a life in which there was so much activity, so much useless talk, so much superficial and needless stimulation, that I could not remember who I was. But the fact remains that my flight from the world is not a reproach to you who remain in the world, and I have no right to repudiate the world in a purely negative fashion, because if I do that, my flight will have taken me not to truth and to God, but to a private, though doubtless pious, illusion.

THOMAS MERTON

It is a weakening and discoloring idea that rustic people knew God personally once upon a time but that it is too late for us. There never was a more holy age than ours, and never a less. There is no whit less enlightenment under the tree by your street than there was under the Buddha's bo tree.

ANNIE DILLARD

You do not need to leave your room.
Remain sitting at your table and listen.
Do not even listen, simply wait,
be quiet, still and solitary.
The world will freely offer itself to you to be unmasked,
it has no choice, it will roll in ecstasy at your feet.

FRANZ KAFKA

Happiness is not a matter of intensity but of balance, order, rhythm and harmony.

THOMAS MERTON

Nothing in all creation is so like God as silence.

MEISTER ECKHART

Blessed is the servant who loves his brother as much when he is sick and useless as when he is well and can be of service to him.

SAINT FRANCIS OF ASSISI

The ordinary activities I find most compatible with contemplation are walking, baking bread, and doing laundry.

KATHLEEN NORRIS

The Buddha was a monastic, but the practice of mindfulness in the context of any lifestyle is one of renunciation. Every moment of mindfulness renounces the reflexive, self-protecting response of the mind in favor of clear and balanced understanding. In the light of the wisdom that comes from balanced understanding, attachment to having things be other than what they are falls away.

SYLVIA BOORSTEIN

It is important that we do not think of self-discipline as being imposed from outside upon us by an irresistible power. Discipline must come from within. It should be based on clear awareness of its value as well as a certain degree of introspection and mindfulness. Once you have such an attitude towards discipline, it will be self-adopted rather than imposed. Being freely chosen, discipline will really help you develop two very important qualities of the mind: alertness and mindfulness. As you develop these two basic factors of awakening, you will have the most powerful tools to attain single-pointedness of the mind.

HIS HOLINESS THE DALAI LAMA

His solitude is neither an argument, an accusation, a reproach or a sermon. It is simply life itself. . . . It not only does not attract attention, or desire it, but it remains, for the most part, completely invisible.

THOMAS MERTON

SACRED WHORE'S MOON
THE BALSAMIC MOON IN LIBRA

As the Libra Moon passes again from the realm of justice to the realm of harmony and love, the Judge cedes domain to the Sacred Whore. This title is controversial, because in our society sex is considered filthy and profane, and the priests and priestesses who provide it as a service are reviled and degraded. Once, long ago, in many cultures, there were women (and a few men) who gave the gift of pleasure in the flesh to any who entered their temple with respect. They embodied the Goddess of Love for the lonely and the wounded, those seeking healing through the flesh. Today, some individuals are relearning the gift of the Sacred Whore and giving a spiritual gift through the many kinds of love.

The Sacred Whore is not the client's personal lover; her job is to give the client the transpersonal love of the Love God or Goddess, to show them divine love on a physically intimate scale that they cannot ignore, that tears them open to the beauty of All That Is. Some people need it to be physical, and to come through a human connection, before they can really accept the love past their wounds and damage. The Sacred Whore is a healer on the front lines of all that the world can do to hurt a person. She must find a way to channel "higher" energies into "lower" activities without glamorizing one and devaluing the other, in a way that bypasses the hurt and salves the wounds. She must balance the qualities that society says are opposites, and learn—and teach others as well—that there is no contradiction.

The Sacred Whore is also concerned with value, and self-value. Other Moons in other signs also struggle with the question of worth—Capricorn and Taurus, for instance—but the Libra Moon's struggle here is more personal. In the question of whether to give to one who can't pay and thus cheat oneself, or to hold to one's price and deny the needy, different Moons fall to different errors. Capricorn and Taurus tend to err on the side of not cheating oneself, while Cancer and Pisces will give it all away if they see enough need. When the Libra Moon comes to this lesson, however, she cannot err in either direction. She must get it exactly right, because she is placing a value not only on her skills, but on her own body as well, and to an extent on her own self.

Also, Libra is the sign of balance. We've traced the Libran mystery as she tilts her scales back and forth between justice and beauty; this is the moment when the two must meet and be even. The Sacred Whore must bring beauty to those who come seeking to her temple, but it must also be a place of justice, where neither she nor they are mistreated, devalued, or damaged through poor judgment. When Libra was Black Knight and Judge, that judgment was turned outward on others. Here it is turned inward, directly on the Whore, and she is in a much more compassionate place to judge those who come to her. It's a challenge worthy of the matured and seasoned Libra Moon, a balance that is perfect divine love when it's done right.

On the Sacred Whore's Moon we revisit our relationship with our bodies and pleasure. It's obviously a good time for sex; it's also a good time for doing any sensual thing with yourself, from long baths to good food to self-pleasuring. If you have a lover, spend time with each other and try to see the divine within, while not getting bogged down by the human needs.

People born under the Sacred Whore's Moon need to develop a strong sense of self-worth that does not depend on the opinions of others, yet takes their feelings into account in a higher, transpersonal way. That's a hard balance. It may be a matter of continually saying, "The way that I present myself and act is a magnet of sincerity that draws the right people, and those who are not attracted are just not the right people at this time." Being clear on what they are worth, and holding to that even when they are told otherwise, is the way to keep their self-esteem from being crushed.

People with the Sacred Whore's Moon are, of all the Libra Moons, the most drawn to the healing of others . . . yet unlike the Pisces Moon, that healing is accomplished through some expression of beauty and harmony, a vibration of Venus so strong that it can break through old wounds and heal the needy. It can be done as an expression of art, or in a relationship—although if it is the latter, they need to strike a balance between personal and transpersonal love, *eros* and *agape,* so that their own needs do not get cheated as well.

Quotes for the Sacred Whore's Moon

My great religion is a belief in the blood, in the flesh, as being wiser than the intellect.

D. H. LAWRENCE

Poor is the man whose pleasures depend on the permission of another.

MADONNA

I truly feel that there are as many ways of loving as there are people in the world and as there are days in the lives of those people.

MARY CALDERONE

Any time I am looking to somebody else as my source, I'm coming from scarcity. I am no longer trusting God, or the Universe, for my harvest. It's reasonable for me to have expectations based on what somebody I trust has committed to. And it's natural for me to feel disappointed when that somebody doesn't come through. But when I feel more than disappointment, when I also feel anger, it's because I deviated from my truth. It's because I compromised my truth to get what somebody else promised. Because when I'm really following my truth, I will be at peace with the consequences—whatever they are. I can accept somebody else's truth, but I must live my own truth. And sometimes that means walking away from a relationship.

JAN DENISE

Love and religion are the two most volcanic emotions to which the human organism is liable, and it is not surprising that when there is a disturbance in one of these spheres, the vibrations should readily extend to the other.

HAVELOCK ELLIS

The whore is despised by the hypocritical world because she has made a realistic assessment of her assets and does not have to rely on fraud to make a living. In an area of human relations where fraud is regular practice between the sexes, her honesty is regarded with a mocking wonder.

ANGELA CARTER

> When authorities warn you of the sinfulness of sex, there is an important lesson to be learned. Do not have sex with the authorities.
>
> MATT GROENING
>
> The sexual embrace can only be compared with music and with prayer.
>
> MARCUS AURELIUS
>
> The way you treat yourself sets the standard for others.
>
> DR. SONYA FRIEDMAN
>
> Don't ask yourself what the world needs, ask yourself what makes you come alive. And then go and do that. Because what the world needs is people who have come alive.
>
> HOWARD WASHINGTON THURMAN

PHOENIX MOON
THE BALSAMIC MOON IN SCORPIO

As the Scorpio Moon passes into the Balsamic phase, the former Madwoman arises from the wreckage of her life to start anew. Many of these stories are named for jobs that we humans bury ourselves in—Artist, Smith, Woodcutter, Scribe—but on the Phoenix Moon, the job that the former Madwoman takes up is irrelevant. It could be almost anything. The point is that it is entirely different from what has gone before. Scorpio rises from the ashes and looks upon a multitude of possibilities.

Any Scorpio planet learns the Plutonian mystery of rebirth—of burning down your life and walking away to become something entirely different. Pluto gives the Scorpio person the inner will to make this transformation, perhaps more than once in a lifetime, and recover. The Moon, however, is the most human of our planets in its own way. It may struggle and heave like the ocean, but it does not like Pluto's scorched-earth policies, even when Scorpio's lens covers it. The Moon wants to hold on to things, to keep memories, to focus on the here and the now. It is the fastest-moving of all our planets, and wants us to live today, not tomorrow or next year or another lifetime. Pluto's promise of death and rebirth frightens the Moon, and she doesn't like it one bit.

That means that the Moon delays the Scorpio death-and-rebirth all the way to the end of the cycle, the Balsamic Moon, where one has to let go and let it all happen the way it's supposed to, where there is an end of struggling to make an impact on the world. The Moon makes Scorpio crawl through every difficult and intense phase, makes them live it and feel it and immerse themselves in it, before they can come to that point of recycling themselves. (This is in contrast to the Scorpio Sun cycle, where the transmutation comes much earlier in the story—but that's a different book!) After all that struggle, the hard labor of rebirthing oneself, the Balsamic Moon moment in the Scorpio cycle is almost easy, the emerging into the open air without all the layers that were shed in such anguish. It's the first breath of the new life.

On the Phoenix Moon, our direction will differ depending on what we've experienced in our lives. If we've had to live that death-and-rebirth—not just a hard change, but a transformation that forced us to recreate our entire identity—we think about that change and find gratitude for the new direction it took us in. If we haven't had such a change, we consider what it would be like for us. What would we give up only with a struggle? What would it feel like death to give up? What can we not even imagine giving up without destroying who we are . . . and who would we be; what sort of self could we build out of what was left? On the practical side, this is a good time to honor and do service for people who have had to walk that road and are still dazed from the aftereffects—the cancer survivor, the battered spouse who escapes and makes a new life, the transsexual fresh from transition, the POW finally released.

People born under the Phoenix Moon have a gift for coping with extreme change in their lives, and this means that extreme change will come and get them, because they can handle it. They are the calmest of the Scorpio Moons, although one can still feel the volcano stirring under the calm . . . but they tend to get more of a handle on their emotions at a younger age. They make good counselors because they are unshockable and put that energy out to people: *I can listen to anything you tell me and not be horrified. It's all just part of the human experience to me, even the awful stuff.* That can be healing to people with strong darknesses. The fact that they are likely to end up emotionally "rebooting" themselves makes them even more effective in that role once they've gained some years and experience. They can seem cold, though, with all that self-control, and they need to remember that compassion is demonstrated through action and not just merely refraining from being judgmental in the moment.

Quotes for the Phoenix Moon

Take the matter of being reborn. What does being reborn mean to most people? Catastrophe unmitigated. Social revolution. The cultured aristocrat yanked out of his hyperexclusively ultravoluptuous super-palazzo, and dumped into an incredibly vulgar detention camp swarming with every conceivable species of undesirable organism. Most people fancy a guaranteed birthproof safety-suit of indestructible selflessness. If most people were to be born twice they'd probably call it dying.

E. E. CUMMINGS

These, then, are my last words to you: Be not afraid of life. Believe that life is worth living and your belief will help create the fact.

WILLIAM JAMES

I have come to think that the great are characterized precisely by the extreme position which they take, and that their heroism consists in holding to that extremity throughout their lives.

HADRIAN

Perfection is reached, not when there is no longer anything to add, but when there is no longer anything to take away.

ANTOINE DE SAINT-EXUPÉRY

And thou wilt give thyself relief, if thou doest every act of thy life as if it were the last.

MARCUS AURELIUS

It is to the interest of the commonwealth of mankind that there should be someone who is unconquered, someone against whom fortune has no power.

SENECA

You must concentrate upon and consecrate yourself wholly to each day, as though a fire were raging in your hair.

TAISEN DESHIMARU

How does one know if she has forgiven? You tend to feel sorrow over the circumstance instead of rage, you tend to feel sorry for the person rather than angry with him. You tend to have nothing left to say about it all.

CLARISSA PINKOLA ESTÉS

If there is a soul, it is a mistake to believe that it is given to us fully created. It is created here, throughout a whole life. And living is nothing else but that long and painful bringing forth.

ALBERT CAMUS

It's best to have failure happen early in life. It wakes up the Phoenix bird in you so you rise from the ashes.

ANNE BAXTER

SHAMAN'S MOON
THE BALSAMIC MOON IN SAGITTARIUS

The Balsamic Moon in Sagittarius brings us around again to a resolution of the human/animal split that is the fated dance of this sign. Where the Hunter kills animals and dons their skins, the Shaman wears the skins of animals and communes with their spirits. He shapeshifts astrally into an animal and learns their ways, their languages. He understands the animal nature and respects it, yet also respects the cycle of life. He eats their flesh and accepts their sacrifice, but also sings to their spirits and visits them in trance. He allies with the spirits of Nature and brings their wisdom back to human society to help human problems. He is the intermediary, the Walker between Worlds, who bridges the mundane sphere and the realm of spirit without contradiction.

Archetypally, Shamans are not necessarily serene and benign types, like the Balsamic Mystics of Pisces or Monks of Virgo. They can be cranky and impatient; they are often fierce and demand that people pay attention. They throw rocks at the scholar who wants to interview them about their alleged spirits, or run at the sick person with a spear, screaming loudly, to frighten the evil out them. They are both pragmatic and fully in contact with the spirit world, and this is a balance that Sagittarius desperately needs to learn. The fiery, idealistic, Jupiter-ruled Moon tends to err either in the direction of skepticism or of fanatical, unquestioning belief. The Shaman finds a middle ground—he believes completely in his worldview, but he also makes it serve reality rather than attempting to force reality to conform to it. He has learned that pragmatism is not necessarily skepticism, and belief is not necessarily naive.

One moment the Shaman might be dancing around his client, drumming and chanting strange songs to stranger spirits, and the next he is counseling him in a matter-of-fact manner about how he needs to change his life. *Wear this herb in a bag around your neck, make an offering of blood and ashes to this spirit, call your mother, stop smoking, learn to balance your budget.* To the Shaman, there is no division between the sacred and the profane; it's all sacred, and therefore one can accept all sorts of different people's profanity without blinking. It's a way out of fanaticism, a higher and wider view, but anchored in the body and physical world in a way that airy theories do not encompass.

On the Shaman's Moon, we become intermediaries between worlds—Nature and civilization, woman and man, human and animal, mind and body—in ways that benefit both sides and bring understanding, and do not whitewash, euphemize, or disrespect either side. This is not an easy task, and the deeper implications of this Moon may slip by a lot of people. If a group decides to honor this Moon, it might be wise to spend a good deal of time simply discussing what such a position might look like and exploring their own biases. During the Shaman's Moon, if someone enters into a position of being an intermediary while secretly favoring one side—even if unconsciously—the Universe will force that person into a position of defending and being immersed in the side that is less acceptable. It's not about Libran balance, it's about Sagittarian vision. Sagittarius's key phrase is *I see*, and to see all sides clearly one must experience them equally.

Those born under the Shaman's Moon are often drawn emotionally to two opposing worldviews, both seeming equally valid and neither tolerating the other well. They will spend their lives either avoiding and longing for one while clinging to and cursing the other or finding a way to inhabit and honor both equally, and bringing the best of each to the other. This will mean continually explaining one to the other—on both sides—until more understanding is reached, as well as a good deal of personal shape-shifting in order to fully inhabit each one by turns. Ironically, this is the least gregarious of the Sagittarian Moons, and this will constitute a part of their reluctance to pony up the necessary communication to make it all work. In the end, only love of both worlds will heal their hearts and open them up to the hearts of others.

Finding the balance between the physical and the spiritual planes is a necessary chore for any Sagittarian Moon, but the natives of this Moon are on the fast track when it comes to that problem. They will be thrust into situations that force them to face the division between the two and see that it exists entirely in their own mind. Bringing these two poles together, they can find themselves grounded deeper into both of them.

Quotes for the Shaman's Moon

The greatest peril of life lies in the fact that human food consists entirely of souls. All the creatures that we have to strike down and destroy to make food and clothes for ourselves have souls, as we have; souls that do not perish with the body and which therefore must be propitiated lest they revenge themselves on us for taking away their bodies.

INUIT SHAMAN, 1929

"Everything is made of light," he said, "and the space between isn't empty."

DON MIGUEL RUIZ

If an Aborigine drafted an IQ test, all of Western civilization would presumably flunk it.

STANLEY GARN

God has appointed that I must wander both beneath and upon the earth, and has bestowed on me such power that I can comfort and cheer the afflicted, and on the other hand I can cast down those who are too happy. The mind of those who are too much given to striving can I likewise change, so that they will love cheerful amusement.

ZAARIN KOGEL KHAN

When you're doing the wrong thing everything is an effort. Your body will suffer and your health will suffer—running up against a brick wall and splatting time and time again. It's always like that if you are not doing what is authentically right for you. It's a real hard lesson because you didn't get your heart's desire and Spirit has another plan for you.

JAMIE SAMS

Let us go to help and take care of the poor people wherever they are. Let us love people and even enemies although it is a one-sided love. . . . Take courage again, and cheer up, when you are exhausted. Overcome all sorrow and ordeals. Look ahead into the future, and keep the right way in your mind. Think big and carefully. When you are very tired, you might fall down. However, you must stand up again even if you keep falling down. You will arrive at your own place some day if you go on, even after failing down. Come closer to me. Come on. Are you all set? Get it.

KOREAN INITIATION SONG FOR MUDANG
(KOREAN SHAMANS)

Why, why, why oh why?
Why do we live, why do we die?
I know I don't know,
and he don't know,
and you don't know.

ERNESTO ALVARADO

The slenderest knowledge that may be obtained of the highest things is more desirable than the most certain knowledge obtained of lesser things.

THOMAS AQUINAS

We all feed the spirits. Your lease agreement on this earth is your death. You agree to die. Nobody is going to escape.

MARTIN PRECHTEL

> They wished to flower, and flowering is being beautiful: but we wish to ripen, and that means being dark and taking pains.
>
> RAINER MARIA RILKE

DRAGON'S MOON
THE BALSAMIC MOON IN CAPRICORN

The Balsamic Moon in Capricorn gives us the Miser still sitting on his hoard, but now he finds wisdom and comes into his own as the Dragon. In Norse mythology, one who sat too long on a hoard of gold thinking greedy and gloating thoughts was changed magically into a dragon; conversely, in Chinese thought the dragon was a creature of wisdom whose hoard was valuable knowledge given out only to a select few.

Dragons hoard more than money; they hoard wisdom, knowledge, and experience. Dragons also set boundaries and remind people about practical wisdom. When the hero comes with his grand plan, the Dragon challenges him not with equal force and glory, but with weapons that he is not prepared to endure. *How are you going to pay for this adventure?* the Dragon asks. *Who funded that sword and armor, and did they get it cheaply enough that it will break in your hand, or did they pay so much for it that if it breaks, you'll be in debt for years? What are you going to do if there's no treasure to plunder or if the local lord relieves you of it on the way out? What if the damsel in distress spits in your face, or is in league with the enemy, or just doesn't think you're worthy of her? What if her father won't reward you because she's no longer a virgin, even though it's not your fault? Which of your loved ones suffer because you've chosen this path? How will you make it up to them? Do you have the energy to keep doing this adventuring, over and over? What about when you get too old to fight? Who will take care of you? Have you made those arrangements? What are you assuming will bite you when you least expect it?*

Dragon wisdom is grounded in the Earth, as are their hoards of gems and gold. They are the Voice of Saturn, the oldest Saturnian Moon, poking holes in dreams the way that a sensei demolishes the would-be martial artist and lays him calmly and firmly on the mat, again and again. Some dragons of legend could fly as well as crawl, which let them see the world from a higher perspective. Likewise, Capricorn Dragons look toward the future in a way that is about more than just their own family and kinship group. People born to this practical Moon can see the impossible and strategize ways to achieve it. Dragons challenge us to do our best in ways that we hadn't even imagined.

On the Dragon Moon, we take a long look at the limits on our lives and consider how we can surpass them. This isn't, however, a Moon of flights of fancy; save that for the Pisces or Gemini Moons. Keep your speculation pragmatic and well within the realm of possibility. What you should be challenging is your courage and ingenuity, not the laws of time, space, and physics. The Dragon Moon challenges us to be more than just an idealistic hero. We have to become a practical, prepared hero as well, or we won't survive.

People born on the Dragon Moon are the ones who poke holes in idealistic plans. If they do it right—not out of fear of losing their hoard, but out of a desire to challenge and inspire—they can get people actually performing better than they would have otherwise. If all (or even most of) the people they advise end up slinking off sadly and never achieving anything, they've missed the point and lost the game. Feeling superior about one's wisdom is not the goal. Actually helping heroes become heroes, not discouraged ne'er-do-wells, is the goal. The world needs more heroes, not more broken people.

That challenge applies equally to them, by the way. If Dragon Moon people are depressed and broken, it's because they are afraid. They cling to their hoarded knowledge and memories and neither use them nor give them out, and they need to learn generosity of spirit. Dragons don't inspire heroes—or become them—by sulking in a back room. They do it by giving out their magical treasures, and only when they have given almost all of them away can they muster the heroic army that will stand behind their goals. The more Dragon Moon people give, the more they achieve. It's an ancient wisdom that they carry in their hearts, if they'll only look for it.

Quotes for the Dragon Moon

It does not do to leave a dragon out of your calculations, if you live near him.

J. R. R. TOLKIEN

I spent most of my childhood being terrified by the question "Am I normal?" I'm relieved now that I know for sure that I am not.

TOM LIMONCELLI

Man is something that is to be surpassed. What have you done to surpass him?

FRIEDRICH NIETZSCHE

Challenge is a dragon with a gift in its mouth . . . Tame the dragon and the gift is yours.

NOELA EVANS

He who fights too long against dragons becomes a dragon himself; and if you gaze too long into the abyss, the abyss will gaze into you.

FRIEDRICH NIETZSCHE

I think somehow we learn who we really are and then live with that decision.

ELEANOR ROOSEVELT

For the North, the direction of Earth, we have the Dragons, who establish and guard the group's boundaries, who keep the group grounded. . . . They may be perceived as throwing a wet blanket on the fires of fresh enthusiasm, but they may win great appreciation from those in the group who are feeling overwhelmed.

STARHAWK

The tragedy and the magnificence of *Homo sapiens* together rise from the same smoky truth that we alone among the animal species refuse to acknowledge natural law.

ROBERT ARDREY

A man is rich in proportion to the number of things he can afford to let alone.

HENRY DAVID THOREAU

To have what we want is riches; to be able to do without is power.

GEORGE MacDONALD

PROPHET'S MOON
THE BALSAMIC MOON IN AQUARIUS

The Balsamic Moon in Aquarius sees the Heretic survive the blast of society's disapproval and sink into oblivion. But eventually people find him again in his last years, and read his works, and are impressed. They come to him, asking what he knows about the future, and he tells them. They take his words and run with them, and the argument starts again. Most don't believe. A few do and promise to remember.

For him, things are different than they were in the days of heresy. The Prophet has aged and seen both the brevity of his own life and the immenseness of time, and he is much more sanguine that the truth will come out, even if he does not see it before his death. He knows, also, that most people will not believe him, and this fact no longer enrages or terrifies. The Prophet can smile and shrug and let it go. He's learned to see things in the long term.

He does live in the future most of the time. Those who think that one can't comfortably live in the future haven't looked through the Prophet's eyes. He sees not one future but many. Some are frightening, certainly, but there are enough that are beautiful that he always has a dream to turn his eyes to. (This, the last phase of Aquarius, has a strange vibration of the oncoming Pisces Moon about it. At the moment, the Pisces energy is still more fantasy than possibility, but that will change as the Moon moves ahead.)

The Prophet sees the sad things to come and cries for them, and sometimes his own personal pain is that he knows no one would have listened had he said something. Even harder are the times when he sees something difficult in the wind and knows that it is necessary as well as painful, and that the best thing he can do is to say nothing and let it run its course. These moments, especially, cause resentment among his followers. "You needed to go through that" is not something anyone wants to hear, and he is sometimes accused of being cold and unfeeling. At his worst he can be cold, or at least thoughtless, but generally he is keenly aware of his own inability to affect the change he sees coming. It is part of his lesson to learn to be entirely at peace with that.

On the Prophet's Moon, we look to the future and think about how it might be. It's also a good time for reading science fiction or writing it, if that's your interest. If you'd rather deal in real life, read about cutting-edge science. On the other hand, there's also the ongoing work of humanitarians, and how they intend to change the world. Stay away from apocalyptic ideas, though. The Prophet's Moon is more relaxed than that.

People born on the Prophet's Moon are generally more easygoing than natives of the other Aquarius Moons. They take things in stride and don't sweat the small stuff. Emotionally, they are happy doing work that will echo through the future, but they aren't driven about it. There is an "older than their years" feel to them. They have the ability to look into their own futures and see them like a tree, branching and forking, but being constantly "pruned" as they make their decisions. The tree may eventually become one straight road, or it may not, but they are at peace with the process. Like all the Aquarius Moons, they do feel a little distant from their partners, but they are wonderfully tolerant.

If they have faults, its being less ambitious than most and preferring to make pronouncements from their porch rocker rather than digging in and doing the work. When they are doing the work, though, it's much more fulfilling to them. They just need the extra prodding to get out of the porch rocker. Those born to more ambitious signs might shake their heads and sigh, but the Prophet's Moon people probably invented the slang saying "It's all good, man." Their heads are in the clouds, but it does mean that your country looks as good as any other to them, and they will appreciate the differences of your unique self as much as any of the other "aliens" in their world, which includes everyone else as well.

Quotes for the Prophet's Moon

Look ahead.
You are not expected to complete the task.
Neither are you permitted to lay it down.

THE TALMUD

The decent moderation of today will be the least human of things tomorrow. At the time of the Spanish Inquisition, the opinion of good sense and of the good medium was certainly that people ought not to burn too large a number of heretics; extreme and unreasonable opinion obviously demanded that they should burn none at all.

MAURICE MAETERLINCK

Once you accept your own death, all of a sudden you are free to live. You no longer care about your reputation. . . . You no longer care except so far as your life can be used tactically—to promote a cause you believe in.

SAUL ALINSKY

It does not pay a prophet to be too specific.

L. SPRAGUE DE CAMP

The best of seers is he who guesses well.

EURIPIDES

Hence it comes about that all armed Prophets have been victorious, and all unarmed Prophets have been destroyed.

NICCOLÒ MACHIAVELLI

Bad will be the day for every man when he becomes absolutely content with the life that he is living, with the deeds that he is doing, when there is not forever beating at the doors of his soul some great desire to do something larger, which he knows that he was meant and made to do, because he is still, in spite of all, the child of God.

PHILLIPS BROOKS

We are going to have to find ways of organizing ourselves cooperatively, sanely, scientifically, harmonically, and in regenerative spontaneity with the rest of humanity around Earth. . . . We are not going to be able to operate our Spaceship Earth successfully much longer unless we see it as a whole spaceship and our fate as common. It has to be everybody or nobody.

BUCKMINSTER FULLER

And though I have the gift of prophecy, and understand all mysteries and all knowledge, and though I have all faith, so that I could remove mountains, but have not love, I am nothing.

THE BIBLE

> The best way to predict the future is to invent it.
>
> ALAN KAY

MYSTIC'S MOON
THE BALSAMIC MOON IN PISCES

The Pisces Moon reaches the Balsamic stage and the Lost Soul reaches upward to save himself . . . and grabs hold of what, up until now, he has touched but felt slip through his fingers. This time, however, he has it . . . or, rather, it has him. He touches All That Is, That Which Is Unspeakable, the place that once you've been there you can never describe properly, the Beingness that cannot be quantified, the Point of Oneness. The Pisces Moon becomes the Mystic, and it saves him from himself. Whatever self-destructive behavior he was resorting to, he pushes it aside. Suddenly nothing else is important, and so much of the old pain falls away. Losing oneself in the bottle or the drug or madness or other people is nothing to losing oneself in All That Is . . . and everything he's tried to merge with before was just part of the training to drop the walls and become One here and now.

The Mystic's Moon is the final Moon in the final sign's cycle, and as the last point it is fittingly the most nebulous. What can one say about a Mystic? It is a path of devotion to something greater, not from a remote place where you scream into the void and hope someone hears, but from a place where the Beloved Mystery is right there with you, all the time, beautiful and terrible, familiar and unknowable. All right, one could go on with such unhelpful metaphors all day. Mystics do, usually. Mostly they succeed in communicating, yet again, that what they do is not something that can be communicated. It must be experienced . . . and this is the ambivalent destiny of the Mystic.

The Mystic, like the Shaman (Balsamic Moon in Sagittarius), is not bound by the rules of society. He moves beyond all those rules, which have just been cobwebs laid on the Pisces Moon anyway, and which he has always wanted to shrug off. He does whatever he needs to do to find the connection he needs, whether that is retreating to a faraway place away from people or wandering around the city park with a dowsing rod. What people think isn't important. If he is healed of the wounds inflicted on his reality and the people who inhabit it, he will attract people who know he's got something and want some of the inner peace that radiates from him. If he isn't quite healed himself, he will tend to push them away. When he's healed enough to look on them with real compassion, he may choose to teach them . . . or he may not. Mystics are not required to be teachers, although we are all better off when they choose to do so.

On the Mystic's Moon, we pray, or meditate, or go to a moving religious ritual, or find some other way to experience All That Is. If this is not something that is part of your life, skip this Moon. There's really no substitute. For many people, religion and spirituality are not something that they are meant to do this time around, and that's all right. So wait for the next Moon—it'll be something in Aries and probably a lot more fun.

Mystic's Moon people need a strong spiritual life. Again, there's really no way around this. The context where they find their spirituality doesn't seem to matter, but it must be the sort of spirituality where they have a "personal relationship" with the Universe in some way. Their hearts seek upward no matter what they do, yearning for something more. If they don't make space in their lives for this, they will walk around hollowly, feeling like something is more important than everything in their lives, but they can't seem to reach it. Eventually they will have to blot the feeling out so hard that their lives become a flat gray shallowness, or else the feeling will reach through and drag them away from everything they have. It's better if they start making room for their spiritual life at an early stage, but it's never too late. A wise partner will support and encourage this, even if it means a lot of time spent apart. This is between them and the Universe, and there's no real way to beat that relationship.

Quotes for the Mystic's Moon

The whole drift of my education goes to persuade me that the world of our present consciousness is one out of many worlds of consciousness that exist.

WILLIAM JAMES

For my part, the longer I live the less I feel the need of any sort of theological belief, and the more I am content to let unseen powers go on their way with me and mine without question or distrust.

JOHN BURROUGHS

Reality isn't all there is, after all.

ISAAC ASIMOV

When a pious visitor inquired sweetly, "Henry, have you made your peace with God?" Thoreau replied, "We have never quarreled."

BROOKS ATKINSON

Mysticism and exaggeration go together. A mystic must not fear ridicule if he is to push all the way to the limits of humility or the limits of delight.

MILAN KUNDERA

As I grow to understand Life less and less, I learn to live it more and more.

JULES RENARD

If we discover a desire within us that nothing in this world can satisfy, we should begin to wonder if perhaps we were created for another world.

C. S. LEWIS

What does mysticism really mean? It means the way to attain knowledge. It's close to philosophy, except in philosophy you go horizontally while in mysticism you go vertically.

ELIE WIESEL

Just as in earthly life lovers long for the moment when they are able to breathe forth their love for each other, to let their souls blend in a soft whisper, so the mystic longs for the moment when in prayer he can, as it were, creep into God.

SØREN KIERKEGAARD

I betook myself to prayer
and in every lonely place
I found an altar.

ELIZABETH, BONDSWOMAN AND MINISTER,
BORN IN MARYLAND, 1766

EPILOGUE

I didn't used to like the Moon much. For some decades, when I did astrology, I was fascinated by the antics of the outer planets—Saturn, Uranus, Neptune, Pluto. I found the Moon's energy too emotional, too vague, too bound up in parent-child issues . . . and, in some ways, too everyday. The placement of my own Moon probably has something to do with that; it's highly afflicted and in an Air sign, so my own first experience of lunar energy was not exactly positive or comforting. It took many decades of other Moons shadowing my own for me to understand the sacred and fulfilling nature of the Moon. Just because my own childhood experience of nurturing was rather horrifying (Moon squaring Saturn, Chiron, Mars, Uranus, and Pluto, and opposing Venus as one arm of a grand cross) didn't mean that it always had to be that way.

I finally came to terms with the Moon by actually watching it in the sky, talking to the spirit of that white sphere that wandered in and out of my sight. It was Mani, the Norse Moon god, who eventually used that focus to make contact with me and tell me some of the secrets that my confused personal astrology had blocked off. In some ways, he straightened me out about lunar energy. I learned that although the Moon rules female endocrine cycles, it is not necessarily female or feminine. I learned that there were many different kinds of nurturing, not just the "good way" and the "bad way." I learned that the Moon is a dancer, and how it dances with the Sun is a reflection of how one's day self should interact with one's night self—one neither ruling nor crowding the other, both having lots of space to do what they do best, but regularly checking in with each other and joining hands to dance. Some of those check-ins are more tense than others—as you'll know by now, having read about the various phases—but never do they part for very long. And that's the way it should be.

The Moon is changeable, by its very nature. That's not a bad thing. It means that the Moon can wear many faces. Some of them are mine. Some of them are yours.

ABOUT THE AUTHOR

Raven Kaldera is a Northern Tradition Shaman who has been an astrologer since 1984 and a Pagan since 1986, practicing the once-lost shamanic tradition of northern Europe (see his website at www.northernshamanism.org).

The author of 25 books under his own name as well as a scant handful under other names, Kaldera is a prolific author who plans to continue writing until he's too decrepit to dictate the words. Included among his many books are *Pagan Astrology* and this volume, *Moon Phase Astrology*.

Kaldera's interest in astrology began at an early age, when he learned astrology from books in junior high and practiced by doing the charts of classmates during lunch. His practice began in earnest in 1984, when he began giving astrological readings professionally. Eventually his interest in astrology and his shamanic practices collided, and the result was the storytelling described in his book *MythAstrology* and the techniques described in his *Pagan Astrology*. In writing *Moon Phase Astrology*, Kaldera communed with the Moon God in his religious tradition, who guided him through the secrets of the ninety-six Moons of this book.

Kaldera's current and ongoing astrological interests lie in such obscure areas as the role of Pallas in the charts of transgendered individuals and the role of black holes in the charts of psychic vampires. He is spiritually researching the lost meanings of the fixed stars in the tradition of his ancestors, with the help of the ancient gods and spirits of his faith.

Kaldera is a musician, a priest and minister of the Neo-Pagan First Kingdom Church of Asphodel, a diviner, a homesteader and keeper of goats and sheep, an Ordeal Master, and a transgendered activist. To find out about all the pies he's got his fingers in, check out his home website at: **www.ravenkaldera.org**. 'Tis an ill wind that blows no minds.

BOOKS OF RELATED INTEREST

Pagan Astrology
Spell-Casting, Love Magic, and Shamanic Stargazing
by Raven Kaldera

Drawing Down the Spirits
The Traditions and Techniques of Spirit Possession
by Kenaz Filan and Raven Kaldera

Shamanic Egyptian Astrology
Your Planetary Relationship to the Gods
by Linda Star Wolf and Ruby Falconer

Aspects in Astrology
A Guide to Understanding Planetary Relationships
in the Horoscope
by Sue Tompkins

Numerology
With Tantra, Ayurveda, and Astrology
by Harish Johari

Cherokee Astrology
Animal Medicine in the Stars
by Raven Hail

Liquid Light of Sex
Kundalini, Astrology, and the Key Life Transitions
by Barbara Hand Clow

Taoist Astrology
A Handbook of the Authentic Chinese Tradition
by Susan Levitt with Jean Tang

INNER TRADITIONS • BEAR & COMPANY
P.O. Box 388
Rochester, VT 05767
1-800-246-8648
www.InnerTraditions.com

Or contact your local bookseller